Microsoft® Office
OUTLOOK 2003
QuickSteps

Microsoft® Office OUTLOOK 2003

QuickSteps

MARTY MATTHEWS

KELLEN DIAMANTI

CURT SIMMONS

McGraw-Hill/Osborne

New York Chicago San Francisco
Lisbon London Madrid Mexico City
Milan New Delhi San Juan
Seoul Singapore Sydney Toronto

McGraw-Hill/Osborne
2100 Powell Street, 10th Floor
Emeryville, California 94608
U.S.A.

To arrange bulk purchase discounts for sales promotions, premiums, or fund-raisers, please contact McGraw-Hill/Osborne at the above address. For information on translations or book distributors outside the U.S.A., please see the International Contact Information page immediately following the index of this book.

This book was composed with Adobe® InDesign®

234567890 WCK WCK 01987654

ISBN 0-07-223227-7

PUBLISHER / Brandon A. Nordin

VICE PRESIDENT & ASSOCIATE PUBLISHER / Scott Rogers

ACQUISITIONS EDITOR / Roger Stewart

ACQUISITIONS COORDINATOR / Jessica Wilson

TECHNICAL EDITORS / Curt Simmons, Kellen Diamanti, Marty Matthews

COPY EDITOR / Jan Jue

PROOFREADER / Chara Curtis

INDEXERS / Kellen Diamanti, Deborah Fisher

LAYOUT ARTISTS / Bailey Cunningham, Keith Eyer

ILLUSTRATORS / Kathleen Edwards, Pattie Lee, Bruce Hopkins

SERIES DESIGN / Bailey Cunningham

COVER DESIGN / Pattie Lee

To Our Spice in Life:

Marty Matthews:

To Carole,
For over 32 years you have been my very best friend, and I could not ask for a better one; you have been my partner in all things from parenting, to business, to life, and I could not ask for a better one; you have been a strong and willing supporter for all that I have wanted to do, and I could not ask for a better one. Thank you my love for being such a wonderful and vital part of my life.

Kellen Diamanti:

To Mike,
We have taken many roads less traveled in our 20 years together, and I am perpetually grateful for having taken the journey with you. Your steadfast support, balanced intelligence, and willingness to take risks and to work hard make you my soul mate, helpmate, and truelove, always.

Curt Simmons:

To Dawn,
Thank you so much for always being so supportive of me as your husband and in my work. Thanks for putting up with the long hours and the frustrations that come with a freelancing career. You are always understanding, my best friend, and the best wife I could have ever hoped for.

About the Authors

Marty Matthews:

Marty has used computers for over 40 years—from mainframes to the most recent PCs. He has done this as a programmer, and as the president of a software firm, and has held many positions in between. As a result, he has firsthand knowledge of most facets of computing. Over 20 years ago, Marty and his wife, Carole, began writing computer books, and they have now written over 60 of them, including *Windows XP QuickSteps, Windows Server 2003: A Beginner's Guide, Windows XP: A Beginner's Guide, FrontPage 2003: The Complete Reference*, and *Outlook 98 Made Easy*, all published by McGraw-Hill/Osborne. Marty, his wife, and son live on an island in the Puget Sound.

Kellen Diamanti:

Kellen explains technical concepts to audiences ranging from first graders to network engineers. She has published or scripted dozens of manuals, movies, magazine articles, interactive training modules, educational curricula, and textbooks. She fell into mainframe documentation in graduate school, back when the *Star Trek* computer still answered to Captain Kirk. Since then, she has gone through six PCs and wrestled with software most people never heard of. From her bucolic paradise in the Puget Sound, she is dedicated to plain speech and the proposition that the ordinary mortal can understand this stuff.

Curt Simmons:

Curt Simmons, MCSE, MCSA, CTT, is a technology author and trainer from Dallas, Texas. Curt is the author of over 40 technology books on a variety of subjects and the best-selling author of *How to Do Everything with Windows XP*, also from McGraw-Hill/Osborne. When Curt is not writing or teaching, he spends his time with his wife and two daughters. Visit Curt on the Internet at http://www.curtsimmons.com.

Contents at a Glance

Contents

Chapter 5 **Scheduling and the Calendar** 87

Chapter 6 **Using Task Lists** 121

Chapter 7   Using a Journal and Making Notes 141

Chapter 8   Managing Files and Folders 159

9

10

Acknowledgments

Although this book has only three names on the cover, it was really produced by a fantastic team of truly talented people. This team, which has only recently been formed, has pulled together to produce a really great series of books in an incredibly short time. They did this by putting in endless hours, working selflessly with each other, and applying a great amount of skill.

Jan Jue, copy editor, who with great skill and a light touch took our poor attempts at writing and made them readable, while also melding three voices into one. Thanks Jan!

Bailey Cunningham, series designer and layout artist, provided equal parts of tremendous skill, endless patience, and great humor to produce a beautiful book. Thanks Bailey!

Keith Eyer, layout artist and prepress expert, jumped in to fill a vital need, working many late and weekend hours. Thanks Keith!

Chara Curtis, proof reader, added to the readability and understandability of the book while always having a smile in her e-mail voice. Thanks Chara!

Deborah Fisher, indexer, performed this most valuable task with both great care and a most pleasant nature. Thanks Deborah!

Roger Stewart, Editorial Director at Osborne, believed in us against substantial odds to sell the series and continued to stand behind us throughout the production process. Thanks Roger!

David Zielonka, Managing Editor at Osborne, provided production guidance and support throughout the project. Thanks David!

To our children, (five in all) who accept (for the most part!) our long hours and need for concentration, and still unconditionally give us the love and joy that only children can do. Thanks to you all!

Introduction

QuickSteps books are recipe books for computer users. They answer the question "How do I…?" by providing quick sets of steps to accomplish the most common tasks in a particular program. The sets of steps are the central focus of the book. QuickSteps sidebars show you how to quickly do many small functions or tasks that support the primary functions. Notes, Tips, and Cautions augment the steps, yet they are presented in such a manner as to not interrupt the flow of the steps. The brief introductions are minimal rather than narrative, and numerous illustrations and figures, many with callouts, support the steps.

QuickSteps books are organized by function and the tasks needed to perform that function. Each function is a chapter. Each task, or "How To," contains the steps needed for accomplishing the function along with relevant Notes, Tips, Cautions, and screenshots. Tasks will be easy to find through:

- The Table of Contents, which lists the functional areas (chapters) and tasks in the order they are presented

- A How-To list of tasks on the opening page of each chapter

- The index with its alphabetical list of terms used in describing the functions and tasks

- Color-coded tabs for each chapter or functional area with an index to the tabs just before the Table of Contents

Conventions Used in this Book

Microsoft Office Outlook 2003 QuickSteps uses several conventions designed to make the book easier for you to follow. Among these are:

- A in the Table of Contents or the How To list in each chapter references a QuickSteps sidebar in a chapter.

- **Bold type** is used for words on the screen that you are to do something with, such as click **Save As** or open **File**.

- *Italic type* is used for a word or phrase that is being defined or otherwise deserves special emphasis.

- <u>Underlined type</u> is used for text that you are to type from the keyboard.

- SMALL CAPITAL LETTERS are used for keys on the keyboard such as **ENTER** and **SHIFT**.

- When you are expected to enter a command, you are told to press the key(s). If you are to enter text or numbers, you are told to type them.

How to...

Chapter 1
Stepping into Outlook

When someone mentions Outlook, the first thought is generally the sending and receiving of e-mail. Outlook does handle e-mail very competently, and it does a lot more, including managing contacts, scheduling activities, tracking tasks, keeping a journal, and using notes. Outlook also provides the means to collaborate with others, can be used with and from other applications, and can be used with a PDA (personal digital assistant).

In this chapter you will familiarize yourself with Outlook; see how to start and leave it; use Outlook's windows, panes, toolbars, and menus; learn how to get help; and find out how to customize Outlook.

Start Outlook

Starting Outlook depends on how Outlook was installed and what has happened to it since its installation. In this section you'll see a surefire way to start Outlook and some alternatives, you'll see how to use the Startup Wizard and how to upgrade from Outlook Express, and finally, you'll see how to leave Outlook.

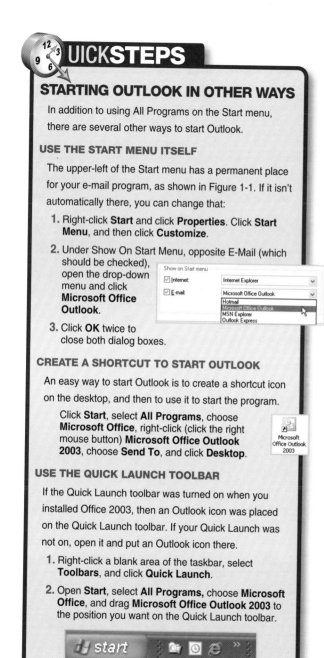

QUICKSTEPS

STARTING OUTLOOK IN OTHER WAYS

In addition to using All Programs on the Start menu, there are several other ways to start Outlook.

USE THE START MENU ITSELF

The upper-left of the Start menu has a permanent place for your e-mail program, as shown in Figure 1-1. If it isn't automatically there, you can change that:

1. Right-click **Start** and click **Properties**. Click **Start Menu**, and then click **Customize**.

2. Under Show On Start Menu, opposite E-Mail (which should be checked), open the drop-down menu and click **Microsoft Office Outlook**.

3. Click **OK** twice to close both dialog boxes.

CREATE A SHORTCUT TO START OUTLOOK

An easy way to start Outlook is to create a shortcut icon on the desktop, and then to use it to start the program.

Click **Start**, select **All Programs**, choose **Microsoft Office**, right-click (click the right mouse button) **Microsoft Office Outlook 2003**, choose **Send To**, and click **Desktop**.

USE THE QUICK LAUNCH TOOLBAR

If the Quick Launch toolbar was turned on when you installed Office 2003, then an Outlook icon was placed on the Quick Launch toolbar. If your Quick Launch was not on, open it and put an Outlook icon there.

1. Right-click a blank area of the taskbar, select **Toolbars**, and click **Quick Launch**.

2. Open **Start**, select **All Programs**, choose **Microsoft Office**, and drag **Microsoft Office Outlook 2003** to the position you want on the Quick Launch toolbar.

Use the Start Menu to Start Outlook

If there are no other icons for or shortcuts to Outlook available on your desktop, you can always start Outlook using the Start menu:

1. Start your computer if it is not already running, and log on to Windows if necessary.

2. Click **Start**. The Start menu opens.

3. Select **All Programs**, choose **Microsoft Office**, and click **Microsoft Office Outlook 2003**, as shown in Figure 1-1.

Figure 1-1: The foolproof way to start Outlook is through the Start menu.

E-mail Accounts

Internet E-mail Settings (POP3)
Each of these settings are required to get your e-mail account working.

User Information

Your Name: Marty Matthews

E-mail Address: marty@matthewstechnolo

Logon Information

User Name: marty

Password: ********

☑ Remember password

☐ Log on using Secure Password Authentication (SPA)

Server Information

Incoming mail server (POP3): mail.matthewstechnology.

Outgoing mail server (SMTP): mail.matthewstechnology.

Test Settings

After filling out the information on this screen, we recommend you test your account by clicking the button below. (Requires network connection)

Test Account Settings ...

More Settings ...

< Back   Next >   Cancel

Figure 1-2: This shows the information that is needed for a POP3 e-mail account.

NOTE

If you have been running Outlook Express and then install Outlook, you may get a message when you run Outlook 2003 Startup Wizard asking if you want to upgrade from Outlook Express and if you want to import your Outlook Express messages and addresses. See "Upgrade from Outlook Express" later in this chapter.

Use the Startup Wizard

The first time you start Outlook on either a new computer with Office 2003 or a new installation of Office 2003, the Outlook 2003 Startup Wizard will open.

1. Click **Next**. Accept the default of **Yes**, you want to configure an e-mail account, and click **Next**.

2. Click the type of mail server you will use. You may have to contact your network administrator or your Internet service provider (ISP) for this choice. Also, Chapter 2 explores the various alternative mail accounts, and Table 1-1 provides further information on the choices in this dialog box. Click **Next**.

3. Fill in the User, Server, and Logon Information that is correct for you, as shown for me in Figure 1-2. Again, you may need to contact your network administrator or ISP for this information.

4. Click **Test Account Settings**. You will get a dialog box showing the steps that were taken and the results, like this:

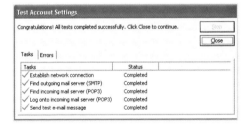

5. Click **Close**. If your results were not satisfactory, contact your network administrator or ISP for the correct entries.

6. Click **Next**. You are congratulated on entering all the information needed to set up an account. Click **Finish**. The wizard will close and Outlook itself will open. See "Explore Outlook" later in this chapter.

TABLE 1-1: TYPES OF E-MAIL SERVERS

E-MAIL SERVER	DESCRIPTION	EXAMPLES OF USE
Exchange Server	Uses Microsoft Exchange Server running on a server on your local area network (LAN)	Used within an organization for both internal and external mail
POP3	Post Office Protocol 3 (POP3) is used by the majority of Internet service providers (ISPs) to download e-mail.	Local or national ISPs
IMAP	Internet Message Access Protocol (IMAP) is used where the mail is to stay on the mail server, unlike POP3. IMAP provides better security and more flexibility than does POP3.	Used within an organization and by more expensive ISP services
HTTP	Hypertext Transfer Protocol (HTTP) is used to transfer information on the World Wide Web (WWW or just "Web").	Used by Web-based e-mail services such as Hotmail

TIP

A *protocol* is an industry standard that is widely accepted and used by many organizations to perform some function, like exchanging e-mail.

Upgrade from Outlook Express

If you have been using Outlook Express and you install Office 2003, when Outlook 2003 Startup Wizard runs, you may be asked if you want to upgrade from Outlook Express, as shown in Figure 1-3. If you choose to upgrade, you will be asked if you want to import your Outlook Express messages and addresses. Click **Yes** and you will see the progress as the files are being imported and will get a summary upon completion.

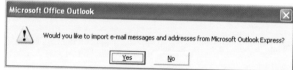

Figure 1-3: You may be asked in Outlook 2003 Startup Wizard if you want to upgrade from Outlook Express.

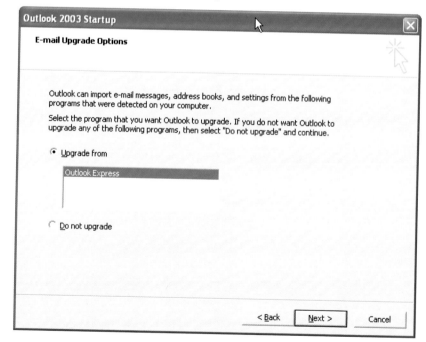

NOTE

If you want to import Outlook Express files from another computer, locate the files by starting **Outlook Express** on the other computer, click the **Tools** menu, choose **Options**, click the **Maintenance** tab, and click **Store Folder**. Select the entire address line, press **CTRL+C** (press **CTRL** and while holding it down, press **C**), click **Start**, click **My Computer**, select the contents of the Address bar, press **CTRL+V**, and press **ENTER**. This will show you the Outlook Express files. Copy these files to the new computer, import them into Outlook Express on that computer, and then use the instructions under "Upgrade from Outlook Express" to import the files into Outlook.

If you have been using Outlook Express and were not asked by the Outlook 2003 Startup Wizard if you want to upgrade, you can still import your Outlook Express files into Outlook.

1. Start **Outlook** in one of the ways described earlier in this chapter.
2. Click the **File** menu and click **Import And Export**.
3. Select **Import Internet Mail And Addresses**, and click **Next**.
4. Click **Outlook Express** and make sure that **Import Mail**, **Import Address Book**, and **Import Rules** are all checked, as shown in Figure 1-4.
5. Click **Next**, choose how you want to handle duplicates, and then click **Finish**.

   You will be told the progress as the files are being imported and will get a summary upon completion.

Outlook Import Tool

Select the Internet Mail application to import from:

Eudora (Pro and Light) 2.x, 3.x, 4.x
Outlook Express 4.x, 5.x, 6.x

☑ Import Mail
☑ Import Address book
☑ Import Rules

< Back   Next >   Cancel

Figure 1-4: You can bring over all of your Outlook Express files to Outlook.

Exit Outlook

When you are done using Outlook, you can shut it down:

- Click the **File** menu and click **Exit**.

  –Or–

- Click **Close** on the right of the title bar.

Explore Outlook

Outlook uses a wide assortment of windows, toolbars, menus, and special features to accomplish its functions. Much of this book explores how to find and use all of those items. In this section you'll see the most common features of the default Outlook window, including the parts of the window, the buttons on the principal toolbars, and the major menus. Also, you'll see how to use the Navigation pane and Outlook Today.

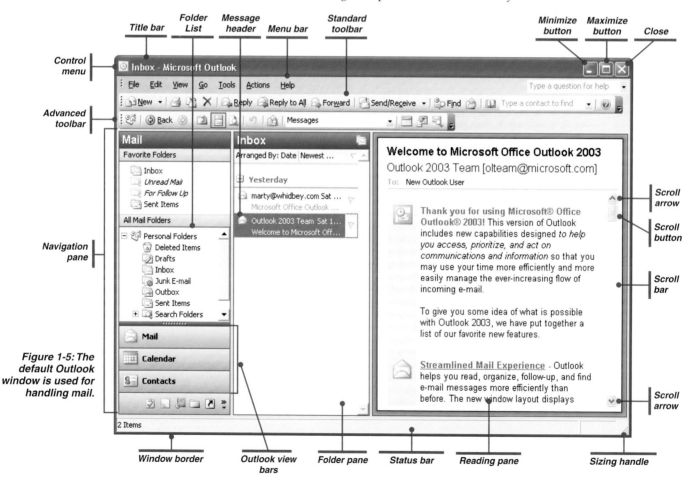

Figure 1-5: The default Outlook window is used for handling mail.

Explore the Outlook Window

The Outlook window takes on a different appearance depending on the function you want Outlook to perform. The initial view when you first start Outlook is for handling mail, as shown in Figure 1-5. The windows for handling other functions are described in the chapters that deal with those functions. The principal features of the Outlook window are described in Table 1-2.

TABLE 1-2: PRINCIPAL FEATURES OF THE OUTLOOK WINDOW

OUTLOOK FEATURES	DESCRIPTION
Title bar	Name of the open folder; contains the controls for the window
Menu bar	Contains the primary controls for Outlook
Standard toolbar	Changes to contain the controls needed for the open folder
Minimize button	Minimizes the window to an icon on the taskbar
Maximize button	Maximizes the window to fill the screen
Close	Exits Outlook and closes the window
Scroll arrow	Moves the contents of the pane in the direction of the arrow
Scroll button	Moves the contents of the pane in the direction it is dragged
Scroll bar	Moves the contents of the pane in the direction it is clicked
Sizing handle	Sizes the window in the direction it is diagonally dragged
Reading pane	Displays the contents of the selected item in the open folder
Status bar	Displays information about what is selected
Folder pane	Displays the contents of the selected folder
Message header	Contains the sender, some part of the date, and some part of the subject
Folder List	Contains the folders within the selected view
Outlook view bars	Provide selection of the various views
Window border	Sizes the window by dragging
Navigation pane	Contains the means for selecting what you want to do and look at
Advanced toolbar	Provides additional controls to those on the Standard toolbar
Control menu	Contains controls for the window itself

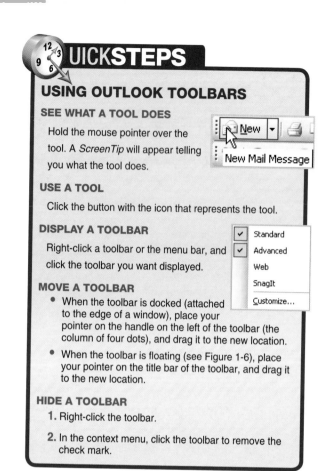

QUICKSTEPS

USING OUTLOOK TOOLBARS

SEE WHAT A TOOL DOES

Hold the mouse pointer over the tool. A *ScreenTip* will appear telling you what the tool does.

USE A TOOL

Click the button with the icon that represents the tool.

DISPLAY A TOOLBAR

Right-click a toolbar or the menu bar, and click the toolbar you want displayed.

MOVE A TOOLBAR

- When the toolbar is docked (attached to the edge of a window), place your pointer on the handle on the left of the toolbar (the column of four dots), and drag it to the new location.
- When the toolbar is floating (see Figure 1-6), place your pointer on the title bar of the toolbar, and drag it to the new location.

HIDE A TOOLBAR

1. Right-click the toolbar.
2. In the context menu, click the toolbar to remove the check mark.

TIP

When you drag a toolbar next to the edge of the window, it automatically attaches itself to the window and becomes docked.

Display the Advanced Toolbar

By default the Advanced toolbar shown in Figure 1-5 is not displayed. You can display it:

1. Click the **View** menu and click **Toolbars**. The Toolbars menu will be displayed.

2. Click the **Advanced** toolbar. A check mark appears next to it, and the toolbar displays on the screen.

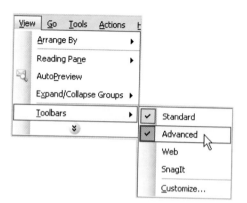

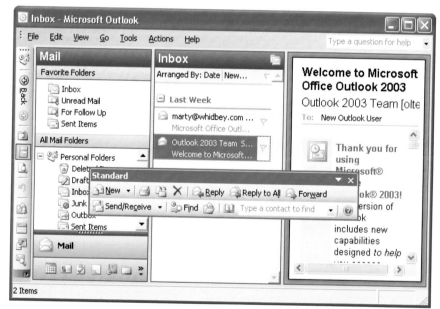

Figure 1-6: A toolbar can be attached to any edge of the Outlook window, or it can be floating in or out of the window.

Use the Navigation Pane

There are three main areas of the Navigation pane, as shown in Figure 1-7:

- **Folder List** at the top where you can select the folder to open
- **Outlook view bars** in the middle where you can select the view in which to work
- **Button bar** at the bottom to hold and access views not in the view bars

SELECT A VIEW

The Outlook view determines which area of Outlook you will work in—for example, Mail, Calendar, or Contacts. To select a view:

- Click the appropriate view bar.

  –Or–

- Click the appropriate button in the button bar.

  –Or–

- Click the **Go** menu, and then click the desired view.

OPEN A FOLDER

The folder that is open determines which specific documents you will work on, for example, incoming messages in the Inbox folder or notes in the Note folder. To open a folder:

- Click the appropriate folder in the Folder List.

  –Or–

- Click the related view in the view bar, button in the button bar, or view in the Go menu.

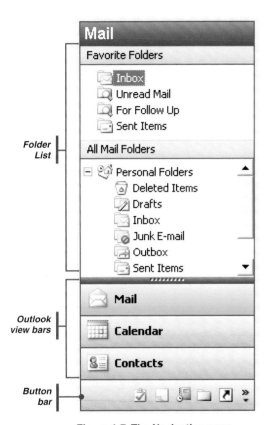

Figure 1-7: The Navigation pane provides the primary control of which area and which folder you are working with.

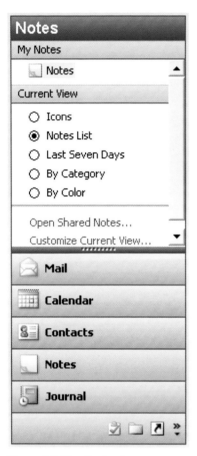

Figure 1-8: The Navigation pane can take on different appearances depending on the current view and how you tailor the Outlook view bars.

DISPLAY VIEW BARS

The number of view bars displayed depends on the size of the Outlook window and the size of the area dedicated to the view bars, as shown in Figure 1-8. To change the number of view bars displayed:

- Drag the bottom window border up or down.

  –Or–

- Drag the handle between the top view bar and the bottom of the Folder List.

DISPLAY BUTTONS

The buttons in the button bar are just an extension of view bars. When you reduce the number of view bars, the options become buttons on the button bar. To change the buttons on the button bar, in addition to changing the number of view bars that are displayed:

1. Click the **button menu** button on the right of the button bar.

2. Click **Add Or Remove Buttons**, and then click the button you want to add or remove.

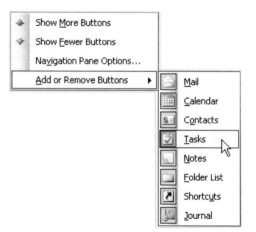

QUICKSTEPS

USING MENUS

Menus are the foundational means of control in Outlook. Many, if not most, of the menu options are also on toolbars or some other control. When you can't find a control, though, look at the menus.

OPEN A MENU WITH THE MOUSE

Click the menu.

OPEN A MENU WITH THE KEYBOARD

Press **ALT+** the underlined letter in the menu name. For example, press **ALT+F** to open the File menu.

File

EXPAND A MENU

By default, when you open a menu, only the most common options are displayed. To see the full menu:

- Click the downward-pointing arrowheads at the bottom of the menu.

Exit
⌄

  –Or–
- Wait a few seconds and the menu will automatically expand.

OPEN A SUBMENU

A number of menu options have a right-pointing arrow on their right indicating that there is a submenu associated with that option. To open the submenu:

Move the mouse pointer to the menu option with a submenu, and the submenu will open.

File	Edit	View	Go	Tools		
New		▶			
Open		▶		Selected Items	Ctrl+O
Close All Items				Other User's Folder...	
Save As...				Outlook Data File...	

SELECT A MENU OPTION

To select a menu option:

Click the menu to open it, and then click the option.

CLOSE THE NAVIGATION PANE

If you need more room to display a folder and its contents, you can close the Navigation pane:

- Click the **View** menu and click **Navigation Pane**.

  –Or–
- Press **ALT+F1**.

Use Outlook Today

Outlook Today gives you a summary of the information in Outlook for the current day. You can see a summary of your messages, your appointments and meetings, and the tasks you are slated to do, as shown in Figure 1-9.

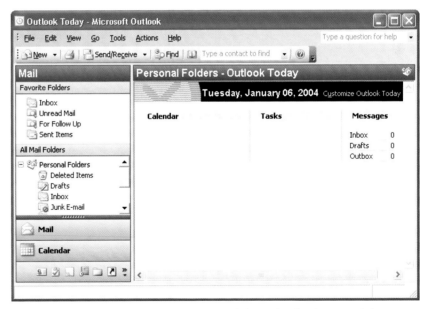

Figure 1-9: Outlook Today provides summary information for the current day.

OPEN OUTLOOK TODAY

- Click the **Go** menu, click **Shortcuts** to open the Short-cuts panel in the Navigation pane, and click **Outlook Today**.

- If the Advanced toolbar is open, click the **Outlook Today** icon.

CHANGE OUTLOOK TODAY

Click **Customize Outlook Today** in the upper-right of the Outlook Today folder. Customize Outlook Today will open as shown in Figure 1-10.

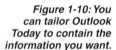

Figure 1-10: You can tailor Outlook Today to contain the information you want.

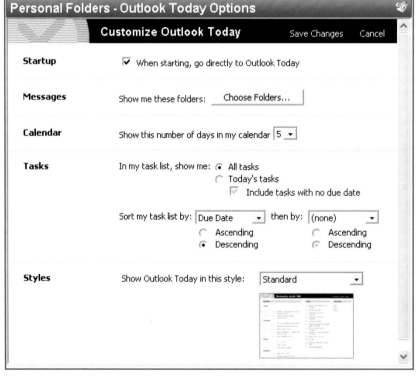

Figure 1-11: The Outlook Help task pane provides links to several avenues of online and offline assistance.

MAKE OUTLOOK TODAY YOUR DEFAULT PAGE

To make Outlook Today the default you see when you open Outlook:

1. In the Customize Outlook Today pane, opposite Startup, click **When Starting, Go Directly To Outlook Today**.

2. Click **Save Changes**.

Get Help

Microsoft provides substantial assistance to Outlook users. Outlook tailors much of the assistance offered to whether you are working online or offline. If you are offline, you will get a quick but more limited help. If you are or can be online, it will be slower, but more comprehensive.

Access Help

Access Help using one of these techniques:

DISPLAY THE OUTLOOK HELP TASK PANE

The Outlook Help task pane, shown in Figure 1-11, provides links to several assistance tools and forums, including a table of contents, access to downloads, contact information, and late-breaking news on Outlook. To display the Outlook Help task pane:

- Click the **Help** menu to open it, and select **Microsoft Office Outlook Help**.

  –Or–

- Click the **Microsoft Office Outlook Help** icon on the Standard toolbar.

  –Or–

- Press **F1**.

QUICKSTEPS

USING HELP

PRINT A HELP TOPIC

Click the **Print** icon in the Help topic dialog box toolbar.

SHOW/HIDE THE OFFICE ASSISTANT

Click the **Help** menu and click **Show The Office Assistant** or **Hide The Office Assistant**, depending on whether you want to show or hide it.

NOTE

When you turn off the Office Assistant or the Type A Question For Help box, you are not deleting it—you are just hiding it.

ASK A QUESTION

Quickly ask a question about Outlook directly from the menu bar without use of the Outlook Help task pane:

1. Type your question in the **Type A Question For Help** text box on the right of the menu bar.

   > Type a question for help ▾

2. Press **ENTER**. The Search Results pane will open, as you can see in Figure 1-12. Click one of the search results, and the Microsoft Office Outlook Help will open and display the requested information.

HIDE THE TYPE A QUESTION FOR HELP BOX

To remove the display of the Type A Question For Help box:

1. Click the **Tools** menu and click **Customize**. The Customize dialog box will open.

2. Right-click the **Type A Question For Help** box on the menu bar.

3. Click the check mark beside the **Show Ask A Question** box, removing the check mark.

4. Click **Close** on the dialog box. When the dialog box is closed, the text box will be removed from the menu bar.

Figure 1-12: From the Search Results pane, you can search both online and offline Help as well as other sources.

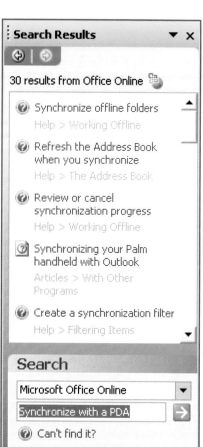

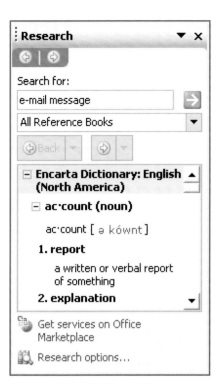

Figure 1-13: In the Research pane, you can search a dictionary, a thesaurus, an encyclopedia, or several other sources.

When you are working offline, only the reference tools provided with Outlook, such as a thesaurus, are available.

Do Research

Doing research on the Internet using Outlook's Research command, which displays the Research task pane, allows you to enter your search criteria and specify references. You can do research both from a message window and from the main Outlook window.

DO RESEARCH FROM THE MESSAGE WINDOW

1. With a message open in the Message window, select the word or phrase you would like to research.

2. Click the **Tools** menu and click **Research**. The Research pane will open, as you can see in Figure 1-13.

3. Beneath the Search For text box, a reference source is selected. To change the reference source, open the list box by clicking its **down arrow**, and click a reference to be searched.

DO RESEARCH FROM THE OUTLOOK WINDOW

1. Open **Help** in one of the ways described earlier in this chapter.

2. In the Outlook Help pane title bar, open the drop-down list and click **Research**. The Research pane will open.

3. Enter your search criteria in the Search For text box.

4. Beneath the text box, a reference source is selected. To change the reference source, open the list box, and click a reference to be searched.

5. Click the **Go** arrow.

Work with the Office Assistant

The Office Assistant provides tips and messages that may be helpful, as well as providing a way to search and access Help.

TURN THE OFFICE ASSISTANT ON OR OFF

Click the **Help** menu and click **Show The Office Assistant** or **Hide The Office Assistant**.

USE THE OFFICE ASSISTANT

The Office Assistant will observe what you are doing and offer tips and alerts as you go along. In addition, you can click the **Office Assistant**, type a question and click **Search** to search online and offline Help, and open the Search Results pane with the results.

CHANGE THE OFFICE ASSISTANT

The Office Assistant has several different characters you can choose to display in place of the paper clip (called "Clippit") and several options in its use.

1. Click the **Office Assistant** and click **Options**. The Office Assistant dialog box will open.

2. Click the **Gallery** tab, and click **Next** and **Back** to scroll through the various characters that are available.

3. Click the **Options** tab and select how you want to use the Office Assistant, as shown in Figure 1-14. Click **OK**.

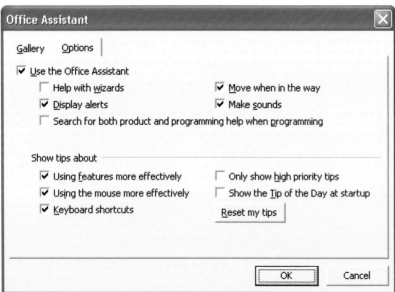

Figure 1-14: The Office Assistant can provide tips and alerts, as well as a means to search Help.

QUICKSTEPS

SETTING PREFERENCES

Setting preferences allows you to adapt Outlook to your needs and inclinations. The Options dialog box provides access to these settings.

1. Click the **Tools** menu and click **Options** to open the Options dialog box.

2. Click the **Other** tab, which opens as shown in Figure 1-15.

HANDLE DELETED ITEMS

If desired, click **Empty The Deleted Items Folder Upon Exiting**.

SET NAVIGATION PANE CONTENTS

1. Click **Navigation Pane Options**.

2. Ensure that the Outlook views you want in the Navigation pane are selected (checked).

3. Move the views you want in the view bars to the top of the list by selecting a view and clicking **Move Up**, or by selecting a view you don't want in the view bars and clicking **Move Down**.

4. When the Navigation pane is the way you want it, click **OK**.

Continued...

Customize Outlook

Outlook provides a number of ways to customize both how it looks as well as how it operates. Some of these ways to customize have already been discussed in this chapter, and others will be discussed in later chapters. Here you'll see how to set general and security preferences, how to customize the toolbars and menus, how to create a user profile, and how to update Outlook.

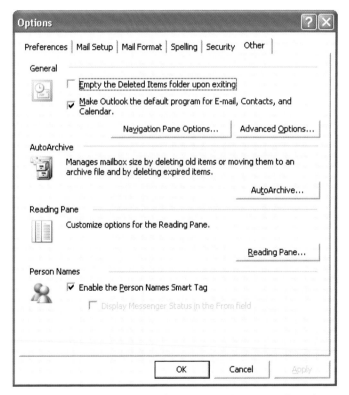

Figure 1-15: The Tools Options Other tab provides a number of general preference settings.

SETTING PREFERENCES *(Continued)*

SET ADVANCED OPTIONS

1. Click **Advanced Options** (see Figure 1-16).

2. Click **Browse**, click the folder you want displayed at startup, and click **OK**.

3. Review and select (check mark) the General and Appearance options that are correct for your situation.

4. When you have set the Advanced Options as you want, click **OK**.

SET SECURITY OPTIONS

1. Click the **Security** tab and click **Zone Settings**.

2. Click **OK** to the message that you are about to change security settings. The Security dialog box will open.

3. Click one of the four security zones at the top of the dialog box, click **Default Level**, and adjust the slider for the level you want applied to that zone, as shown in Figure 1-17.

4. Click **Sites**, select or enter the information required for that zone, and click **OK**.

5. When all of the sites you want have been entered and all of the zones have been handled, click **OK** twice.

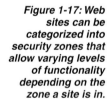

NOTE

Preferences in each of the major areas—Mail, Calendar, Tasks, Contacts, and Notes—are set in the chapters that discuss those subjects. Here you'll see how to set general and security preferences.

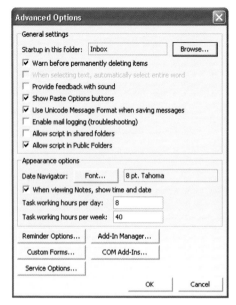

Figure 1-16: Many of the basic preferences in using Outlook are set in the Advanced Options dialog box.

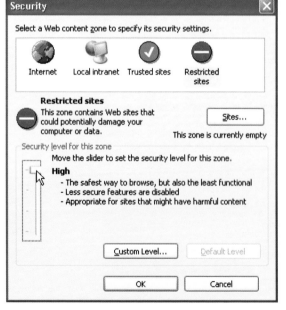

Figure 1-17: Web sites can be categorized into security zones that allow varying levels of functionality depending on the zone a site is in.

Customize Outlook Toolbars

You can customize a toolbar by adding commands or menus to an existing toolbar, or by creating a new toolbar and adding commands or menus to that.

ADD COMMANDS TO THE TOOLBAR

If you find the buttons on the toolbars are not as convenient as you would like, or you frequently use a feature that is not on one of the toolbars, you can rearrange the buttons or add commands to a toolbar.

1. Click the **Tools** menu, click **Customize**, and click the **Commands** tab.

2. Under Categories select the category where the command will be found.

3. Under Commands find the command, and drag it from the dialog box to the location on the toolbar where you want it (see Figure 1-18).

4. Click **Close** when you are finished.

Figure 1-18: You can drag commands from a number of categories both to existing and to new toolbars.

NOTE

As you drag the command from the dialog box to the toolbar, it will initially drag a small rectangle containing an "X," signifying it can't be placed where it is. The rectangle will change into a plus sign, signifying a copy, when the pointer is over the toolbars, and then into an I-beam icon over the individual icons. This I-beam icon marks the insertion point where the command icon will be inserted between the adjoining icons in the toolbar.

TIP

Don't worry about messing things up. You can always click **Reset Menu And Toolbar Usage Data** on the Options tab of the Customize menu to restore the menus and toolbars to default settings.

CREATE A CUSTOM TOOLBAR

You can create a custom toolbar, such as the one shown in Figure 1-19, with the commands on it that you most frequently use, avoid displaying several toolbars, and make more open space for the presentation.

1. Click the **Tools** menu, click **Customize**, and click the **Toolbars** tab.

2. Click **New**. The New Toolbar dialog box will be displayed:

3. Enter the name of the new toolbar, and click **OK**. A small toolbar will appear on the screen with the first few letters of its name in the title bar.

4. Use the steps in the preceding "Add Commands to the Toolbar" to build the toolbar with the commands you want.

DRAG A MENU TO A TOOLBAR

Outlook provides several menus you can add to a custom or existing toolbar.

1. Click the **Tools** menu, click **Customize**, and click the **Commands** tab.

2. Select **Menu Bar** from the Categories list.

3. Drag the menu you want to the destination toolbar. See "Add Commands to the Toolbar," earlier in this chapter, for steps on how to move commands.

DELETE A TOOLBAR

You can delete only custom toolbars that you created.

1. Click the **Tools** menu, click **Customize**, and click the **Toolbars** tab.

2. Click the check box next to the toolbar you want to delete.

3. Click **Delete**. You will be asked if you really want to delete the toolbar.

4. Click **OK** and click **Close**.

Figure 1-19: Here is a custom toolbar that is a mixture of menus and tools that might be used to replace the existing menu and toolbars and allow them to be turned off.

Customize Outlook Menus

Customizing a menu is very similar to customizing a toolbar. It can be done by adding commands to an existing menu, or by creating a new menu and adding commands to it.

ADD COMMANDS TO A MENU

If you find the options on a menu are not as convenient as you would like, or if you frequently use a feature that is not on one of the menus, you can rearrange the options or add commands to become new options on a menu.

1. Click the **Tools** menu, click **Customize**, and click the **Commands** tab.

2. Under Categories select the category where the command will be found.

3. Under Commands find the command, and drag it from the dialog box to the location on the menu where you want it, as shown in Figure 1-20.

4. Click **Close** when you are finished.

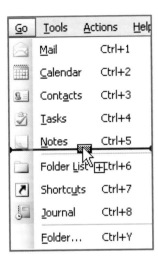

Figure 1-20: An obvious additional menu option is the addition of Outlook Today to the Go menu.

CREATE A CUSTOM MENU

You can create a custom menu with the options on it that you most frequently use.

1. Click the **Tools** menu, click **Customize**, and click the **Commands** tab.

2. Under Categories click **New Menu**. Under Commands drag **New Menu** to the menu bar at the location where you want the new menu.

3. Right-click the new menu, opposite Name enter the name of the new menu, and press **ENTER**.

4. Use the steps in the earlier "Add Commands to a Menu" to build the menu with the commands you want.

USING MULTIPLE USER PROFILES

When you went through the Startup Wizard, as described earlier in this chapter, a default Outlook user profile was created. This profile, which can have multiple mail accounts, as described in Chapter 2, may be the only profile you need. If you wanted to completely separate all of your Outlook folders and files into, let's say, separate personal and business entities, then you want to create multiple user profiles.

CREATE AN ADDITIONAL USER PROFILE

1. If it is open, close **Outlook**.

2. Click **Start**, click **Control Panel**, and in Classic View double-click **Mail**.

Mail

3. In the Mail Setup – Outlook dialog box that opens, click **Show Profiles**, as you can see in Figure 1-21.

4. Click **Add**. Enter the name you want to use for this profile, and click **OK**. The Outlook Setup Wizard will open and ask if you want to add or change an e-mail account.

5. Select **Add A New E-Mail Account**, and click **Next**. Continue as described in "Use the Startup Wizard" earlier in this chapter.

6. When you have completed the Outlook Setup Wizard and returned to the Mail dialog box, click **Prompt For A Profile To Be Used**, and click **OK**.

COPY A USER PROFILE

1. In the Mail Setup – Outlook dialog box, click **Show Profiles**.

2. Click the profile to copy, and click **Copy**.

3. Enter the name of the new profile, and click **OK** twice.

Continued...

DELETE A MENU

You can delete only custom menus that you created.

1. Click the **Tools** menu, click **Customize**, and click the **Commands** tab.

2. Drag the menu off the menu bar and out of the window.

3. Click **Close**.

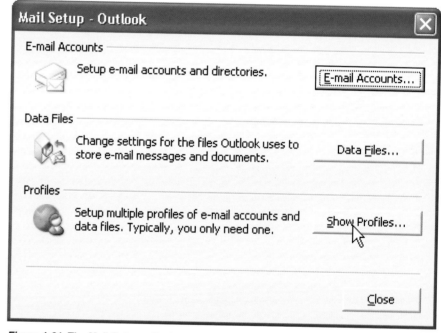

Figure 1-21: The Mail Setup – Outlook window lets you add and modify e-mail accounts, change the location and/or name of the file Outlook uses, or set up multiple user profiles.

Update Outlook

Periodically, Microsoft comes out with updates for Office and Outlook. You can check on available updates, download them, and install them from the Microsoft web site.

1. In the Address text box, type www.office.microsoft.com, and press **ENTER**. Microsoft Office Online will open, as shown in Figure 1-22.

2. Click **Check For Updates** and follow the instructions. Your system will be checked for any necessary updates, and you will be given the opportunity to download and install them if you choose.

3. When you have downloaded the updates you want, close your web browser.

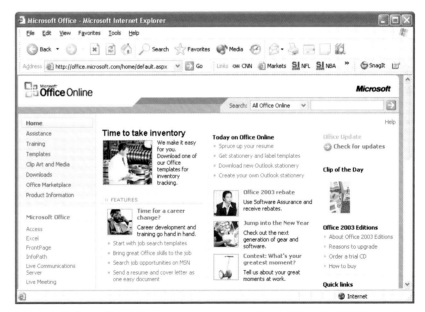

Figure 1-22: One of the primary reasons to check for and download Office and Outlook updates is to get needed security patches.

Chapter 2

Receiving and Handling E-Mail

Most people get Outlook so they can send and receive e-mail. For anyone who has Internet access, e-mail has essentially replaced letter writing. As great as e-mail is, it's possible to get overwhelmed by the amount of mail that arrives, much of it *spam,* or mass-mailed junk. In this chapter, you'll learn how to create e-mail accounts, receive e-mail, and deal with the messages that come in.

Set Up E-Mail

The Internet provides a global pipeline through which e-mail flows; therefore, you need a connection that lets you tap into that pipeline. Both local and national Internet service providers (ISPs) offer e-mail with their Internet connections. At your work or business, you may have an e-mail account over a local area network (LAN) that also connects to the Internet. You can also obtain e-mail accounts on the Internet that are independent of the connection. You can access these Internet accounts (Hotmail, for example) from anywhere in the world. These three ways of accessing Internet e-mail—ISPs, corporate connections, and Internet e-mail—use different types of e-mail systems:

- **POP3** (Post Office Protocol 3), used by ISPs, retrieves e-mail from a dedicated mail server and is usually combined with SMTP (Simple Mail Transfer Protocol) to send e-mail from a separate server.
- **MAPI** (Messaging Application Programming Interface) lets businesses handle e-mail on Microsoft Exchange Servers and LANs.
- **HTTP** (Hypertext Transfer Protocol) transfers information from servers on the World Wide Web to browsers (that's why your browser's address line starts with "http://") and is used with Hotmail and other Internet mail accounts.

Get Online

Whether you choose dial-up or a high-speed service like DSL (digital subscriber line) or cable Internet, getting online requires hardware, software, and some system configuration. It's possible that everything you need is already installed, or that your computer came with extra disks for getting online. First, find an ISP:

- **Get a recommendation** from satisfied friends.
- **Look in the phone book** yellow pages under "Internet Service Providers" or "Internet Access Providers."
- **Find out if ISP software is already loaded**. Click **Start**, click **All Programs**, and then click **Online Services** to see if any software is listed.
- **Check Microsoft Referral Service**, which is a database of large ISPs that Microsoft searches to find the ones that are available in your area code. (You'll need a modem hooked to a phone line for this one; see "Use the New Connection Wizard" next.)

If you find what you want in the Online Services folder, double-click the provider icon and follow the instructions. If you have a disk that came with your computer or from an ISP, pop it in and follow the instructions. If you use a local provider, their tech support people will usually walk you through the entire setup process on the phone. To create a local dial-up connection yourself, or to check with the Microsoft Referral Service, you need to use the New Connection Wizard.

NOTE

In the Control Panel, you can switch between Category view and Classic view by clicking **Switch To Category View** (or **Classic View**) in the Navigation pane.

Control Panel

Switch to Classic View

USE THE NEW CONNECTION WIZARD

1. Click **Start** and click **Control Panel**.

2. In Category view click **Network And Internet Connections**, and then click **Internet Options**.

   –Or–

   In Classic view double-click **Internet Options**. The Internet Properties dialog box will open.

3. Click the **Connections** tab, and then click **Setup**. The New Connection Wizard opens.

4. Click **Next**, choose **Connect To The Internet**, as shown in Figure 2-1, and click **Next** again.

5. Choose how you want to connect to the Internet, and click **Next**.

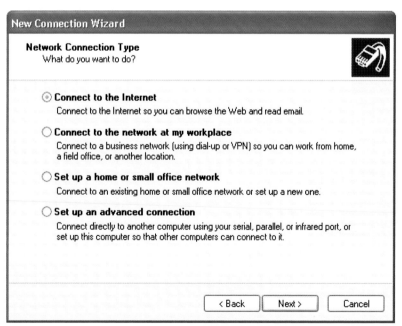

Figure 2-1: Windows XP is designed to make a variety of common network connections easy to create.

6. Depending on your choice, proceed as follows:

- If you selected Choose From A List Of Internet Service Providers, choose between MSN and seeing a list of other ISPs, and then click **Finish**. If you choose MSN, it will begin the process to use that connection, so follow the instructions. If you choose to see a list of other ISPs, the Online Services folder will open. Double-click **Refer Me To More Internet Service Providers**. The Internet Connection Wizard will open, make a call to the Microsoft Referral Service, and then list the national ISPs available in your area; follow the instructions.

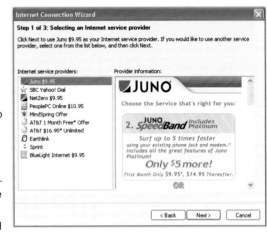

–Or–

- If you chose Set Up My Connection Manually, enter the information you got from your ISP in the remaining pages of the wizard, and click **Finish**.

–Or–

- If you selected Use The CD I Got From An ISP, click **Next**, click **Finish**, insert the CD into your CD drive, and follow the instructions.

NOTE

To get a Hotmail account, you must already have a way to get on the Internet, and the instructions here assume you can do that.

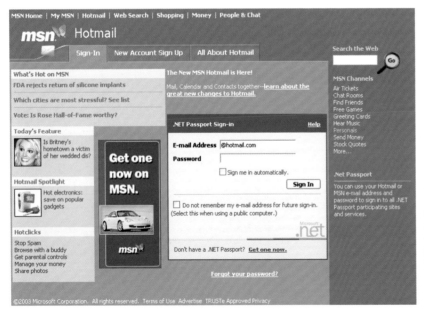

Figure 2-2: The .NET Passport lets you remember a single user name and password to log on to many secure web sites.

COLLECTING ACCOUNT INFORMATION

The information needed to install an e-mail account in Outlook depends on the type of e-mail you choose.

ISP ACCOUNTS
- Type of server: POP or IMAP
- E-mail address
- User name
- Password
- Incoming mail server name
- Outgoing mail server name

HTTP ACCOUNTS (LIKE HOTMAIL)
- Type of server: HTTP
- E-mail address: .NET Passport
- User name
- Password
- Your mail service Internet address—if not Hotmail or MSN, which are provided

Use Hotmail

Hotmail, one of many Internet-based HTTP services, is free, and you can access it from any Internet connection in the world, so you don't even need to own a computer. The easiest way to set up Hotmail is to get a .NET Passport just for Hotmail—even if you already have one using your ISP e-mail address (see Figure 2-2).

SET UP HOTMAIL

1. Click **Start**, click **Internet**, and/or follow any other steps needed for you to get on the Internet and to open your Internet browser. In your browser type www.hotmail.com in the Address text box.

2. Ignore the .NET Passport Sign-In box, and click the **New Account Sign Up** tab.

3. Fill in every field on the registration form. At E-Mail Address enter the name you want for the account, leaving out the "@hotmail.com" part.

4. When you see the message that your account has been created, click **Continue**.

5. Click **FREE E-Mail** at the bottom of the page.

6. Work your way through a few pages of pitches, checking any items you want popping into your Inbox, scrolling to the bottom of the page, and clicking **Continue** until you see that your Hotmail account has been created.

Install Accounts in Outlook

Once you have an e-mail account, you need to tell Outlook where to find the server that stores your mail. As you proceed through the E-Mail Accounts Wizard, you will need some information about the account. See the earlier QuickSteps, "Collecting Account Information," for the information you'll need to enter.

1. Click **Start**, select **All Programs**, choose **Microsoft Office**, and click **Microsoft Office Outlook 2003**. (From now on, we'll assume that you already have opened Outlook.)

2. Click **Tools** and click **E-Mail Accounts**.

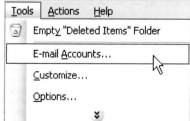

3. Select **Add A New E-Mail Account**, and click **Next**.

4. Select the type of e-mail server used by your provider, and click **Next**.

5. Type your name under User Information, and supply the remaining connection information.

6. Check the **Remember Password** check box if you want to avoid typing your password every time.

7. If it is available to you, click the **Test Account Settings** button to see if everything's working correctly (recommended).

8. If the Test Account Settings dialog box congratulates you, click **Close**, and then, in any case, click **Finish**. If you get an error message and you are sure you typed all the information correctly, contact your e-mail provider's technical support.

TIP

To remove an e-mail account, click **Tools** and click **E-Mail Accounts** to open the wizard. Click **View Or Change Existing E-Mail Accounts**, click **Next**, click the account, click **Remove**, click **Yes**, and click **Close**.

Act on selected message

Simultaneously send and receive e-mail

Show/hide Find bar

Open address book

Search address book

Find bar

Create message

Select a folder

Selected message

Folder pane

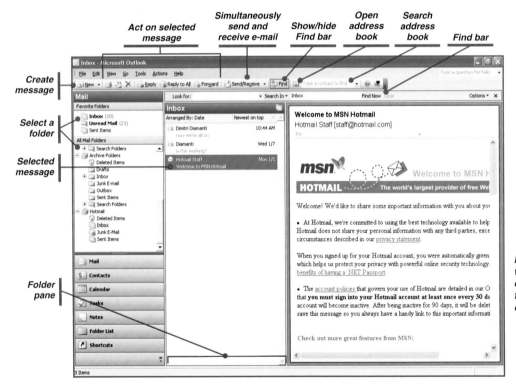

Receive E-Mail

With at least one e-mail account installed in Outlook, you're ready to receive mail. Everything is done from the Outlook Mail folder, shown in Figure 2-3. Be sure to share your e-mail address with the friends you'd like to hear from.

Figure 2-3: The Mail workspace provides one-click access to the most common operations.

Check for E-Mail

Once you are set up, it is very easy to download mail:

1. Make sure you're connected to the Internet or can be automatically connected, and that **Mail** is selected in the Outlook Navigation pane.

2. Click **Send/Receive** on the toolbar.

3. Click the **Inbox** mail folder icon in the Navigation pane, and watch the mail come in.

RECEIVE E-MAIL AUTOMATICALLY

Not only can Outlook periodically check your e-mail provider for you, but it also can do it automatically. Desktop alerts, new to Outlook 2003, are pleasantly subtle, quietly fading in and out.

1. Click **Tools** and click **Options** (see Figure 2-4).

2. Click the **Mail Setup** tab, and click **Send/Receive**.

3. Under the section Setting For Group..., check **Schedule An Automatic Send/ Receive Every**, type or click the spinner to enter the number of minutes to elapse between checking, and click **Close**.

4. If you also want to create a desktop alert telling you when mail arrives, click the **Preferences** tab, click **E-Mail Options**, and click **Advanced E-Mail Options**. Check **Display A New Mail Desktop Alert**, and click **OK** twice.

5. Click **OK** to close the Options dialog box.

TIP

If you like where the old Preview pane was located in earlier versions of Outlook, you can place the Reading pane beneath the Folder pane: click the **View** menu, point at **Reading Pane**, and click an option.

NOTE

If you don't see the Send/Receive button on your toolbar, click **Toolbar Options** at the right end of the toolbar, and click the **Send/Receive** button you see there. After you do that once, it will appear in its normal place.

TIP

You can download messages from a particular e-mail provider if you prefer. Click **Tools**, point to **Send/Receive**, and click the desired account.

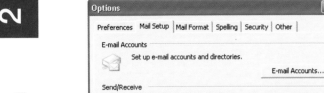

Figure 2-4: The Options dialog box is where you can customize many Outlook processes.

Read E-Mail

Besides being easy to obtain, e-mail messages are effortless to open and read. There are two ways to view the body of the message:

- Double-click the message and read it in the window that opens, as shown in Figure 2-5.

  –Or–

- Click the message and read it in the Reading pane, scrolling as needed.

Of course, you can also control which accounts you check, what kinds of e-mail you let in, and how it is presented to you.

Figure 2-5: An e-mail message window contains all the information and tools you need to respond.

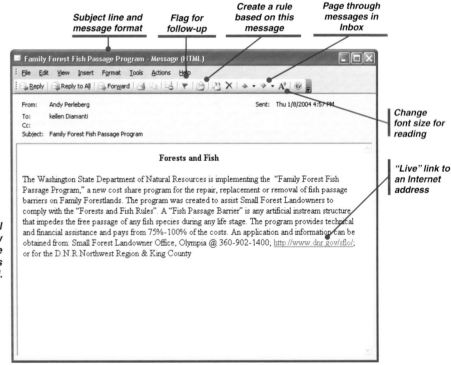

Download Sender and Subject Only

If you are inundated with e-mail or if messages contain really large files (like lots of photos), you might want to choose among your messages for specific ones to download to Outlook. This only works on your POP server e-mail (not on HTTP server e-mail, such as Hotmail).

RECEIVE HEADERS MANUALLY

1. Click **Inbox** (or whatever folder you prefer).

2. Click the **Send/Receive down arrow** on the toolbar, and click **Download Headers In This Folder**.

   –Or–

   Click the **Tools** menu, point at **Send/Receive**, and click **Download Headers In This Folder**. Headers are marked with a special icon.

3. Right-click a header-only message in the folder to open the context menu.

   –Or–

   Double-click a header-only message in the Inbox folder to open the Remote Item Header dialog box.

4. In either case, click one of these options:

   - **Mark To Download This Message** will bring in the whole message next time you click Send/Receive.

   - **Mark To Download This Message And Leave A Copy...** will bring in the whole message next time and still leave the original on the server (handy for checking e-mail on the road).

   - **Mark To Delete This Message...** will cause it to be deleted from the server and from Outlook next time you Send/Receive.

   - **Unmark This Header** Item lets you change your mind about the fate of the message.

5. Repeat the process for all headers, and click **Send/Receive** to perform the actions selected.

RECEIVE HEADERS AUTOMATICALLY

If you want to download only headers from your POP-server accounts every time, you can set up Outlook to do so:

1. Click the **Send/Receive down arrow** on the toolbar, point at **Send/Receive Settings**, and click **Define Send/Receive Groups**.

   –Or–

   Click the **Tools** menu, point at **Send/Receive**, point at **Send/Receive Settings**, and click **Define Send/Receive Groups**.

2. Make sure **All Accounts** is selected, and click **Edit**. All your e-mail accounts are listed on the left.

3. Click on the desired POP account.

4. Under Folder Options, click **Download Headers Only**, as shown in Figure 2-6, click **OK**, and click **Close**.

Figure 2-6: Outlook can be set up to download only headers for all messages.

FILTERING OUT SPAM

Begin by closing the Junk E-Mail folder:

1. Click the **Tools** menu and click **Options**.

2. Click the **Preferences** tab and click **Junk-E-Mail**.

CHOOSE LEVEL OF PROTECTION

Click the **Options** tab and click the desired level of protection.

BUILD ADDRESS LISTS

The Safe Senders, Blocked Senders, and Safe Recipients tabs let you manually create lists of e-mail addresses and domain names.

For each entry, click **Add**, type the information, and click **OK** twice.

UPDATE LISTS QUICKLY

Sender and recipient addresses can be added quickly to the Safe Senders, Blocked Senders, and Safe Recipients lists from an Outlook folder:

Right-click a message whose sender you want to list, select **Junk E-Mail**, and click the appropriate option.

UNBLOCK PICTURE DOWNLOADS

By default picture downloads are blocked to speed e-mail downloading. To change that for specific items:

- **Single message**, click **Click Here To Download Pictures** in the info bar at the top of the message
- **All mail from source** of message, add to Safe Senders list
- **All HTML mail** (not recommended)

Head Off Junk Mail

Outlook can automatically filter out a lot of annoying spam before you ever see it, and it can set aside suspicious-looking messages in a Junk E-Mail folder. It does this in two ways: by analyzing message content based on a protection level you choose, and by having you identify good and bad senders.

Outlook also bars pictures and sounds from being downloaded into messages that contain HTML formatting. Up to now, savvy spammers have been able to design messages that only download images when you open or preview the message. They plant *web beacons* in the messages, which tell their server that they have reached a valid address so that they can send you even more junk. Outlook now blocks both the external content, as shown in Figure 2-7, and the beacon unless you tell it to unblock it.

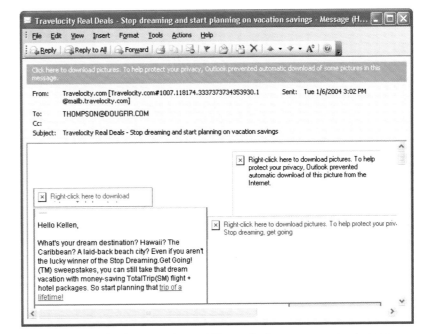

Figure 2-7: Blocking image and sound files protects your computer, but you can easily unblock a message if you want to.

CHOOSE A PROTECTION LEVEL

The amount of junk e-mail you receive suggests the level of protection you need. By default, Outlook sets the level at Low, but you might decide that another option would work better for you. Table 2-1 shows some considerations in choosing a level.

TABLE 2-1: JUNK E-MAIL PROTECTION LEVEL OPTIONS

OPTION	RESULT	PROS	CONS
No Automatic Filtering	Only mail from blocked senders goes to the Junk E-Mail folder.	You have total control.	Your Inbox could be stuffed; you or others might see unsolicited pornography.
Low (default)	Outlook scans messages for offensive language and indications of unsolicited commercial mailings.	The worst of the junk gets caught.	Some canny spammers will still find ways around the protections.
High	Pretty much all the junk e-mail gets caught.	Considerably fewer rude shocks in the Inbox.	Some regular mail will inadvertently get sent to the junk folder.
Safe Lists Only	Only mail from Safe Senders and Safe Recipients lists goes to the Inbox.	Complete protection.	Lots of friendly mail will be junked.
Permanently Delete Suspected Junk E-Mail...	Filtered junk mail never gets onto your computer.	You never have to inspect the Junk E-Mail folder.	Unless you chose the No Automatic Filtering option, you are sure to lose some friendly mail.

ADD ADDRESSES TO FILTER LISTS

The three other tabs in the Junk E-Mail Options window provide means for you to specifically identify good and bad e-mailers:

- **Safe Senders** contains your contacts, so Outlook never identifies their messages as junk, no matter how silly their jokes are. If you subscribe to a newsgroup or some other mass mailing, you might need to specifically add it to the list.

- **Blocked Senders** sends undesirable messages straight to the Junk E-mail folder. It's especially useful to add obnoxious domains to this list so that no address from that source makes it to your Inbox.

- **Safe Recipients** ensures that mailing lists you subscribe to treat you as a safe sender when you contribute messages to the list.

TIP

If you aren't satisfied with the way junk e-mail filtering is being handled, click **Help** and type <u>troubleshoot junk</u> in the **Search** text box (offline is fine), and you'll get an article explaining easy solutions to common issues.

Deal With E-Mail Messages

E-mail has a way of building up fast. Outlook lets you sort your messages just about any way you want. You will learn all about managing folders in Chapter 8, "Managing Files and Folders." For now, we'll consider ways to sort and mark messages so they don't get lost in the crowd.

Mark Messages as Read or Unread

As soon as you select a message so that its contents display in the Reading pane, Outlook marks it as read, and changes it from boldface to plain type. A message can get lost in the pile if it's accidentally selected (all it takes is a single click). You can easily mark it as unread again:

Right-click the message and click **Mark As Unread**.

Flag Messages for Follow-Up

Place colored flags beside messages you want to do something with later. Start by selecting the message, and do one of the following:

- Click in the flag column. A red flag displays.

- Press **INSERT** on the keyboard.

Inbox

⊠ ! ☐ ⬯	Received	From	Subject	Size	▽
	Tue 12/30/2003...	janjacobs1@...	Hubble Photos	12 KB	▽
	Thu 12/25/2003...	gc-orders@a...	Aunt Becky and Uncle David sent you an A...	26 KB	▽
	Thu 12/25/2003...	gc-orders@a...	Aunt Becky and Uncle David sent you an A...	26 KB	▽
	Fri 1/9/2004 12:...	Susan Stoddard	Seattle Times	7 KB	▽
	Fri 1/9/2004 11:...	SELO SELO	Re: RMAP workshops	6 KB	▽

TIP

You're going to receive e-mail tagged with an exclamation point to get your attention. If you disagree with the priority the sender gave it, right-click the message, click **Options**, and pick another level of importance. Click **Close**.

NOTE

Drag over means to drag from one end to the other of some text you want to replace or to highlight.

This places a red flag beside that message and also puts a copy in the For Follow Up folder (look for it in the Search Folders folder). To pick another flag color:

⊟ 🔍 Search Folders
   🔍 **For Follow Up** [2]
   🔍 Large Mail
   🔍 **Unread Mail** (26)

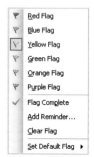

Right-click the flag and click another color.

COLOR-CODE YOUR FLAGS

You can dictate different types of follow-up actions and associate them with specific flag colors. The actions appear as reminders on the info line of the flagged message.

1. Choose one of the following to open the Flag For Follow Up dialog box:

   - In the Folder pane, right-click the flag column and click **Add Reminder**.

   - In the open message window, click **Follow Up** (the flag) on the toolbar.

2. Click the **Flag To** drop-down list, and click an action.

   –Or–

   Type your own action in the **Flag To** text box.

3. Click the **Flag Color** drop-down list, and pick one to associate with the action.

4. Click the **Due By** drop-down list, click a date, and, next to that, choose a time if desired.

5. Click **OK** when you have the flags the way you want them.

NOTE

Whenever a menu displays the expansion button at the bottom of the list, pointing at it will expand the list.

NOTE

A plus (+) or minus (–) sign to the left of an item indicates that you can expand or contract a list by clicking the sign.

TIP

You can assign multiple items to a category at one time, by pressing and holding **CTRL** while you click on each item. Then right-click one of the items, click **Categories**, and assign them. If some in the group are already assigned, a checked box will be shaded gray. To add them to the category anyway, click the check mark until there is no shading behind it. To remove all selected items from the category, click the check mark until the box is clear.

Arrange the Inbox

Outlook contains 13 types of Inbox arrangements. You can have Outlook organize messages by the date they were sent, which Outlook uses by default; alphabetically by who sent them or by first word in the subject line; or by clustering those with attachments, colored flags you give them, or categories you created for your own use. Outlook can even group *conversations*, e-mail exchanges in which senders clicked Reply, thus preserving the subject line. To arrange messages:

1. Click **Inbox** or the specific mail folder in the navigation bar on the left side.

2. Click the **View** menu, point to **Arranged By**, and click one of the kinds listed.

ADD CATEGORIES

Mail is only one kind of item that you can categorize. You can assign categories to whatever you create in Outlook—tasks, appointments, contacts, notes, journal entries, and documents. You can also create new categories in the list:

1. Right-click a message (or other item), and click **Categories**. The Categories dialog box opens.

2. Do one of the following:

    ● Check one or more categories for the item.

    ● Type a name in the **Item(s) Belong To These Categories** text box, and click **Add To List**. When you have selected or added the categories you want, click **OK**.

3. View items sorted into categories by clicking the **View** menu, selecting **Arrange By**, and clicking **Categories**.

Make Up Your Own Rules

When it comes to sorting e-mail, you can make up the rules as you go along, and Outlook will follow them. Or you can pick from a list of predefined rules for common situations, like having Outlook send a message to your cell phone if you win an eBay auction, or flag all messages from your daughter at college for follow-up. (This only works for POP3 server accounts.)

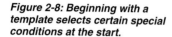

Figure 2-8: Beginning with a template selects certain special conditions at the start.

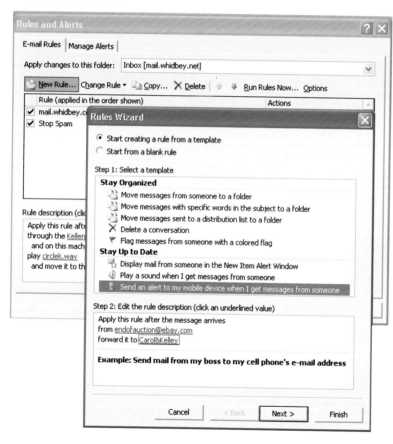

1. With Mail selected click the **Tools** menu, and click **Rules And Alerts**. Click **OK** to acknowledge that HTTP mail cannot be filtered.

2. Click the **Apply Changes To This Folder** drop-down list, and select a folder (such as the Inbox).

3. Click **New Rule** and click one of the options:

   - Click **Start Creating A Rule From A Template**, which abbreviates the remaining steps by combining some components and letting you enter the details earlier, as shown in Figure 2-8.

   - Click **Start From A Blank Rule**, which lets you build a completely custom rule.

4. Click an opening scenario in the upper box (it displays in the description box below it), and click **Next**.

5. Click all conditions under which you want the rule applied, clicking any underlined value and changing it as needed. The information is added to the scenario.

6. Step through the wizard, selecting circumstances and actions, changing values as needed, and clicking **Next**.

7. Type a name for the rule where requested, click an option specifying when the rule goes into effect, click **Finish**, and click **OK**.

UICKSTEPS

MANIPULATING THE RULES

The first page of the Rules Wizard lists current rules under the names you gave them.

LEARN THE RULES

Select a rule in the list, and review it in the description pane below it.

CHANGE THE RULES

1. Click a rule in the list, click **Change Rule**, and click an action from the drop-down list.

   –Or–

   Double-click the rule to open the wizard.

2. If you opened the wizard, change the contents as needed, click **Finish**, and click **OK**.

3. If you selected an option with a picture beside it, add any requested information or fill in any new underlined variable in the description, and click **OK** as many times as it takes to close the window.

MAKE A SIMILAR RULE

1. Click a rule in the list, click **Copy**, and click **OK**.

2. Double-click the copy.

3. Step through the wizard, tweaking settings as necessary.

4. Give the rule a new name, and click **Finish**.

CANCEL A RULE

1. Select a rule in the list, and click **Delete**.

2. Click **Yes**.

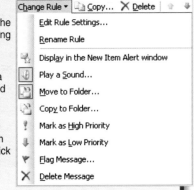

Continued...

Find a Message

No matter how many messages your e-mail folders contain, Outlook can help you find a specific one. You can narrow the search by having Outlook search only certain folders, but you can choose as many of them as you like.

1. Click **Find** in the Standard toolbar.

   –Or–

   Click the **Tools** menu, choose **Find**, and click **Find**.

2. In the **Look For** text box, type any words that you know the message contains.

3. Click **Search In** and click a selection to narrow the search.

4. If you clicked **Choose Folders**, check all the specific folders and subfolders, expanding the lists by clicking ⊞ on the left, and click **OK**.

5. Click **Find Now**. The Reading pane will list all messages that fit the criteria you entered.

6. If necessary, click **Clear** to start over.

Archive Messages

Archiving is for people who have a hard time throwing things away. Outlook is set up on a schedule, which you can see:

Click **Tools**, click **Options**, click the **Other** tab, and click **AutoArchive**.

MANIPULATING THE RULES
(Continued)

REORDER THE RULES

You might want rules to be applied in a certain order:

1. Select a rule in the list.
2. Click the **Move Up** or **Move Down** button until the rule resides where you want it in the sequence.

BASE A RULE ON A MESSAGE

1. Right-click the message and click **Create Rule**.
2. Check the desired options in the Create Rule dialog box.
3. To use the more detailed specifications in the wizard, click **Advanced Options**, step through the wizard with information from the dialog box supplying some of the underlined values, and click **Finish**.
4. If using the Create Rule dialog box, click **OK** twice.

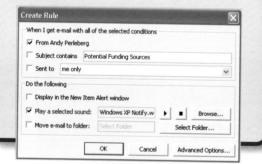

NOTE

Remember to delete the contents of the Sent folder. It can get huge.

When you see the polite little note asking if you are ready to archive files, you can click **Yes** and be assured of finding the messages later. They are saved in a file structure that mirrors your Personal folders yet compresses the files and cleans up the Inbox. To open archived files, use one of these methods:

- Click ⊞ beside Archive Folders in the Navigation pane, and click a folder.
- Click the **File** menu, point to **Open**, click **Outlook Data File**, and click a file.

Either way, archived files, saved in .pst format, display in the Reading pane. You can search them to find the message you want.

Delete Messages

Outlook creates two stages for deletion by providing a Delete folder, which holds all the things you deleted from other folders.

DELETE MESSAGES FROM THE INBOX

Start by clicking a message in the Inbox, and then:

- **Delete one message** by selecting a message and clicking **Delete** on the toolbar.
- **Delete a block of messages** by clicking on the first message, pressing and holding **SHIFT**, clicking on the last message (all the messages in between are selected as well), and clicking **Delete** on the toolbar.
- **Delete multiple unconnected messages** by pressing **CTRL** while clicking on the messages to be removed; then click **Delete** on the toolbar.

EMPTY THE DELETE FOLDER

1. Click the **Deleted Items** folder.
2. Choose one:
   - Select files to delete permanently as you did earlier, click **Delete**, and click **Yes**.
   - Press **CTRL+A** to select the entire folder, click **Delete**, and click **Yes**.

Manage Attachments

Messages that contain extra files, such as pictures and documents, display a paper clip in the Reading pane to show that there's more to see. In the message itself, attachments are listed below the subject line, as shown in Figure 2-9. Since computer vandals like to broadcast debilitating viruses by way of attachments, you should be sure that you are dealing with a trusted source before you open one. An important protection, of course, is antivirus software added to your system, as well as provided by your ISP. Make sure you have it, and keep your virus definitions up to date.

When a message comes in with an attachment, you can open it right away or save it first.

OPEN ATTACHMENTS

Either in the opened message or in the Reading pane:

Double-click the attachment icon, and click **Open**.

Figure 2-9: A single message can contain one or many attachments consisting of all kinds of files.

SAVE ATTACHMENTS

If you have My Computer or Windows Explorer open to the folder where you want to save the attachment, you can drag the attachment there. Otherwise:

1. Right-click the attachment icon, and click **Save As**.

2. Use the Save In dialog box to navigate to the desired folder.

3. Type a name in the File Name text box, and click **Save**.

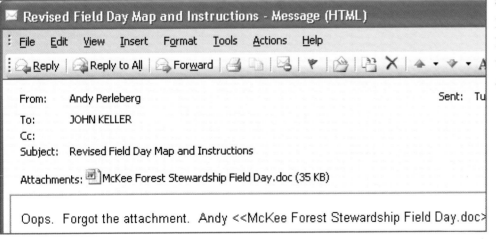

SAVE EMBEDDED ATTACHMENTS

If a photo or other file shows up in the e-mail message body, as shown in Figure 2-10, you can still save it separately.

> Right-click the item in the message, click **Save Picture As**, and save as you would other attachments.

OPEN SAVED ATTACHMENTS

1. Navigate to the folder where you saved the file.
2. Double-click the file.

Figure 2-10: You can choose to save just one picture in the message if you like.

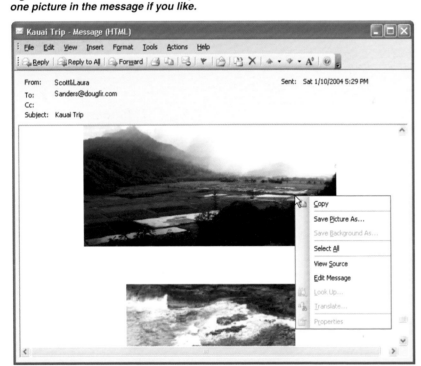

Figure 2-10: You can choose to save just one picture in the message if you like.

Print Messages

Occasionally you get something that you want to print and pass around or save as a hard copy. Outlook lets you print in a hurry with the default print settings or control certain parts of the process.

PRINT IN A HURRY

Right-click the message or an attachment, and click **Print**.

CHOOSE PRINT SETTINGS

1. Select or open the message.
2. If the message is selected, click **Print** on the Outlook toolbar. If it's opened, click **Print** on the message toolbar.
3. Enter your preferences in the Print dialog box.
4. If desired, click **Properties**, dictate the layout or quality, and click **OK**.
5. Click **OK** to begin printing.

Chapter 3
Creating and Sending E-Mail

As the saying goes, you have to send mail to get mail. The beauty of Outlook e-mail is that the messages are so easy to send and respond to that you can essentially carry on conversations. Outlook also makes it just as easy to send a message to one person or to 50, bedeck messages with fancy backgrounds known as *stationery,* insert links to Internet sites, include pictures, and even add a distinctive signature. In this chapter you will learn how to create and enhance messages, as well as how to send copies, respond to others, restrict access, and control how and when e-mail is sent.

Write Messages

Creating an e-mail message can be as simple as dispatching a note or as elaborate as designing a marketing poster. It's wise to get used to creating simple messages before making an art project of one. Without your having to impose any guidelines, however, Outlook is set to create an attractive basic e-mail message.

Create a Message

One click starts a message, and the only field you have to complete is the address of the recipient. Normally, at least three fields are filled in before you send the message:

- **Recipient**   One or more e-mail addresses or names in your address book
- **Subject**   Words indicating the contents of the message (used by the Find tool in a search)
- **Message body**   Whatever you want to say to the recipient

To start a message:

Click the **New** button on the toolbar. The new message window opens as shown in Figure 3-1.

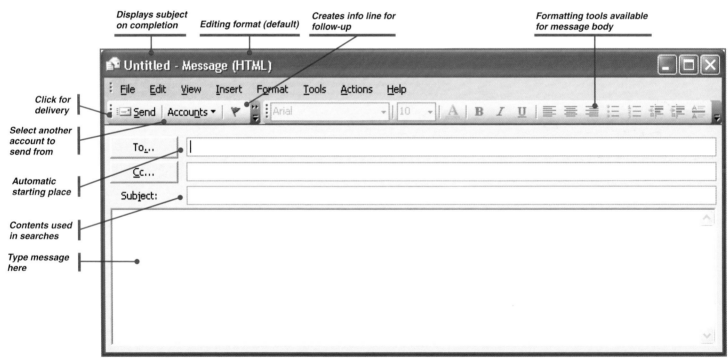

Displays subject on completion

Editing format (default)

Creates info line for follow-up

Formatting tools available for message body

Click for delivery

Select another account to send from

Automatic starting place

Contents used in searches

Type message here

Figure 3-1: The window for creating a message contains important differences from the one in which you read them.

Address a Message

Outlook is the lazy person's dream for addressing messages. Of course, the address itself is simple: *username@domain.suffix* (such as "com"). Once you have entered names in the Contacts workspace, however, you can address your messages with almost no typing. See Chapter 4, "Managing Contacts," for a complete explanation of filling out the address book. In this chapter we will focus on what happens to the e-mail itself. The following alternatives come into play as soon as you create a new message by clicking **New** on the toolbar.

TYPE THE ADDRESS

This is the most basic addressing technique. As soon as you click **New**, the cursor blinks in the To field on the message, and for:

- **A single recipient**, type the address
- **Multiple recipients**, type each address, separating them with semicolons (;)

SELECT FROM THE ADDRESS BOOK

1. Click **To**. The Select Names dialog box displays your address book.

2. Choose one of the following:

   - Type the first letter of the recipient's name in the Type Name Or Select From List text box, and double-click the name when it displays in the table.

   - Scroll the table and double-click the name when it displays.

3. For multiple names, choose one:

   - Repeat either method as needed until all desired names are listed below at To.

   - Press and hold **CTRL** while you click all desired names, and then click **To**.

4. Click **OK**.

COMPLETE ADDRESSES AUTOMATICALLY

Outlook runs AutoComplete by default. So as soon as you type the first letter of an address, Outlook begins searching for matches from among names and addresses you've typed in the past.

NOTE

Even if a name appears in your address book, the name won't be suggested by AutoComplete unless you have used it to send e-mail.

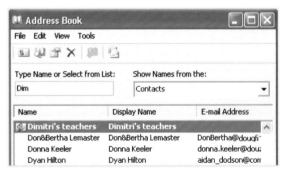

1. Begin typing a name or address after To in the message window.

2. If the name you want appears in the list, press **DOWN ARROW** until the name is highlighted.

3. Press **ENTER** to accept the address. The name displays, a semicolon follows it, and the cursor blinks where the next name would appear.

4. If you wish to add another recipient, begin typing another name, and repeat the process as needed.

5. Press **TAB** to go to the next desired field.

Use a Distribution List

If you group your contacts into distribution lists (see Chapter 4), you will have an even quicker way to add multiple addresses to messages. Use any of the preceding procedures, and enter or select the name of the distribution list as it appears in the address book. When you send it, the message will go to everyone on the list.

Add Carbon and Blind Copies

You may never have seen a real carbon copy, but Outlook keeps the concept alive by way of this feature located just below To in the new message window. Persons who receive a message with their e-mail address in the *Cc* (carbon copy) line understand that they are not the primary recipients; they got the message as an FYI (for your information). All other recipients can see to whom the copy was sent. A *Bcc* (blind carbon copy) hides addresses entered in that line from anyone else who receives the message, as shown in Figure 3-2.

NOTE

You can turn AutoComplete off if you wish. Click **Tools**, click **Options**, and click the **Preferences** tab. Then click the **E-Mail Options** button, click **Advanced E-Mail Options**, and deselect (click to remove the check mark) **Suggest Names While Completing To, Cc, And Bcc Fields**. Click **OK** three times to close.

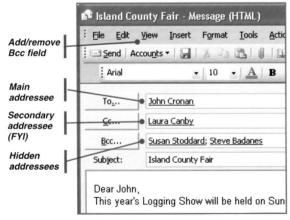

Add/remove Bcc field

Main addressee

Secondary addressee (FYI)

Hidden addressees

Figure 3-2: The way a message is addressed suggests different roles for the various recipients.

INCLUDE BCC FIELD ON NEW MESSAGES

1. Click **New**.

2. Click **View** in the new message window, and select **Bcc Field**.

REMOVE THE BCC FIELD FROM NEW MESSAGES

Deselect **Bcc Field** in the View menu on a new message.

ADDRESS THE COPIES

Type addresses in the Cc and Bcc fields completely or with the aid of AutoComplete. Use the address book by clicking **Cc** or **Bcc** in the message window and clicking the name(s) in the address book.

Edit a Message

E-mail can be created in any of three formats and with the additional option of using the powerful formatting capability of Microsoft Word for composing messages. Outlook handles all of them quite easily, but sometimes you need to consider your recipients' computer resources and Internet connections.

- **HTML** (Hypertext Markup Language), the default format, lets you go crazy with design elements like colors, pictures, links, animations, sound, and movies—though good taste and the need control the size of the message file might suggest a little discretion.

- **Plain Text** format lies at the other extreme, eliminating embellishments so that any computer can manage the message.

- **Rich Text Format** (RTF) takes the middle ground, providing font choices—including color, boldface, italics, and underlining—basic paragraph layouts, and bullets.

With Outlook you can edit messages you create as well as those you receive. Regardless which of the three formats you choose, some editing processes are always available, as shown in Table 3-1.

TABLE 3-1: *Standard Editing Operations*

To		Do This	
Insert new text in message body		Click where new text belongs, and type new text.	
Indent the start of a paragraph		Click before the first letter of the paragraph, and press **TAB**.	
Replace a	Word	Double-click the word.	Type new text.
	Line	Click left of the line.	
	Paragraph	Double-click left of the paragraph.	
Move a	Word	Double-click the word.	Drag to a new location in the message.
	Line	Click left of the line.	
	Paragraph	Double-click left of the paragraph.	

Using HTML or Rich Text provides a wide range of options for enhancing the appearance of a message. See the "Formatting Messages" QuickSteps for a rundown of common formatting selections. (You can also create the message in another program and copy and paste it into a message body. HTML will preserve the formatting exactly, and Rich Text will come close.)

SELECT A MESSAGE FORMAT

The message format displays on the upper edge of the new message window. To set the default message format:

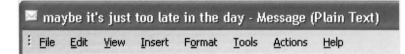

1. In Outlook (not in a message), click the **Tools** menu, select **Options**, and click the **Mail Format** tab, as shown in Figure 3-3.

2. Click the **Compose In This Message Format down arrow**, and select one of the choices.

3. Click **OK** to close the Options dialog box.

SELECT MICROSOFT WORD TO EDIT MESSAGES

If you are used to composing documents with Microsoft Word, selecting that application as your message editor creates a comfortable continuity in the daily work flow by adding to the toolbar such features as automatic corrections, formatting, spelling and grammar checking, as well as Word themes and tables.

1. Click **Tools | Options** and click the **Mail Format** tab.

2. Check **Use Microsoft Office Word 2003 To Edit E-Mail Messages**.

3. Click **OK** to close the Options dialog box.

Provides most powerful format by default

Turns new message window into MS Word document

Preserves formatting upon receipt of Rich Text messages

Helps design custom messages

Creates personalized message closings

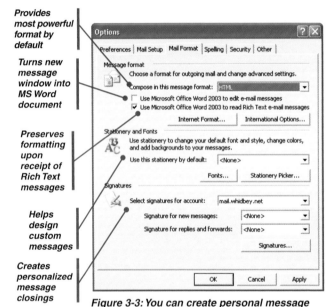

Figure 3-3: You can create personal message designs that distinguish you as the sender.

FORMATTING MESSAGES

You can use the Format menu or the Formatting toolbar in the message window to set up most of the formatting before you start typing, or you can select text and do the formatting once you are finished composing.

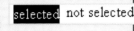

APPLY FORMATTING

To apply formatting to existing text, first see Table 3-1 for a list of selection methods, then for:

- **Fonts**, select a word or line, and use one of the font tasks described next

   selected not selected

- A **paragraph**, click anywhere in the paragraph, and use one of the paragraph tasks

  the cursor

CHOOSE A FONT AND ITS SIZE

A font can immediately set the tone of your message.

1. Click the **Font down arrow**, and select a font.
2. Click the **Font Size down arrow** next to the font, and select a type size.

CREATE BOLD, ITALIC, OR UNDERLINED FONTS

Click the desired effect on the toolbar.

Continued...

TIP

Choose a default font for all messages (until you change it). In Outlook click **Tools | Options**, click the **Mail Format** tab, and click **Fonts** in the Stationery And Fonts panel. Choose any typeface, style, size, and color you desire, and click **OK**.

Use Stationery

Choosing the stationery for a message is fast. You can pick a different type of stationery for every message or set a default style for all messages (until you change it). The default style will be applied to Word mail documents as well.

SET A STANDARD STATIONERY

The first time you click **Use This Stationery By Default**, you might get a message saying that the design hasn't been installed yet. When asked if you want to install it, click **Yes**, and Microsoft Office will install the pattern (no CD necessary).

1. Click **Tools | Options** and click the **Mail Format** tab.
2. Make sure that HTML has been selected as the message format.
3. If you know what you want, click the **Use This Stationery By Default down arrow**, and select a type.
4. If you need to examine what's available, click the **Stationery Picker** button, click any designs listed under Stationery, view them in the Preview pane, and when the one you want appears, click **OK**.
5. Click **OK** to close the Option dialog box.

CHANGE A STATIONERY DESIGN

Designs you create and most designs contained in Outlook can be changed to suit your taste. If the selected design is not available for editing, the Edit button will not be available.

1. Click **Tools | Options**, and click the **Mail Format** tab.
2. Select the design you want to change at Use This Stationery By Default, and click **Stationery Picker**.
3. Click **Edit**. The Edit Stationery dialog box opens.

FORMATTING MESSAGES *(Continued)*

COLOR THE FONT

Click the **Font Color down arrow**, and select a color.

ALIGN PARAGRAPHS

Click an alignment for a straight left margin, centered text, or a straight right margin.

ITEMIZE PARAGRAPHS

If you turn this on before you start typing your list, you will need to turn it off—that is, click the button again—when you finish.

Click the **Bullets** or **Numbering** button on the toolbar.

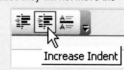

SHIFT THE PARAGRAPH

The Increase Indent and Decrease Indent buttons move the selected paragraph in fixed increments. You can alternate clicking them until you are satisfied with the location. However, because they will not move the paragraph beyond the message margins, they have no effect on centered paragraphs.

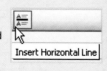

INSERT A HORIZONTAL LINE

Set off paragraphs with lines, to which you can add color for dramatic effect.

* Click where the separation is desired (usually at the end of a paragraph).
* Click the **Insert Horizontal Line** button.
* To add color, click the line to select it. Then click the **Font Color down arrow**, and select a color.

4. To change the typeface, click **Change Font**, make selections as described in the "Formatting Messages" Quick-Steps, and then click **OK**.

5. To add or change a background picture, choose **Picture**, and choose one:

   * Select an Outlook option with the down arrow.

   * Click **Browse**, find the file you want, and click **Select**.

6. To select a solid background color, choose **Color**, click the **Color down arrow**, and select a color.

7. Click **OK** three times.

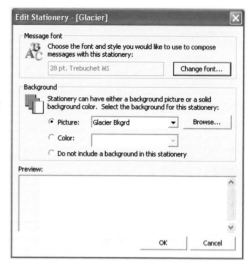

APPLY STATIONERY TO A SINGLE MESSAGE

1. Click the **Actions** menu in the Outlook window, and select **New Mail Message Using**.

2. Choose one:

   * Click the name of the stationery that you or someone else has previously used.

   * If no one has used stationery in Outlook yet or you want more selections, click **More Stationery**, click the designs listed under Stationery, view them in the Preview pane, and when the one you want appears, click **OK**.

REMOVE STATIONERY

To remove stationery from a single message:

Click **Actions | New Mail Message Using**, and select **HTML (no stationery)**.

To stop having standard stationery:

Click **Tools | Options | Mail Format** tab, select **<None>** at Use This Stationery By Default, and click **OK**.

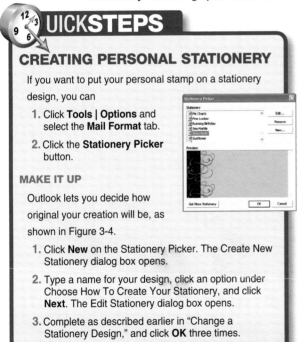

Becomes option in Stationery Picker

Begins with empty page

Provides a design that can be altered

Bases design on a saved HTML page

Goes to Edit Stationery dialog box

Figure 3-4: Starting with blank stationery ensures that backgrounds you choose aren't cluttered by "canned" graphic elements.

QUICKSTEPS

CREATING PERSONAL STATIONERY

If you want to put your personal stamp on a stationery design, you can

1. Click **Tools | Options** and select the **Mail Format** tab.
2. Click the **Stationery Picker** button.

MAKE IT UP

Outlook lets you decide how original your creation will be, as shown in Figure 3-4.

1. Click **New** on the Stationery Picker. The Create New Stationery dialog box opens.
2. Type a name for your design, click an option under Choose How To Create Your Stationery, and click **Next**. The Edit Stationery dialog box opens.
3. Complete as described earlier in "Change a Stationery Design," and click **OK** three times.

Continued...

Include Hyperlinks

You can add hyperlinks by typing them into the message body or by copying and pasting them. Outlook creates a live link, which it turns to a blue, underlined font when you type or paste any kind of Internet protocol (http://, mailto:, www.*something*, Outlook:), regardless what mail format you use. Only HTML, however, will make a live link out of an e-mail address: *something@something*. Also, only in HTML can you substitute different text for the actual URL or e-mail address and still retain the link—by dragging to select the hyperlink and typing something different.

Attach Files

Sometimes you will want to send or receive a message accompanied by other files: pictures, word-processed documents, sound, or movie files, for example. Creating attachments is like clipping newspaper stories and baby pictures to a letter. If you are editing or otherwise working on the item you want to attach, make sure you save the latest version before you proceed. After that:

Click **New** to open the new message window, and use one of the following attachment procedures.

DRAG A FILE INTO A MESSAGE

Find the file to be attached by using My Computer or Windows Explorer, and drag it onto the message.

INSERT A FILE

This procedure gives you the option to enter the contents of some text-based documents directly into the body of the message. The insertion methods available are:

- **Insert** and **Insert As Attachment** both create an Attachment field on the message, insert the file name and an icon representing the file type, and open the Attachment Options dialog box.

- **Insert As Text** enters the file content of certain file types, such as .txt and .eml, and the source code of others, such as HTML or HTA. Everything else—documents, pictures, sound—would just generate nonsense characters in the message body.

QUICKSTEPS

CREATING PERSONAL STATIONERY (Continued)

MAKE IT YOURS

If you like a design you see on e-mail you receive, you can use it—f it hasn't been copyrighted. This process automatically removes the message text and makes a design ready to be used for other messages.

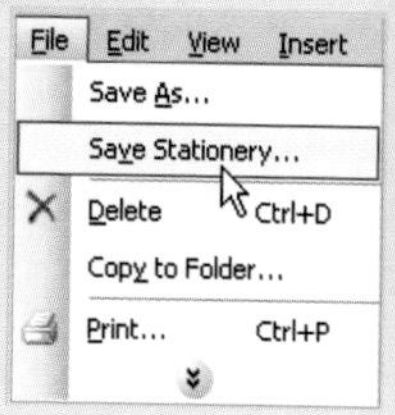

1. Double-click the message to open it.

2. Click **File** and select **Save Stationery**.

3. Type a name for the design, and click **OK**.

File	Edit	View	Insert
Save As...			
Save Stationery...			
✕ Delete	Ctrl+D		
Copy to Folder...			
🖶 Print...	Ctrl+P		
�»			

TAKE A THEME FROM WORD

If Microsoft Office Word 2003 is your e-mail editor, you can use one of the packaged themes in your e-mail.

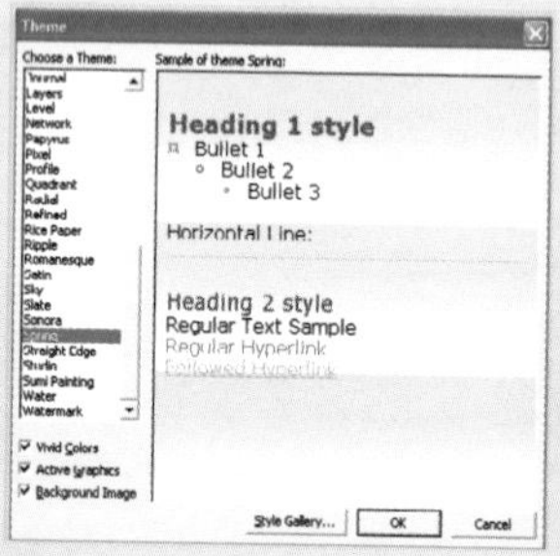

1. Click **New** to open the new message window, and click in the message body.

2. Click the **Format** menu and click **Theme**. The Theme dialog box opens.

3. Select and preview themes until you find one you want, and click **OK**.

NOTE

The Insert menu also allows you to insert an Item, which refers to anything saved in an Outlook folder, such as notes, tasks, contacts, documents, and appointments.

---

1. Choose one:
   - Click the **Insert** menu and then click **File** in the message window.
   - Click the **Insert** icon on the toolbar.

2. Find the saved file by using the Insert File dialog box, and choose one:
   - Click **Insert**.
   - Click the **Insert down arrow**, and select a type of insertion.

Insert

Insert as Text

Insert as Attachment

3. If the Attachment Options dialog box opens, as shown in Figure 3-5, either choose an option and close it, or simply close it.

4. Complete and send the e-mail message.

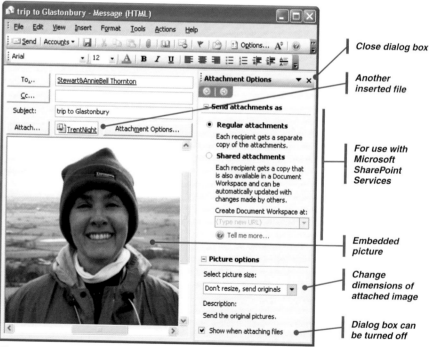

Figure 3-5: The Attachment Options dialog box refers to the item (in this case a picture) that is listed in the field.

EMBED PICTURE INTO MESSAGE

Though any kind of file you save on your computer or on a disk can be sent by following the previous steps, you have the added option of placing pictures (.gif, .jpg, .bmp, .tif, and so on) right into the message body.

1. Click in the message body to set the insertion point.

2. Click the **Insert** menu and click **Picture**. The Picture dialog box opens.

3. Click **Browse**, find the picture, click **Open**, and click **OK**.

4. Complete and send the e-mail message.

Sign Messages

You can create closings, or signatures, for your e-mail messages. Outlook signatures can contain pictures and text along with your name. You can create signatures in different styles for the different kinds of messages you write: friendly, formal, or business.

CREATE A SIGNATURE

1. Click **Tools | Options** and click the **Mail Format** tab.

2. Click **Signatures** and then click **New**.

3. Enter a name for your signature, and click **Next**.

4. Type (or paste from another document) any text you want to include in your closing, including your name.

5. To apply formatting, select the text, click **Font** or **Paragraph**, and make selections as described earlier in the "Formatting Messages" QuickSteps. Plain Text messages, by definition, cannot be formatted.

6. To include a vCard, do one of the following:

- Click the **Attach This Business Card (vCard)... down arrow**, and select a vCard from the list.

USING SIGNATURES

You can use certain signatures for certain accounts, and you can pick a different one for a particular message.

Click **Tools | Options** and click the **Mail Format** tab.

ASSIGN SIGNATURES TO ACCOUNTS

1. Select an account at Select Signatures For Account.

2. Select the name of a signature at Signature For New Messages.

3. Optionally, select the name of a signature at Signature For Replies And Forwards.

4. Click **Apply**.

5. Repeat Steps 1–4 for each of your accounts, and then click **OK**.

INSERT A SPECIAL SIGNATURE

(This is not available if you are using Word as your e-mail editor.)

1. Create an e-mail message.

2. Click in the body of the message where you want the special closing.

3. Click **Insert**, select **Signature**, and click one.

You can also click the signature button on the toolbar and select a signature from the drop-down list.

- Click **New vCard From Contact**, double-click a name in the Select Contacts To Export As vCards list, and click **OK**.

7. Click **Finish** and preview the card.

8. To make changes, click **Edit**, make the changes, and click **OK**.

9. Click **OK** twice to close.

DESIGN A SIGNATURE IN WORD

If you create a signature in Microsoft Office Word 2003, you automatically will be able to use it in Outlook. The advantage is that Word provides options for decorating signatures with pictures and links. Check it out by opening Word; click **Tools | Options**; on the General tab, click **E-Mail Options**; click the **E-Mail Signature** tab and then click **OK** twice to close..

Use Digital Certificates

A *digital signature* certifies that everything contained in the message—documents, forms, computer code, training modules—originated with the sender. Computer programmers and people engaged in e-commerce use them a lot. To embed a formal digital signature, you need to acquire a *digital certificate* (akin to a license) from a certification authority, such as Wells Fargo or VeriSign, Inc.

Alternatively, you can create your own digital signature, though it is not administered by a certification authority. A self-signed certificate is considered unauthenticated and will generate a Security Warning if the recipient has security set at High.

ACQUIRE A DIGITAL CERTIFICATE

If you do not already have a digital certificate, Outlook can lead you to a web site where you can find a commercial certification authority who will issue one. Make sure you are online before you begin.

1. Click **Tools | Options** and click the **Security** tab.

2. Click **Get A Digital ID**.

3. Follow the instructions on the Digital ID web page to obtain a certificate.

CREATE A SELF-SIGNED CERTIFICATE

1. Click **Start**, point to **All Programs | Microsoft Office | Microsoft Office Tools**, and click **Digital Certificate For VBA Projects**. The system will attempt to locate the software.

2. If a message tells you that the file was not found, insert your Microsoft Office CD into the CD drive, or browse to the network location from which you installed Office, and click **OK**. The system will begin configuring the program.

3. Type a name for the certificate in the Create Digital Certificate dialog box, and click **OK**.

4. When a message tells you that the certificate has been created, click **OK**.

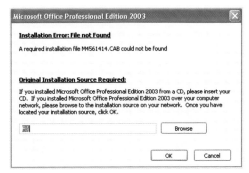

ADD A DIGITAL SIGNATURE

1. In the message window, click the **View** menu and then click **Options**. The Message Options dialog box opens.

2. Click the **Security Settings** button.

3. Check the **Add Digital Signature To This Message** check box.

4. To make sure that recipients can read the message if they don't have S/MIME security, check **Send This Message As Clear Text Signed**.

5. To receive an Inbox message confirming that your message got to the recipient, check **Request S/MIME Receipt For This Message**.

6. Click **OK** and **Close**.

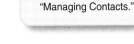

Find out how to save the Digital ID you receive from a sender by reading "Add a New Contact," in Chapter 4, "Managing Contacts."

You can make a backup copy of your digital ID. Click **Tools | Options**, click the **Security tab**, and click **Import/Export**. Choose **Export Your Digital ID To A File**, click **Select**, click the ID to back up, and click **OK**. Type a name at Filename, browse to the desired location, type a password twice, and click **OK** twice.

Spelling

Not in Dictionary:	cribbige
Change to:	cribbage
Suggestions:	cribbage

Ignore | Ignore All
Change | Change All
Add | Suggest
Options... | Undo Last | Cancel

Keep spelling as is

Accept spelling suggestion

Keep spelling and add word to personal dictionary

Reverse last change

Open Spelling tab on Options dialog box

Fwd: HCHY List: Sad Ne

How you doin?

maybe it's just too late

The annual **cribbige** tournament starts tomorrow.

Figure 3-6: The default spelling dictionary contains everyday words rather than technical or scientific terms.

Check Spelling

For all the hip abbreviations that have emerged with e-mail and instant messaging, unintentional spelling errors still mark a person, however unfairly, as uneducated. You can have Outlook spell check your message when you finish, or you can have it automatically search messages before you send them.

CHECK A MESSAGE

1. Create a message and keep the cursor in the body when you are finished.

2. Click the **Tools** menu and then click **Spelling**.

3. If the checker finds an error, decide what action to take (see Figure 3-6).

4. When the spell check is done, click **OK**.

CHECK MESSAGES BEFORE SENDING

1. Click **Tools | Options** and select the **Spelling** tab.

2. Click **Always Check Spelling Before Sending**, and click **OK**.

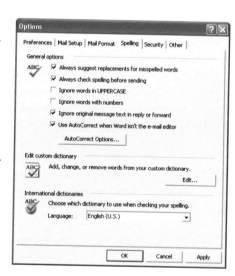

TIP

The personal, or custom, dictionary can get long, and misspellings can be added accidentally. To edit the dictionary from Outlook, click **Tools | Options**, click the **Spelling** tab, and click the **Edit** button. To remove a word, double-click it and press **DELETE**; to correct it, type over the selected word. Click **File | Save**, click **Close**, and click **OK**.

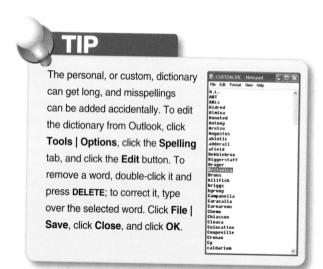

Send Messages

No extra postage, no trip to the post office, no running out of envelopes. What could be better? Once a message is ready to go, you can just click a button. Outlook provides features that let you exercise more control over the process than you could ever get from the postal service, or "snail" mail.

Make sure that your message is complete and ready to send, and then:

Click **Send** on the message toolbar.

The next easiest thing is to send a message from a particular account. Again, make sure that your message is complete, and then:

Click **Accounts** on the message toolbar, select an account as sender, and click **Send**.

Reply to Messages

When you receive a message that you want to answer, it's often best to reply immediately, before you're interrupted by something else. You have three ways to initiate a reply:

- Open the message and click **Reply**.

  –Or–

- Right-click the message in the folder pane, and select **Reply**.

  –Or–

- Click the message in the folder pane, and click **Reply** on the Outlook toolbar.

Whichever way you use, a reply message window opens in the same format the sender used, with Re: and the original subject in the Subject line. By default, the cursor blinks in the message body above the original message and sender's address (see also "Change the Reply Layout," later in this chapter). Treat it like a new message window: type a message, add attachments or links, and click **Send**.

NOTE

The Re: inserted in a reply stands for "in reference to," not "reply" or "response."

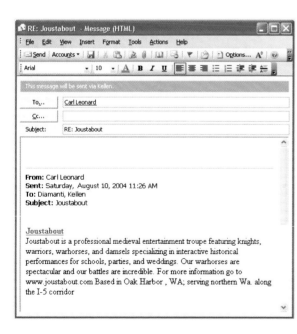

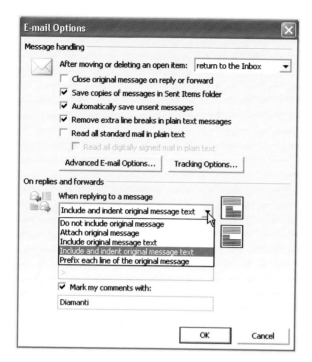

REPLY TO ALL RECIPIENTS

If the To field in the message contains a number of recipients, all of whom should read your reply, Outlook makes it simple. Using any of the three ways just listed, select **Reply To All**. The reply message window will list all original recipients in the To field. Send as usual.

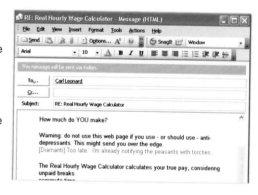

CHANGE THE REPLY LAYOUT

You can select from five different ways to incorporate the original message. Also, if you'd rather just insert your responses into the original text, Outlook lets you decide how to identify your remarks.

1. Click **Tools | Options** and click the **E-Mail Options** button.

2. Click the **When Replying To A Message down arrow**, and select how you want the original message included.

3. Check **Mark My Comments With**, and type the label you want.

SET AUTOMATIC REPLY

Businesses that use Microsoft Exchange Server e-mail can create an automatic reply for when you are not available to answer messages. Each sender will receive only one notification, no matter how many messages he or she sends before you return.

1. Click **Tools** and click **Out Of Office Assistant**.

2. Choose **I Am Currently Out Of The Office**.

3. In the Auto Reply Only Once... panel, type the message you want in your reply.

4. To turn it off, click **Tools**, click **Out Of Office Assistant**, and choose **I Am Currently In The Office**.

5. Click **OK** to close the assistant.

TIP

Even if you use regular e-mail, you can automate a reply with a rule. Turn off Word as your e-mail editor if you're using it. Create a reply message with a suitable subject. Click **File**, click **Save As**, select **Outlook Template** at Save As Type, and click **Save**. Finally, create a new rule as explained in Chapter 2. Start from a blank rule, check messages when they arrive, and click **Next**. Then check and complete any other relevant conditions, and click **Next**. Check **Reply Using A Specific Template**, select the user template, click **Open**, and click **Next**. Complete the rule as usual.

Forward Messages

You can send messages on to new recipients, using the same three ways described earlier in "Reply to Messages." The difference, of course, is that you select **Forward**, instead of Reply. A Forward message window opens, with the cursor blinking in the To field and a space above the original message for you to type your own. Once the forward message window opens, the simplest action is to:

Enter the recipient address(es), insert attachments as needed, and send as usual.

FORWARD MULTIPLE MESSAGES

Rather than forward a bunch of messages one by one, you can bundle them and forward them in one message.

1. Press **CTRL** while click each message in the message list that you want forwarded in the group.

2. Right-click and select **Forward Items**. A new mail message opens with the messages included as attachments.

3. Complete the message and send as usual.

Set Priority

If your recipient gets a lot of messages, you might want to identify your message as important so that it will stand out in his or her Inbox. Outlook sticks a red exclamation point in the message list to call attention to messages set with high importance and a blue down arrow to indicate low importance. In the message window, the info line spells out some details.

1. Create a message.

2. Click **Importance: High** or **Importance: Low** on the Standard toolbar.

   –Or–

   Click **Options** on the message window toolbar, click the **Importance down arrow**, select a level, and click **Close**.

3. Send the message as usual.

> This message was sent with High importance.

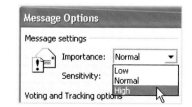

TIP

If the original message had an attachment, you can forward the message without it but keep the attachment with the original. Drag to highlight the attachment, and press **DELETE**.

SENDING MESSAGES

You can fire off your messages now or later or on a schedule.

SEND MANUALLY

As long as you are connected to the Internet, clicking **Send** in the message window posts the completed message.

SEND AT A CERTAIN TIME

1. Create the message and click **Options**.
2. Check **Do Not Deliver Before**.
3. Click the **date down arrow**, and select a day on the calendar.
4. Click the **time down arrow**, and select a time.

SEND AUTOMATICALLY

1. Click the **Send/Receive down arrow** on the toolbar, point to **Send/Receive Settings**, and if Disable Scheduled Send/Receive is checked, click it to deselect.
2. Repeat Step 1 to point to **Send/Receive Settings**, and click **Define Send/Receive Groups**.
3. Select a group (probably All Accounts), and check **Schedule An Automatic Send/Receive Every**.
4. Click the spinner to select the time interval, and click **Close**.

Set Security

Outlook can impose a fairly sophisticated form of security. For most users it's enough to send the message with a notice about its sensitivity, but for some business users confidential messages need to be encrypted.

Once you have a digital ID, you can send encoded messages that only can be deciphered at the other end by a recipient who has the encryption key; therefore, you must first exchange digital IDs with one another.

CLASSIFY MESSAGE SENSITIVITY

A message can be labeled private, personal, confidential, or normal. If either of the first three is selected, notification will display on the info bar when the message is opened.

1. Create a message.
2. Click the **Options** button on the message window toolbar.
3. Click the **Sensitivity down arrow**, and select a level.

   Please treat this as Confidential.

4. Click **Close** and send the message as usual.

EXCHANGE DIGITAL IDS

Both the sender of encrypted files and the recipient exchange digital IDs as follows:

1. Send a digitally signed e-mail.
2. Right-click the From name on the message you receive, select **Add To Contacts**, and click **Save And Close**.
3. If a message says that the person already is a contact, select **Update New Information From This Contact...**, and click **OK**.

ENCRYPT ALL MESSAGES

1. Click **Tools | Options** and select the **Security** tab.
2. Check **Encrypt Contents And Attachments For Outgoing Messages**.

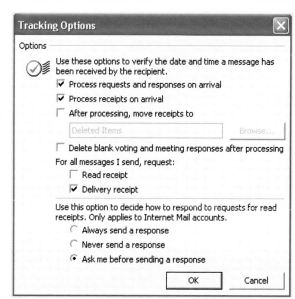

3. To impose additional restrictions, click **Settings**, select from the options, and click **OK**.

4. Click **OK** again to close the Options dialog box.

ENCRYPT A SINGLE MESSAGE

1. Click **Options** in the message window.

2. Click the **Security Settings** button.

3. Check **Encrypt Message Contents And Attachments**.

4. To impose additional restrictions, click **Change Settings**, select from the options, and click **OK**.

5. Click **OK** again and click **Close**.

Request Receipts

Anyone who has sent an important message and has not heard a peep from the recipient can appreciate receipts. When the addressee receives or reads the message, you are notified. You can request receipts for all your messages or on a message-by-message basis.

OBTAIN RECEIPTS FOR ALL MESSAGES

1. Click **Tools | Options** and click the **E-Mail Options** button.

2. Click **Tracking Options**.

3. Check **Read Receipt**, **Delivery Receipt**, or both.

4. If you like, choose an option for responding to other senders' requests for a receipt.

5. Click **OK** three times.

OBTAIN A SINGLE RECEIPT

1. Create a message and click **Options**.

2. Check **Request A Delivery Receipt For This Message**, **Request A Read Receipt For This Message**, or both.

3. Click **Close**.

Delay Delivery with a Rule

You can create a rule to control when messages leave your system after you click **Send**.

1. Click **Tools | Rules And Alerts**, and click **New Rule**.

2. Choose **Start From A Blank Rule**.

3. Select **Check Messages After Sending**, and click **Next**.

4. Check any desired conditions that limit which messages the rule applies to, specify them in the description panel (as you can see in Figure 3-7), click **OK**, and click **Next**.

5. Under Select Action(s), check **Defer Delivery By A Number Of Minutes**.

6. In the description box, click **A Number Of** and enter the total minutes (up to 120) that you want messages delayed, click **OK**, and click **Next**.

7. Check any exceptions, specify them in the description panel, click **OK** if necessary, and click **Next**.

8. Type a name for the rule, and click **Finish**. You are returned to the Rules And Alerts dialog box, which will now show your new rule, as shown in Figure 3-8.

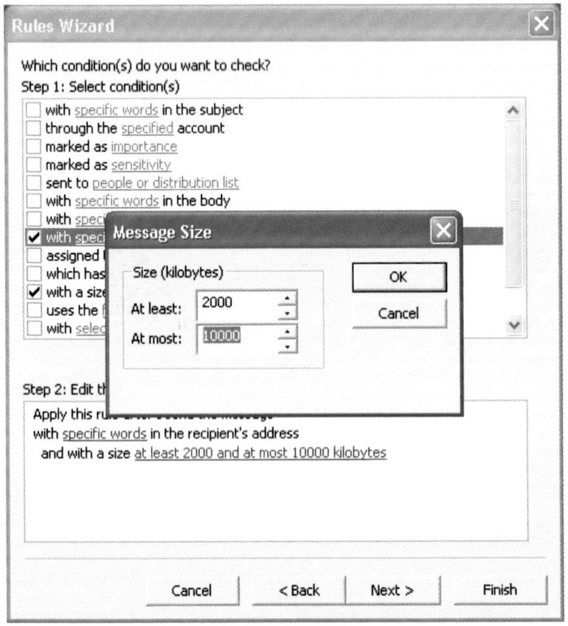

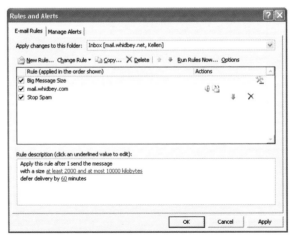

Figure 3-7: Outlook's rule-making feature has a large number of conditions that you can organize into rules.

Figure 3-8: The Rules And Alerts dialog box, opened from the Tools menu, provides for the creation and management of rules.

Chapter 4
Managing Contacts

Taking a moment to create contacts can save you from typing—and later correcting—the whole e-mail address every time you send a message. Once you've entered a name as a contact, you can add business or personal information—like phone numbers, addresses, or an important anniversary—at your convenience. In this chapter you will learn how to create and maintain your contacts, as well as different ways to use contact information. If you are using Microsoft Office Outlook 2003 with Business Contact Manager, you'll find out how to set up Business Contact Manager to manage accounts and individual contacts.

Create Contacts

The kind of address books that fit in the pocket have spaces so tiny that phone numbers can trail down the margins. In mine, lots of entries are scratched out and replaced because the people moved. Other listings are almost unreadable because family members now have multiple phone numbers.

Outlook Contacts provides a satisfying alternative, helping you keep everything straight and up to date, even information for acquaintances who don't have e-mail. After you open Outlook, simply click **Contacts** in the Navigation pane; the Contacts workspace will open, as shown in Figure 4-1.

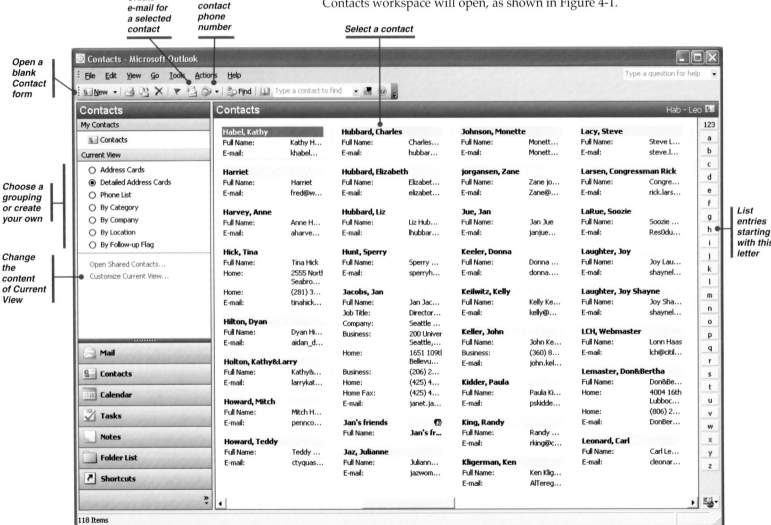

Figure 4-1: Creating detailed contacts can save you a lot of time looking up birthdays and postal addresses later.

Add a New Contact

A name is all you need to save a contact. The Contact form, however, provides a flexible layout that can store an immense amount of information that you can use later for professional and social purposes. The form sorts information onto five tabs:

- **General** contains basic information for identifying and getting in touch with the person (see Figure 4-2).

- **Details** provides office and personal data as well as the means of setting up NetMeeting sessions.

- **Activities**, a search tool, lists Outlook items (e-mail messages, notes, tasks, and so on) associated with the person.

- **Certificates** imports and maintains a contact's digital ID. (See Chapter 3, "Creating and Sending E-Mail," for an explanation of digital certificates.)

- **All Fields** lets you quickly look up the contents of a variety of fields completed for that contact.

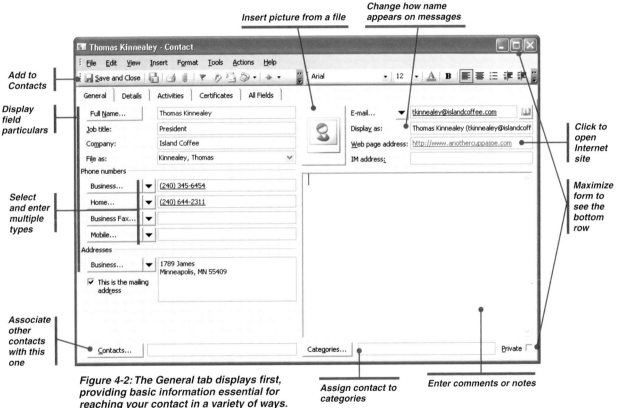

Insert picture from a file
Change how name appears on messages
Add to Contacts
Display field particulars
Select and enter multiple types
Associate other contacts with this one
Click to open Internet site
Maximize form to see the bottom row

Figure 4-2: The General tab displays first, providing basic information essential for reaching your contact in a variety of ways.

Assign contact to categories
Enter comments or notes

1. Click **New** on the Standard toolbar.

2. Enter information on the General tab, pressing **TAB** or clicking to select desired fields:

   - **Full Name** Click the button to provide the complete name, or type a name in the text box. This is all that is required to create a contact.

- **Job Title** Type any title that you need to remember.

- **Company** Type the name of the company or organization the person is connected with.

- **File As** Click the **down arrow** beside the text box to select the combination of name and company that will dictate its place in the Contact listing (you need to enter the name and company first).

- **Phone Numbers** Click the **down arrow** beside each button to select among 19 number types, and then click the label button to enter detailed information about it, or type the number in the text box.

- **Addresses** Click the **down arrow** beside the button to select among three types of addresses, and then click the button to enter detailed information, or type the address in the text box.

- **Contacts** (available after saving this record) Click the button and select other names to associate with this one.

- **E-Mail** Click the **down arrow** to select up to three e-mail addresses to be associated with the person, and for each one, type an address in the text box.

- **Display As** Press **TAB** or drag to enter and highlight the default display, and if desired, type a new name.

- **Web Page Address** Type the person's URL.

- **IM Address** Type the Internet mail address that the person uses for instant messaging.

- **Comments** (unlabeled) Type any comments or notes in the large text box.

- **Categories** Click the button and assign the contact to categories as described in Chapter 2, "Receiving and Handling E-Mail."

3. Click the **Details** tab to open it and enter information.

- **Specific office information** Complete text fields as needed.

- **Personal information** Type information, selecting from drop-down date boxes as appropriate.

- **Online NetMeeting Settings** At Director Server, type the NetMeeting ILS server name. At E-Mail Alias, type the person's NetMeeting e-mail alias, and click **Call Now** when you want to initiate a NetMeeting.

- **Internet Free-Busy** Type an Internet address that presents information about the person's availability.

Thu 12/16/2004	▼

◄	December 2004					►
S	M	T	W	T	F	S
28	29	30	1	2	3	4
5	6	7	8	9	10	11
12	13	14	15	16	17	18
19	20	21	22	23	24	25
26	27	28	29	30	31	1
2	3	4	5	6	7	8

Today	None

General	Details	Activities	Certificates	All Fields	

Show: E-mail

!	D	▽	ⓘ	From	Subject	Received	In Folder
				Andy Perleberg	Forestry Tools	Tue 12/2/2003 4:41 PM	Inbox
				Andy Perleberg	Successful Reforestation: An overview	Tue 12/2/2003 4:33 PM	Inbox
			ⓘ	Andy Perleberg	Washington Tree Seed Transfer Zones	Mon 3/10/2003 11:10...	Forestry stuff
			ⓘ	Andy Perleberg	Low Impact Development	Mon 1/27/2003 9:37 AM	Forestry stuff

1
2
3
4
5
6
7
8
9
10

TIP

The quick way to create an e-mail from the Contacts area is to right-click the contact and select **New Message To Contact**.

4. Click the **Activities** tab, click the **Show down arrow**, and select an area from which to list items related to the person. The search can take quite a while before producing a list.

5. Click the **Certificates** tab; click **Import** to browse for the person's digital certificate. Click a certificate in the list, and click **Properties** to review details. Click **Set As Default** to use the selected certificate by default.

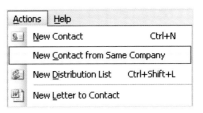

6. Click the **All Fields** tab, select a type of field from the drop-down list, and review the contents of the associated fields.

7. Click **Save And Close** when finished.

ADD A CONTACT FROM THE SAME COMPANY

If you already have a contact for someone in a company and you want to add another, Outlook helps you out by filling in the company information.

1. Open an existing contact from the company.

2. Click **Actions** and select **New Contact From Same Company**. A new Contact form displays with the company data.

3. Complete, save, and close as usual.

Actions	Help	
8⃞	New Contact	Ctrl+N
	New Contact from Same Company	
🖳	New Distribution List	Ctrl+Shift+L
🗎	New Letter to Contact	

Add Multiple Contacts

Outlook is designed to save a step here and there when you are repeating the same task. When you are entering many contacts at once, you can tell Outlook to save the one you just created and start a new one, all at the same time.

COMBINE SAVE WITH NEW CONTACT

In this case, you *don't* use Save And Close as usual. Instead, saving opens a blank form.

1. Create a contact.

2. In the Contact form window, click **File** and select **Save And New**.

   –Or–

   Click **Save And New** on the toolbar.

3. When you've created all the contacts you need for now, click **Save And Close**.

ADD MULTIPLE COMPANY CONTACTS

You can add to the toolbar a command that, with one click, saves business contact information and opens another business contact form with the previous contact's corporate information included.

1. Click **New** and double-click the blank area outside of a toolbar.

   –Or–

   Click the right end of a toolbar, choose **Add Or Remove Buttons**, and click **Customize**. The Customize dialog box opens.

2. Click the **Commands** tab and select **File** in the Categories list.

3. Scroll to locate **Save And New In Company**, and drag it next to Save And Close in the Contact toolbar.

4. Right-click **Save And New In Company**, click **Begin A Group** to insert a separation bar in the toolbar, and click **Close** in the Customize dialog box.

5. Complete the new Contact form, and click **Save And New In Company**. The new contact is saved, and a new Contact form opens with the company information already completed.

6. Create the remaining contacts.

7. Click **Save And Close** when finished.

TIP

To remove Save And New In Company from the toolbar, right-click it on a Contact form, select **Customize**, right-click it on the Contact form again, select **Delete**, and click **Close** in the Customize dialog box.

EDITING CONTACTS

Once you have created a contact, you can change the information as much as you want. Just open the contact and change or enter new information. The following tasks all begin with an open contact and end with clicking **Save And Close**.

ADD A PICTURE

Put a face to the name in Contacts.

Click the picture button, find the photo file on your computer, and click **OK**.

ADD A FILE

Place a copy of a photo, document, spreadsheet, or any other kind of file in the contact.

1. Click the **Insert** menu and click **File**.
2. Find the file by using the Insert File dialog box, and click **Insert**. The link to the file displays in the comments box on the General tab, as shown in Figure 4-4.

ADD A MAP

This requires you to be online, but it saves a map to the contact address that you can print offline.

1. Click **Actions** and select **Display Map Of Address**. The web site MSN Maps & Directions opens and presents the map.
2. Click **Save To Pocket PC** above the map. The map displays as a picture.
3. Move the cursor onto the map, click **Save This Image**, use the Save Picture dialog box to browse to the desired folder, type a file name, and click **Save**.

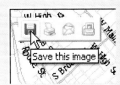

4. See preceding "Add a File" to add the map to the contact comments box.

Continued...

Copy Contacts from E-Mail

When you copy an address off the From, Cc, and Bcc e-mail message fields, the Contact form displays with the name and e-mail address fields filled in.

1. Open an e-mail message.
2. Right-click the name in the message window, and select **Add To Outlook Contacts** (see Figure 4-3).
3. Click **Save And Close**. The name and address are added to your contacts.

Figure 4-3: The context menu that opens for names on received messages presents a complete selection of options for incorporating the information.

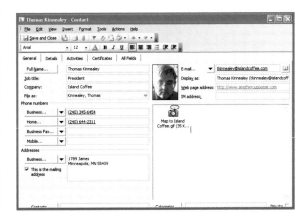

Figure 4-4: In the comments box, double-click the file to open it, and, in this case, to print the map when needed.

EDITING CONTACTS (Continued)

ADD AN ITEM

Place a copy of an Outlook item (e-mail message, task, appointment, and so on) in the contact.

1. Open the contact, click the **Insert** menu, and click **Item**. The Insert Item dialog box opens.

2. Select the subfolder in Look In if necessary, choose **Insert As Attachment** to avoid losing the content if deleted elsewhere, and double-click the desired item.

DRAG INTO CONTACTS

Any Outlook item turns into a contact if you drag it onto the Contacts view bar in the Navigation pane. This is especially useful with important e-mail messages whose senders you need in your contacts. The name and e-mail address go into their respective fields, and the important message displays in the Contact form comments text box.

CREATE A CONTACT FROM A VCARD

Electronic business cards, called vCards, pack contact information into a small, easy-to-share package. If another Outlook user sends you a vCard, you can turn it into a contact for your own records.

1. Open the e-mail message.

2. Double-click the vCard attachment. The Contact form displays.

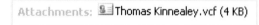

3. Click **Save And Close**.

Create a Distribution List

Avoid entering the address for each member of a group to which you send messages. Instead, create and name a distribution list for the group, as shown in Figure 4-5. It will appear as an entry of its own in your Contacts, so sending a message to the group will send a message to each member. Review Chapter 3, "Creating and Sending E-Mail," to see how to send e-mail messages using a distribution list.

1. Click the **New down arrow**, and select **Distribution List**. The Distribution List dialog box opens.

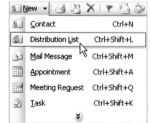

2. Type a name for the list in the Name text box, and click **Select Members**. The Select Members dialog box displays your contacts.

3. Double-click each name to add to the list, and click **OK** when done.

4. If you need to add a name that is not in Contacts, click **Add New**, type a display name and e-mail address in the Add New Member dialog box, and click **OK**.

5. Optionally, click the **Notes** tab to type comments or insert files.

6. Click **Save And Close**.

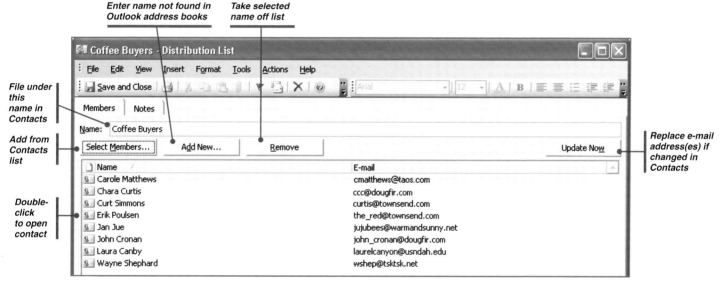

Enter name not found in Outlook address books

Take selected name off list

File under this name in Contacts

Add from Contacts list

Double-click to open contact

Replace e-mail address(es) if changed in Contacts

Figure 4-5: Distribution lists ensure that your e-mail message goes to every member of the group.

MAKE A DISTRIBUTION LIST FROM A MESSAGE

Use this shortcut if you received an e-mail message with the addresses of group members that you'd like to contact from time to time.

1. Open the message in Mail.

2. Right-click the group of names you want to use in the distribution list, choose **Select All**, right-click again, and choose **Copy**.

3. Click **File** in the message, select **New**, and click **Distribution List**. The Distribution List dialog box opens.

4. Type a name for the list, click **Select Members**, click in the Members text box, and press **CTRL+V** to paste the list you copied.

5. Click **OK** and click **Save And Close**.

Change a Distribution List

You can count on change affecting the people in your list. To keep your messages going to the right places:

1. Open your Contacts folder, locate and double-click the distribution list, and make your changes. To:

- **Add contacts**, click **Select Member** and choose as you did in creating the list

- **Add names**, click **Add New**, enter information, and click **OK**

- **Remove members**, click a name, and click **Remove**

- **Refresh e-mail addresses** with new information from individual contacts, click **Update Now**

2. Click **Save And Close**.

Use Contacts

Once you have put together the details on a contact, you can do a lot with it besides fill in e-mail addresses quickly and accurately—though that alone makes it worth far more than any effort involved. You can share contact information, sort contacts, flag them for future action, use an automated telephone dialer built into the contact, and even create a postal service letter by using the contact.

Add Contacts to E-Mail

The information you have may be very useful to someone else. Whether it's a business associate or a relative, sharing the information by way of e-mail prevents typos, copying errors, and tedium. You can send the contact as an Outlook contact record (.msg file) to other Outlook users or as a vCard (.vcf file), which is readable by systems that don't use Outlook. Either way, the recipient treats the contact like any other attached file.

TIP

When you send e-mail to a distribution list, you don't have to let the members see who's on it—enter the name of the list into the Bcc field. You will need to put somebody in the To field, but it can be yourself.

SEND CONTACTS TO OUTLOOK USERS

Right-click a contact, select **Forward**, and create and send the message as usual.

SEND CONTACTS TO OTHER E-MAIL SYSTEMS

Select the contact, click **Actions**, select **Forward As VCard**, and create and send the message as usual.

SEND A DISTRIBUTION LIST

Select the distribution list, press **CTRL+F**, and create and send the message as usual.

–Or–

Click **Actions**, select **Forward As VCard**, and create and send the message as usual.

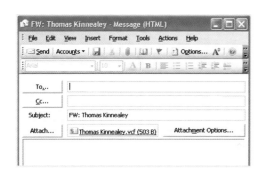

Arrange Contacts

You probably created contacts for different reasons, to serve various purposes, and with some more important than others. Therefore, Outlook provides different ways for you to organize and look at them.

CLASSIFY CONTACTS BY CATEGORIES

Like e-mail messages and all other Outlook items, contacts can be sorted into categories. (See Chapter 2 for a complete explanation, including how to create new categories.) When you create a contact, you might want to assign the person to a category right away:

In the Contact form, click the **Categories** button, choose the desired categories, and click **OK**.

After you have created a lot of contacts, you might want to group them into categories. If you have many contacts, you can simplify selection by using the filter described next in "Take a Different View" or the search feature described later in "Use the Find Tool":

Select all the contacts for a category, click **Edit**, click **Categories** in the Outlook window, check desired categories, and click **OK**.

NOTE

Select contacts using the keyboard and mouse. Press and hold **CTRL** while you click all desired contacts. Or press and hold **SHIFT** while you click the first contact in a sequence and then click the last contact.

Clustering contacts makes it easy to send an e-mail message or appointment request to all contacts in a particular group. Click the category heading, click **Actions**, click **New Message To Contact**, click **OK**, and complete the message.

TAKE A DIFFERENT VIEW

Just as you can select and customize the view in other parts of Outlook, Contacts provides seven standard views, which you can change to suit your needs:

- **Address Cards** show name, e-mail address, phone, and mailing address.
- **Detailed Address Cards,** in addition to the preceding, present a condensed version of the whole contact.
- **Phone List** gives each contact one line in a table with headings you can click to use for sorting the table.
- **By Category** clusters contacts that have been assigned to categories.
- **By Company** groups contacts for which companies have been entered.
- **By Location** clusters contacts for which a country or region has been entered.
- **By Follow-Up Flag** groups contacts that have been flagged.

It's easy to try the various views to find which one might work best for you and then to customize that view:

1. Click a Current View option in the Navigation pane.
2. Click **View | Arrange By | Current View**, and click **Customize Current View**. The Customize View dialog box opens.
3. Click a button to edit the elements of the view (availability depends on the view), and click **OK** after editing.

    - **Fields** displays available fields on the left, fields actually used on the right, and their display order.
    - **Group By** bases a sort on the selected Contact field.
    - **Sort** sequences the contents—as a secondary sort if Group By is used.
    - **Filter** uses the Advanced Search dialog box to limit the contacts listed.
    - **Other Settings** controls how the data looks.
    - **Automatic Formatting** affects time-sensitive contents.
    - **Format Columns** lets you change layouts of table views.
    - **Reset Current View** restores the default settings.

4. Click **OK** when finished.

FLAGGING CONTACTS

Sure, you could create an appointment, but maybe you just want a reminder to call or to write out a batch of thank-you notes. Contacts keeps it simple.

PICK YOUR COLORS

In any of the table views, such as Phone List and By Company, click the Flag column for a contact, and select a color.

DEFINE THE COLOR

Color-code your flags, if you like:

1. Click **By Follow-Up Flag** in the Current View panel.
2. Click the **Follow Up Flag** column for a contact, and type an activity.

CHECK WHAT A COLOR MEANS

After you've associated specific flag colors with specific actions, you might forget what each color means by the time you're ready to use your system again. To check:

Click the **By Follow-Up Flag** option, and see the colors and the actions for them.

FLAG THE CONTACT FORM

1. Click the **Flag** on the Standard toolbar, type an action in the Flag To text box, or select one from the drop-down list box.
2. Type a date at Due By, or select one from the drop-down calendar. Press **TAB** to enter or select a time, and click **OK**. An info line appears on the form.
3. Pick and define colors as described earlier.

Continued...

Find a Contact

Though you'll use the address book that appears in the new message window for e-mail messages, you need to know how to find a contact for the other information it contains or to use it to perform actions mentioned earlier. The method you use will probably depend on how many contacts you have (see the lower-left corner of the Contacts window).

USE THE SCROLL BAR

If you have fewer than 50 contacts, scrolling will probably work just fine. With the Address Cards view selected in the Navigation pane, the contacts move horizontally when you drag the scroll button or click the scroll arrows. Other views also may include a vertical scroll bar, which works the same way.

USE THE ALPHABET BAR TO FIND A CONTACT

If you have a hundred or so contacts and the current view is one of the Address Cards views, you'll find the alphabet bar handy. The alphabet bar searches by the File As name.

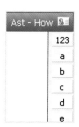

Click a letter button on the alphabet bar to place the first name beginning with that letter at the top of the list.

USE THE FIND TOOL

With the Find tool, you don't have to be sure of the contact's whole name to get the tool started sifting through your contacts. This can be comforting when you are talking about hundreds of contacts.

1. Click **Find** in the Standard toolbar. The Find bar will display.
2. Type the contact's first or last name in the Look For text box, and click **Find Now** or press **ENTER**. The search results display in the Contacts window.

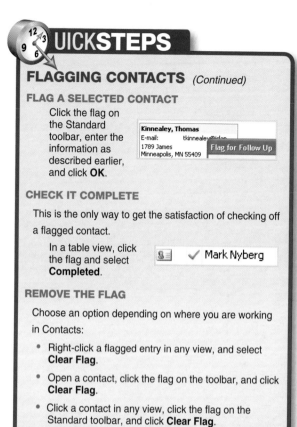

QUICKSTEPS

FLAGGING CONTACTS *(Continued)*

FLAG A SELECTED CONTACT

Click the flag on the Standard toolbar, enter the information as described earlier, and click **OK**.

> **Kinnealey, Thomas**
> E-mail: tkinnealey@islan...
> 1789 James
> Minneapolis, MN 55409
> Flag for Follow Up

CHECK IT COMPLETE

This is the only way to get the satisfaction of checking off a flagged contact.

In a table view, click the flag and select **Completed**.

> ✓ Mark Nyberg

REMOVE THE FLAG

Choose an option depending on where you are working in Contacts:

- Right-click a flagged entry in any view, and select **Clear Flag**.

- Open a contact, click the flag on the toolbar, and click **Clear Flag**.

- Click a contact in any view, click the flag on the Standard toolbar, and click **Clear Flag**.

USE ADVANCED FIND

The Advanced Find dialog box is useful when you have zillions of contacts (or you want to search a huge pile of e-mail messages).

1. Click **Tools**, select **Find**, and click **Advanced Find**.

2. Define the search by using specified criteria, as shown in Figure 4-6.

3. Click **Find Now**.

4. To alter the search, click **New Search**, click **OK**, modify the criteria, and click **Find Now** again.

5. Click to open any results listed.

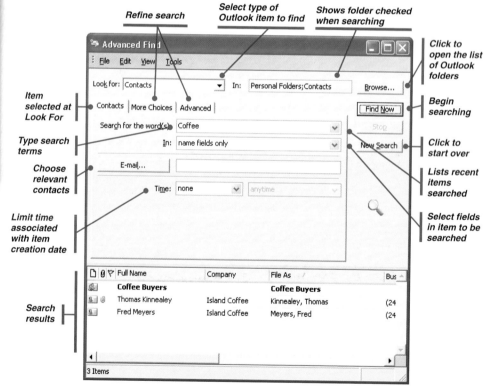

Figure 4-6: The Advanced Find dialog box allows you to impose limits on the search for Outlook items.

Print Contact Information

Outlook lets you print contacts to fit a variety of standard organizers, as well as to fit a billfold.

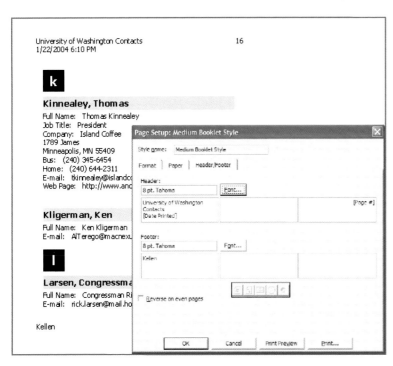

Figure 4-7: A header and footer make the pages look like they were professionally printed, and they can help you track the age of the data.

1. Sort and filter your contacts, as described earlier, so that you print only the group you want in the order you want.

2. Choose one view option:

   - **Table** views for printing contacts in a tabular format
   - **Address Card** views for printing booklet style (presents the most information)

3. Click **File** and select **Print**. The Print dialog box opens.

4. Explore your options by clicking a print style, clicking **Page Setup**, and experimenting with the options in the Print Setup dialog box. Go to the:

   - **Format** tab to choose printing order and fonts (deselect **Contact Index On One Side** to keep from printing the alphabet bar, although this is a handy feature)
   - **Paper** tab for page specifications, including by type of organizer
   - **Header/Footer** tab to create your own header/footer, as shown in Figure 4-7

5. To see how your Contacts will appear printed, click **Preview,** and when you're finished, click **Close**.

6. When ready, click **Print** and click **OK**.

PRINT A SINGLE CONTACT

1. Double-click a contact to open it in the Contact form.

2. Click **File | Print**. The Print dialog box opens.

3. To add a header and/or footer, click **Page Setup**, click the **Header/Footer** tab, and select and type what you need.

4. To see how the contact will appear printed, click **Preview**, and click **Close**.

5. When ready, click **Print**, and click **OK**.

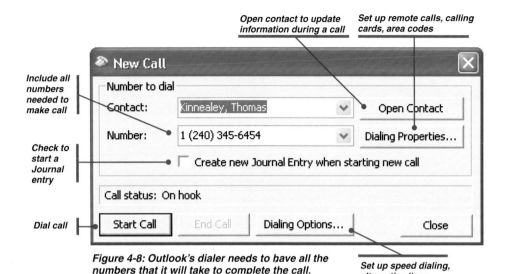

Open contact to update information during a call

Set up remote calls, calling cards, area codes

Include all numbers needed to make call

Check to start a Journal entry

Dial call

Figure 4-8: Outlook's dialer needs to have all the numbers that it will take to complete the call.

Set up speed dialing, alternative lines

Phone a Contact

If your computer is sharing a line with a telephone, you can have Outlook dial your contacts. This means that the modem is connected to a regular voice line. If you use e-mail, then the modem is probably set up for automatic phone dialing. Give it a try and find out:

1. Make sure you are not online.

2. Select a contact for whom you have entered a phone number, and click the **Dial** button on the toolbar. The New Call dialog box opens (see Figure 4-8).

3. To use a different phone number, choose one:

   ● Click the **Number down arrow**, and select an alternative number.

   ● Type a phone number in the Number text box.

4. Click **Start Call**.

5. While the computer is dialing, pick up the receiver connected to that line, and click **Talk** in the Call Status dialog box.

6. When finished, hang up the phone and click **End Call** in the New Call dialog box.

TIP

For impatient people, there's speed dialing. Of course, you first need to enter the numbers: click any contact, click the **Dial** button on the toolbar, click **Dialing Options** in the New Call dialog box, type a name and phone number in the text boxes, click **Add**, click **OK**, and click **Close**. You're all set. Click the **Dial down arrow**, select **Speed Dial**, click a number, click **Start Call**, and proceed as described in "Phone a Contact."

TIP

Check **Create New Journal Entry...** in the New Call dialog box if you want Outlook to time the call while you type notes. When you are finished, just click **Save And Close**.

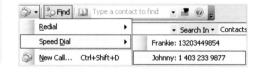

Compose a Letter to a Contact

Using contact information, Outlook supplies just about everything except the actual content of the letter, which you then print and post the old-fashioned way.

1. Select a contact, click **Actions**, and select **New Letter To Contact**. Microsoft Office Word opens a new document and the Letter Wizard.

2. Work your way through the wizard, selecting components and clicking **Next** to proceed through each section:

   ● Layout and design

   ● Recipient information

   ● Identification elements

   ● Sender information

3. Click **Finish**. The letter displays, ready for content, as shown in Figure 4-9.

4. Type the body of the letter, and then save and print as usual.

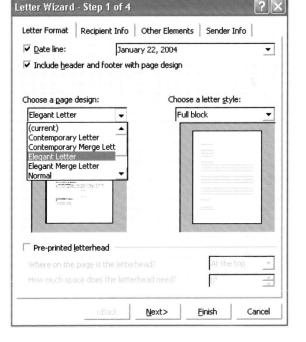

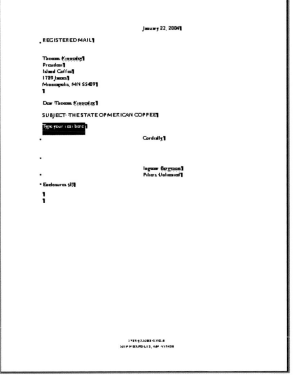

Figure 4-9: Outlook triggers Word to display the letter, and you finish it in Word.

Keyboard Shortcuts for Contacts	
Create new	**CTRL+N**
Create new from another Outlook workspace	**CTRL+SHIFT+C**
Find a contact	**F11**
Save and close	**ALT+S**
Delete	**CTRL+D**
Create distribution list*	**CTRL+SHIFT+L**

*Caution: Does not apply when working in the body of a message, at which time it produces a bullet

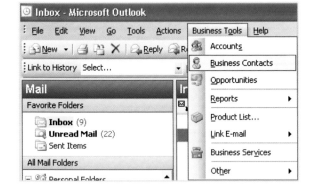

Use Business Contact Manager

Office 2003 Professional includes a new component called Business Contact Manager. It assists you in maintaining good client relationships and in employing the best practices in marketing your products and services. By adding this tool to Outlook, you create three new components—Accounts, Business Contacts, and Business Opportunities—with which you can:

- **Link** e-mail, notes, documents, faxes, and scanned items.
- **Consolidate** all customer data, connecting opportunities with contacts.
- **Maintain** product lists.
- **Create** marketing materials.
- **Generate** reports for tracking, planning, and analysis.

Set Up Business Contact Manager

Business Contact Manager is not installed with the rest of Office 2003 and comes on a separate CD. When the installation finishes, a number of Business Contact Manager options will be added to the Outlook Help and other menus. Take the time to watch the animated overview and summaries of the five main areas in Business Contact Manager Tours. Also, be sure to review the Business Contact Manager Quick Start Guide, which contains animated training modules for common procedures as well as a glossary of terms used in the application.

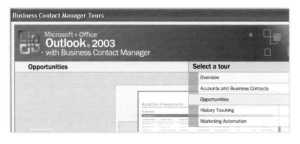

Furthermore, a new menu will appear in Outlook—Business Tools—and a specialized toolbar will display. Once you have completed installation, all remaining procedures will assume that Outlook has been opened and that you have navigated to the Contacts workspace.

When you're ready to begin installation, close Outlook, and have handy your Windows XP disk in case the setup wizard calls for it.

1. Insert the Business Contact Manager CD into the CD-ROM drive on your computer.

2. If you get a message saying you first need to install .NET Framework 1.1, click **OK**, choose **I Agree** on the Microsoft License Agreement, click **Install**, and when finished, click **OK**. The .NET Framework will install, and Business Contact Manager Setup Wizard will begin.

3. Click **Next**, choose **I Accept…**, click **Next** twice, click **Install**, and click **Finish** when done.

4. Start **Outlook**, and, when the message asks if you'd like to use Business Contact Manager with your current profile, click **Yes**.

Create Contact Records

You will generate contact records for both the account and representatives of the organization. The *account* is the company or group you do—or plan to do—business with, regardless of whether they are your customer or you are their customer (like your insurance company). Within the account, you maintain individual contacts.

ADD AN ACCOUNT

1. Click **Accounts In Business Contact Manager** in the Navigation pane under My Contacts, and click **New** on the toolbar. A blank account record form opens.

2. On the General tab, type a name for the account at Account Name, and enter any other information you currently possess, as shown in Figure 4-10.

3. Click the **Details** tab and enter any information you possess:

- **Type Of Business** Click the **down arrow** and select a legal description.
- **Territory** Click the **down arrow** and select a region of the country.
- **Source Of Lead** Click the **down arrow** and make a selection.
- **Referred By** Type the name of the person who referred this account.
- **Comments** Type any notes.

4. Click **Save And Close**.

NOTE

At this writing, because of a bug in the program, the Primary Contact button does not work on the Account record window.

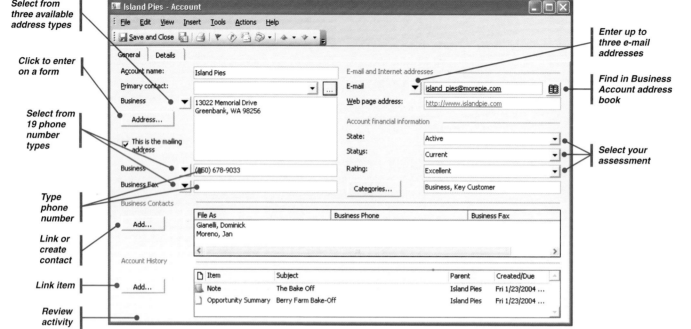

Select from three available address types

Click to enter on a form

Select from 19 phone number types

Type phone number

Link or create contact

Link item

Review activity

Enter up to three e-mail addresses

Find in Business Account address book

Select your assessment

Figure 4-10: Information from records is automatically saved in the Business Contact Manager database.

CAUTION

This is a new application, and it has a few glitches. You may find that you need to restart Outlook more than once to get the Business Contact Manager components synchronized properly.

CREATE INDIVIDUAL BUSINESS CONTACTS

Business contact records are constructed like Account records.

1. Click **Business Contacts In Business Contact Manager** in the Navigation pane under My Contacts, and click **New** on the toolbar. A blank Business Contact record form opens.

2. On the General tab, type the person's name, and enter any other information you currently possess.

3. To link a contact to an account, click the button beside the Account Name text box, and select one:

   ● **Add Existing Account**, and then double-click an account in the list

   ● **Create New Account**, and then type the organization's name

4. Add specific information about this person on the Details tab.

5. Click **Save And Close**.

PREPARING REPORTS

The Business Contact Manager reports you generate with two clicks of the mouse look like you put a lot more into them.

GENERATE A REPORT

Click **Business Tools**, select **Reports**, select a type of report, and click the desired title. The report opens as shown in Figure 4-11.

Note: It may take a few moments for your system to generate the report from the Business Contact Manager database.

CUSTOMIZE A REPORT

1. In a Business Contact Manager report window, click **Modify Report**. The Modify Report dialog box displays.

2. Click the **General** tab to change the sort criteria, date range, and any other available organizational criteria.

3. Click the **Filter** tab to refine the record and data selection.

4. Click the **Header/Footer** tab to enter information to appear on every page.

5. Click **OK**.

SAVE THE REPORT

Click the **Save Report** button on the toolbar, and save the report as a Word, RTF, Excel, or HTML file.

PRINT THE REPORT

Click the **Print** button and generate a hard copy.

CHANGE OR REMOVE ACCOUNT RECORDS

1. Click **Accounts...** or **Business Contacts...** in the Navigation pane under My Contacts.

2. To view and change information, double-click the desired record, change as needed, and then click **Save And Close**.

3. To delete a record, click the record, and click **Delete** on the toolbar.

Track Accounts

Once you have established account and contact records, Business Contact Manager creates a History log (associated with the Outlook Journal) for each record and automatically links it to any related e-mail messages, notes, tasks, and appointments. History can be sorted and filtered so that you can track issues and monitor open tasks.

Track the activity on the accounts in either of two ways:

1. In Contacts click **Accounts In Business Contact Manager** in the Navigation pane under My Contacts, and double-click an account.

   –Or–

   Click **Journal** in the Outlook view bars at the bottom of the Navigation pane, and click **Business History In Business Contact Manager** under My Journals.

2. In either the Account History at the bottom of the Account window or in the Journal's Business History, click the column heading by which you want the information sorted, and double-click specific items to open them.

3. Click **Save And Close** as many times as needed to return to the workspace.

Journal

My Journals
- Journal
- Business History in Business Contact

Current View
- ○ [By Created By]
- ○ [By Parent]
- ● [Chronological]

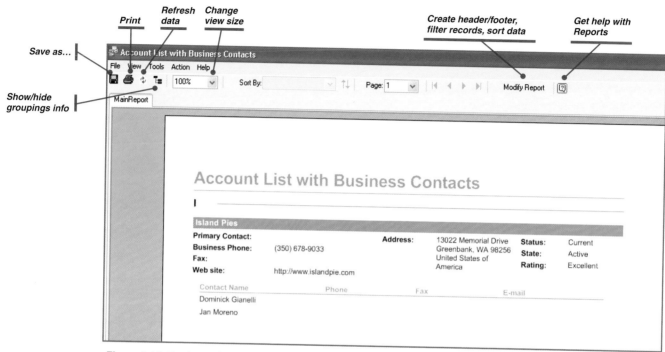

Figure 4-11: Business Contact Manager offers nearly two dozen special reports.

Chapter 5

Scheduling and the Calendar

The Calendar is second only to Mail in its importance in Outlook. The Calendar works closely with Contacts and Tasks to coordinate the use of your time and your interactions with others. The Calendar lets you schedule appointments and meetings, establish recurring activities, and tailor your calendar to your area, religion, and workdays.

In this chapter you will see how to use and customize the Calendar, schedule and manage appointments, and schedule and track meetings and resources.

Use the Calendar

The Calendar has four unique items in its Outlook window: the customized Standard toolbar, an appointment area, the Date Navigator, and the TaskPad, as you can see in Figure 5-1.

Explore the Calendar

The Calendar is designed for you to keep track easily of appointments, meetings, events, due dates, anniversaries, birthdays, and any other date-related happening. Open the Calendar and see the areas in which that is done.

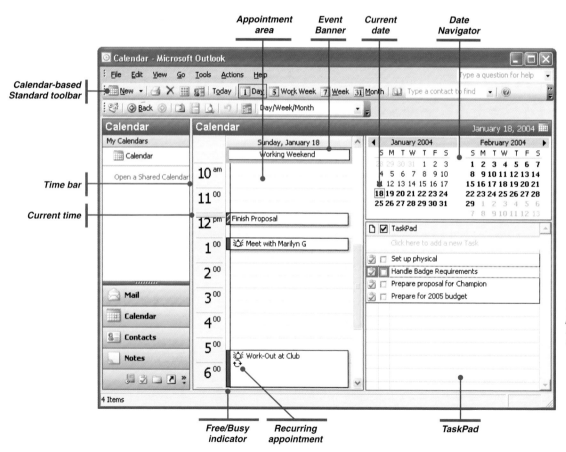

Figure 5-1: The Calendar provides an easy way to track meetings, appointments, and due dates.

1. Start **Outlook** in one of the ways described in Chapter 1.

   - Click the **Go** menu and click **Calendar**.

     –Or–

   - Press **CTRL+2** on the keyboard.

     –Or–

   - Click **Calendar** in the Outlook view bars.

Go	Tools	Actions	Help
Mail			Ctrl+1
Calendar			Ctrl+2
Contacts			Ctrl+3
Tasks			Ctrl+4
Notes			Ctrl+5

2. Double-click in the center appointment area. A new Appointment window will open, as shown in Figure 5-2. Here you can enter all the information about an appointment. Close the Appointment window.

3. Double-click in the TaskPad in the lower-right. A new Task window will open where you can enter all the information about a task. When you are ready, close the Task window.

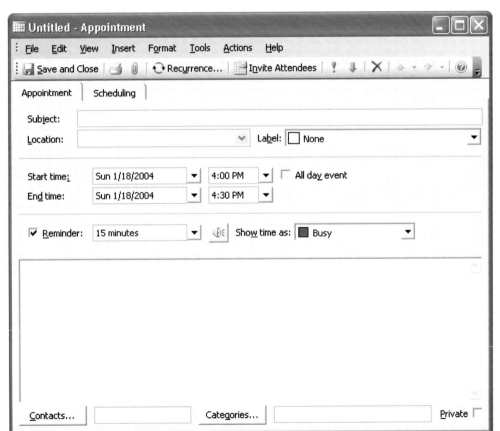

Figure 5-2:
An "appointment"
can be any date-
related event,
including meetings,
due dates, and
anniversaries.

QUICKSTEPS

NAVIGATING THE CALENDAR

The Date Navigator, which by default is in the upper-right corner of the Calendar window, allows you to pick any date from April 1, 1601, to August 31, 4500. To cover this almost 2,900-year span, Outlook provides several efficient tools. To:

◀		January 2004				▶
S	M	T	W	T	F	S
28	29	30	31	1	2	3
4	5	6	7	8	9	10
11	12	13	14	15	16	17
18	**19**	**20**	**21**	**22**	**23**	**24**
25	**26**	**27**	**28**	**29**	**30**	**31**
1	2	3	4	5	6	7

- **Display a day**, click the day in the Date Navigator
- **Display a day with appointments**, click a boldface day in the Date Navigator
- **Display several days**, hold down **CTRL** while clicking the days
- **Display a week**, click to the left of the first day of the week
- **Display several weeks**, hold down **CTRL** while clicking to the left of the weeks
- **Display a month**, drag across the weeks of the month
- **Move an activity to another date**, drag the activity to the new date in the Date Navigator
- **Change the month from one to the next**, click the left and right arrows in the month bar
- **Display several months**, drag the month bar down (into the TaskPad area)
- **Scroll through a list of months**, drag the heading up or down for an individual month
- **Directly display any date**, click the **Go** menu and click **Go To Date,** or press **CTRL+G**

4. Click a date in the Date Navigator to see that date displayed in the appointment area.

5. Click an arrow on either side of the top bar in the Date Navigator to change the dates that are displayed.

6. Click **7 Week** in the Standard toolbar to display a seven-day view of your week, which is shown in Figure 5-3.

7. Click **Today**, which simply highlights the current date, and then click **1 Day** to return to the default view.

This gives you a brief taste of the many facets of the Calendar.

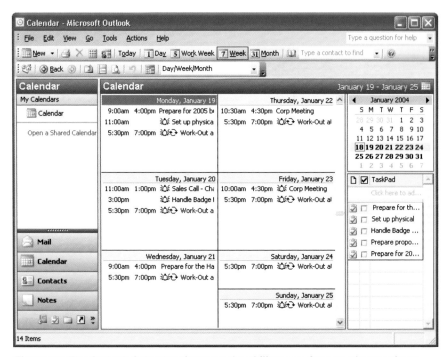

Figure 5-3: The Outlook Calendar gives you the ability to go from an almost minute-by-minute view to a month-at-a-glance view of your appointments.

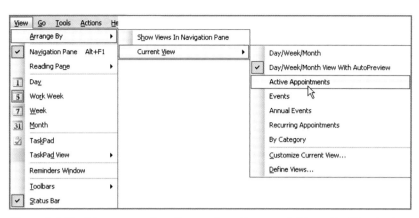

Figure 5-4: The View menu primarily repeats options available on the Standard and Advanced toolbars.

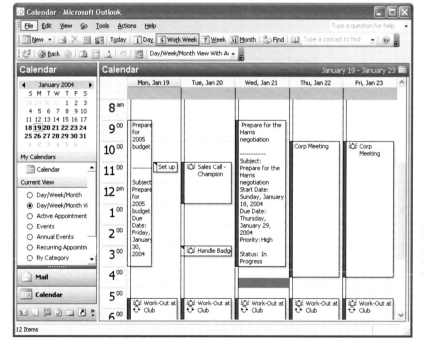

Customize the Calendar

As you have seen with the rest of Outlook, there are many facets of the Calendar that can be customized and several ways to do it. Most important of the methods are the View menu and the Standard and Advanced toolbars.

CUSTOMIZE WITH VIEW MENU

The View menu, shown in Figure 5-4, includes most of the options in the two toolbars. Click the **View** menu and click **Arrange By | Current View** to open the same menu you get from the Current View drop-down list on the Advanced toolbar. The Day, Week, and Month view options are all on the Standard toolbar. These options will be discussed with the toolbars. The two unique options on the View menu with the Calendar are:

- **Arrange By | Show Views In Navigation Pane** This takes the Current View options that are on both the View menu and Advanced toolbar and adds them to the Navigation pane.

- **TaskPad** This turns the TaskPad area in the lower-right of the default Calendar window on or off. When it is off, the Date Navigator moves over to the Navigation pane, as shown in Figure 5-5.

Figure 5-5: When the TaskPad is turned off, the Date Navigator moves to the Navigation pane, where you can also display the Calendar's Current View options.

CHANGE VIEWS WITH THE STANDARD TOOLBAR

The Standard toolbar has seven buttons unique to Calendar, although only the View Group Schedules button is available all the time. The other six buttons only appear in the Day/Week/Month view. All of the Standard toolbar buttons are described in Table 5-1.

TABLE 5-1: CALENDAR STANDARD TOOLBAR BUTTONS

ICON	NAME OF BUTTON	DESCRIPTION
	Calendar Coloring	Provides colors that can be attached to appointments
	View Group Schedules	Creates and opens a group schedule
Today	Go To Today	Returns Calendar display to today's date
1 Day	Day	Displays one day's activities
5 Work Week	Work Week	Displays one work week's activities
7 Week	Week	Displays seven days' activities
31 Month	Month	Displays a month's activities

NOTE

See "Creating a Group Schedule" QuickSteps later in this chapter. Group scheduling either requires a Microsoft Exchange Server network or the Microsoft Office Internet Free/Busy service to gather other group members' information.

CHANGE VIEWS WITH THE ADVANCED TOOLBAR

The Advanced toolbar contains the Plan A Meeting button, which opens the Plan A Meeting dialog box to schedule a meeting. In addition, the Advanced toolbar contains the Current View drop-down list with the default Day/Week/Month view, as well as five other built-in views that you can

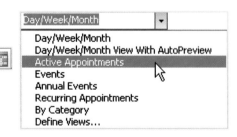

Day/Week/Month
Day/Week/Month
Day/Week/Month View With AutoPreview
Active Appointments
Events
Annual Events
Recurring Appointments
By Category
Define Views...

select. All of the other five views are tabular, as shown in Figure 5-6, and they display various sets of activities (appointments, events, or meetings) using these views:

- **Active Appointments** displays a list of appointments and events that are currently active. All appointments and events, regardless of date, are displayed. Thus, any appointment *not* complete will be listed in this view.

- **Events** lists the events, not the appointments, that are currently on your calendar. An event is an activity that lasts at least 24 hours, such as a conference or a trade show, and is not tied to a specific time.

- **Annual Events** displays only the events that are tied to specific dates, such as birthdays.

- **Recurring Appointments** lists the appointments that occur repeatedly, such as your tennis lessons or weekly management reviews.

- **By Category** lists the appointments by category. You must enter a category code for this to be effective.

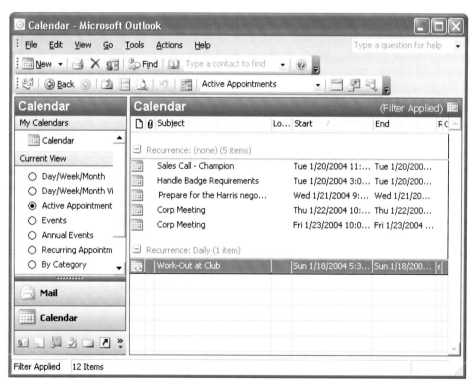

Figure 5-6: The Calendar has five tabular views that allow you to see the detail behind your schedule.

Customize Calendar Views

As with Mail and Contacts, you can create customized views either by modifying an existing view or by creating a new one.

MODIFY AN EXISTING VIEW

1. Select the view you want to change.

2. Click the **View** menu and then click **Arrange By | Current Views | Customize Current View**. The Customize View dialog box will open, as shown in Figure 5-7.

3. Select how you want to change the view, click the appropriate button, and make the change.

4. When you are done, click **OK**.

If you want to undo a change you made to the current view, click **Reset Current View** in the Customize View dialog box.

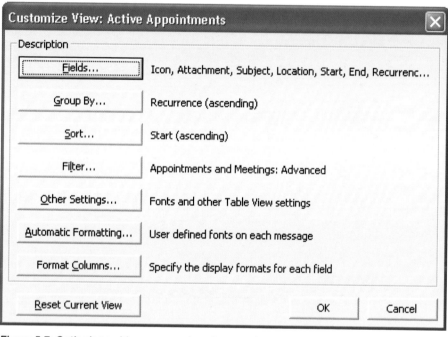

Customize View: Active Appointments

Description

Fields...	Icon, Attachment, Subject, Location, Start, End, Recurrenc...
Group By...	Recurrence (ascending)
Sort...	Start (ascending)
Filter...	Appointments and Meetings: Advanced
Other Settings...	Fonts and other Table View settings
Automatic Formatting...	User defined fonts on each message
Format Columns...	Specify the display formats for each field

Reset Current View   OK   Cancel

Figure 5-7: Outlook provides a comprehensive set of tools to modify what you see on the screen so that it can fit almost any need.

CREATE A NEW VIEW

1. Click **View | Arrange By | Current Views | Define Views**. The Custom View Organizer will open, as you can see in Figure 5-8.

2. Click **New** to open the Create A New View dialog box. Type a name, select a type of view, choose the folder it can be used in, and click **OK**. The Customize View dialog box will open, as shown earlier in Figure 5-7.

3. Select how you want to change the view, click the appropriate button, and make the change.

4. When you are done, click **OK**.

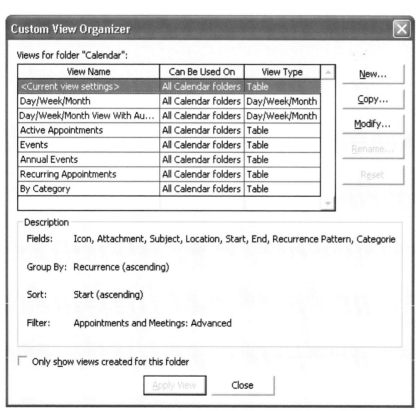

If you want to undo a change you made to the current view, click **Reset Current View** in the Customize View dialog box.

Figure 5-8: The Custom View Organizer gives you a list and summary of the current view as well as the ability to modify the current views and create new ones.

Set Up the Calendar

The Calendar allows you to define your normal work week in terms of the days it contains and when it starts, the normal start and end of your working day, the holidays you observe, and what you consider the first week of the year. To set up your Calendar:

1. With Outlook loaded and the Calendar folder open, click the **Tools** menu and click **Options**. In the Options dialog box, click **Calendar Options**. The Calendar Options dialog box opens, as shown in Figure 5-9.

2. Select the days of the week that you want considered as workdays if they are different from the default of Monday through Friday. (On the daily schedule, workdays are by default a light yellow, while non-working days are light yellow-orange.)

Figure 5-9: You can set Calendar options, such as defining your work week and displaying week numbers, the time zone, and holidays.

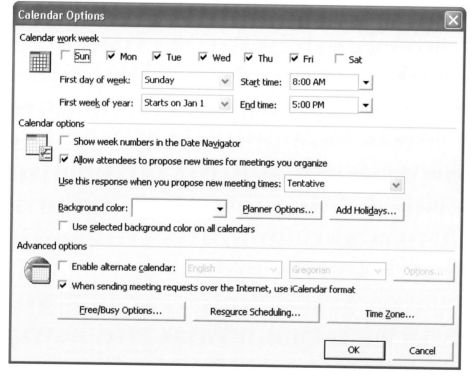

3. Select the day of the week that you want considered as the first day of the week if it is other than Sunday. (The weeks in the Date Navigator will begin with this day.)

4. Select the definition you want to use for the first week of the year if it doesn't begin January 1. (If you turn on week numbering, week number 1 is defined in this manner.)

5. Select the normal start and end times for your working day if they are other than 8 A.M. and 5 P.M. (On the daily schedule, work hours are by default light yellow, and non-working hours are light yellow-orange.)

6. If you want anything other than the defaults, turn on week numbers, decide whether attendees can propose new meeting times, select the response when proposing a new meeting, determine what you want to use for a background color, choose if you want an alternative calendar, and decide on the format to use for calendar information over the Internet.

PLANNER OPTIONS

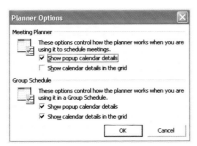

The Planner Options button on the Calendar Options dialog box allows you to determine how the Meeting form and Group Schedule work.

1. From Calendar Options, click **Planner Options**. The Planner Options dialog box opens.

2. For both the Meeting form and the Group Schedule, determine if you want the calendar details to appear in pop-up form and/or be displayed in the grid.

3. When you have set the Meeting form and Group Schedule options, click **OK**.

ADDING HOLIDAYS

You can add holidays to your calendar, both by country and by religion.

1. In the Calendar Options dialog box, click **Add Holidays** to open the Add Holidays To Calendar dialog box. This displays both countries and national and religious sets of holidays from which you can choose.

2. Place a check mark next to the holiday(s) you would like to have in your calendar.

3. When you are done, click **OK** to return to the Calendar Options dialog box. Your system will pause to add the holidays you selected.

SETTING FREE/BUSY OPTIONS

If you and your coworkers are on a Microsoft Exchange network, are willing to share your schedules over the Internet, or can all access a common server, you can store your free/busy times and make them available to each other to schedule meetings and other times together. In this case, requests for meetings will be handled automatically. The request will be matched against the group's free/busy schedule, and meetings will be scheduled at available times. For an individual to set up his or her free/busy options:

Setting up a group schedule is discussed in the QuickSteps "Creating a Group Schedule," later in this chapter.

1. From the Calendar Options dialog box, click **Free/Busy Options**, and the Free/Busy Options dialog box will open, as shown in Figure 5-10.

2. In the first text box, type the number of months of Calendar free/busy information you want to store on the server.

3. In the second text box, type the interval of minutes between free/busy time updates.

4. Select **Publish And Search Using Microsoft Office Internet Free/Busy Service** to direct that your free/busy times be published on a free Internet server maintained by Microsoft.

5. Select **Request Free/Busy Information In Meeting Invitations** to search the Microsoft Server when setting up meetings.

Figure 5-10: Publishing your free/busy schedule allows others to make appointments with and for you without interrupting you.

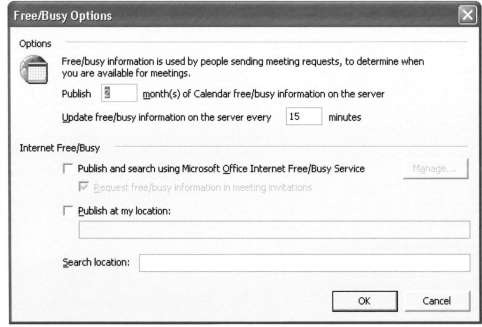

6. Click **Manage** to open the Microsoft Office Internet Free/Busy site, as shown in Figure 5-11. If you have a Microsoft .NET Passport, type your e-mail address and password, if needed, and click **Sign In**. Otherwise, register for a new one by clicking **Get One Now**. Agree to their terms and click **Continue**. Then either enter a list of e-mail addresses separated by semicolons of the individuals you want to see your free/busy times, or choose to have all Microsoft Office Internet Free/Busy Service members see your times. Separately you can invite nonmembers to join and to access your information. When you are ready, click **OK**. Sign out of Microsoft .NET Passport, and close your browser to return to the Free/Busy Options dialog box.

7. Select **Publish At My Location**, and type the URL of the server to publish your free/busy information on a local server.

8. Enter the URL of servers you want searched for the free/busy information of others.

9. Click **OK** to return to the Calendar Options dialog box.

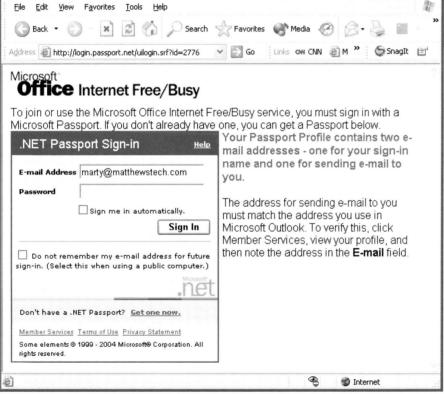

Figure 5-11: Microsoft provides a free service on the Internet to allow the sharing of free/busy information.

SET RESOURCE SCHEDULING OPTIONS

Outlook's resource scheduling can be used in two ways. If you are responsible for scheduling a business resource, such as a conference room or company car, you can automatically accept or reject requests depending on whether the calendar slot has already been reserved. An e-mail message will be sent to the requester either accepting the request or not. You can also use this feature to schedule meetings automatically for yourself by accepting or rejecting meeting requests sent to you, depending on your own schedule commitments.

1. From the Calendar Options dialog box, click **Resource Scheduling**. The Resource Scheduling dialog box will be displayed.

2. Click **Automatically Accept Meeting Requests And Process Cancellations** to automatically accept a scheduling request for yourself or a resource. An e-mail message will be returned to the requester telling him or her that the request has been accepted.

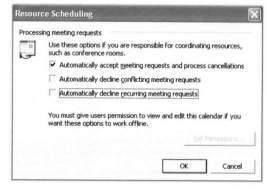

3. Click **Automatically Decline Conflicting Meeting Requests** to automatically decline a request that conflicts with a meeting of your own or with a resource's scheduling. An e-mail message will be returned to the requester telling him or her that the request has been turned down.

4. Click **Automatically Decline Recurring Meeting Requests** to prevent someone from scheduling a recurring meeting that would always tie up your time or a resource's availability at a certain time. An e-mail message will be returned to the requester telling him or her that the request has been declined.

5. Click **OK** to return to the Calendar Options dialog box.

NOTE

The automatic response to resource and meeting requests only works if Outlook is running.

You can choose up to two time zones to display. You can define and name your current time zone—as well as an additional one, if you choose.

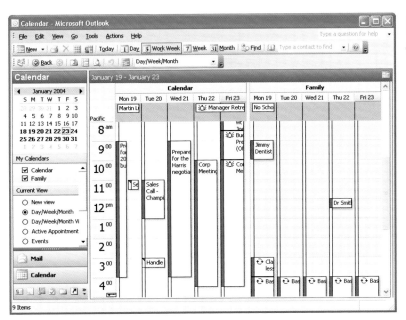

1. From the Calendar Options dialog box, click **Time Zone**. The Time Zone dialog box opens.

2. If you will be using two time zones, type a name in the Label field to identify the current time zone appearing in the Time Zone drop-down list box.

3. Select **Show An Additional Time Zone**, enter a label, and select the time zone from the drop-down list box.

4. Choose **Adjust For Daylight Saving Time** if it applies for either or both time zones.

5. When you are done, click **OK** to accept your changes and to close the Time Zone dialog box, and then click **OK** twice more to close both the Calendar Options and Outlook Options dialog boxes.

Maintain Multiple Calendars

If your calendar is becoming cluttered and hard to use, you might try separating it into two side-by-side calendars. For example, create one for business appointments and one for family appointments.

1. In Outlook, with the Calendar open, right-click in the Navigation pane under My Calendars, and click **New Folder**. The Create New Folder dialog box will open.

2. Type a name for the new calendar, accept **Calendar Items** for the folder contents, and click **Calendar** to select where to place the folder. Click **OK**.

3. Click opposite the new Calendar to display it, as shown in Figure 5-12.

Figure 5-12: By displaying two calendars side-by-side, you separately can show appointments that may only tangentially affect you.

Share a Calendar

You can share your Calendar—not just your free/busy time—with other users on a Microsoft Exchange network, just as you can share your Tasks and your Journal information. You can also access the Calendar information of others if they have granted you permission.

1. In the Calendar Navigation pane, click **Share My Calendar**.
2. To give anyone access, in the Name dialog box, select **Default**. Under the Permissions menu, choose **Read**.
3. To restrict access to certain persons, in the Name dialog box, click **Add**.
4. In the Type Name Or Select From List box, type the network name of the person you want to give access, or you can select the person from the list.
5. Click **Add** and then click **OK**.
6. In the Name box, select the name of the person you added. Then, under Permissions, select the **Read** option.
7. Click **OK**.

NOTE

If **Share My Calendar** is not available in the Navigation pane, then you are not connected to a Microsoft Exchange network.

ACCESS ANOTHER PERSON'S CALENDAR

If you want to access another person's Calendar, you can do so directly within Outlook. You must have permission to access another person's Calendar before you can do so, and you must be connected to a Microsoft Exchange network in order for this option to work.

1. In the Navigation pane, click **Open A Shared Calendar**.
2. In the Name dialog box that appears, enter the network name of the person whose Calendar you want to access.
3. Click **OK**.
4. The user's Calendar is added to the Navigation pane.

The Outlook Calendar allows you to enter dates and times as text and convert that text to numeric dates and times. For example, you can enter next tue and be given next Tuesday's date, or you can enter sep ninth and see that date. You can type this way in any date or time field in Outlook, such as the Go To Date dialog box, reached by clicking the **Go** menu and then clicking **Go To Date** (must be in a Day/Week/Month view). Likewise, you can type in the Start and End date and time fields in the appointment and event forms and in the Plan A Meeting dialog box. Some of the things you can do:

- Abbreviate months and days (for example, *Dec* or *fri*).
- Ignore capitalization and other punctuation (for example, *wednesday, april,* and *lincolns birthday*).
- Use words that indicate dates and times (for example, *noon, midnight, tomorrow, yesterday, today, now, next week, last month, five days ago, in three months, this Saturday,* and *two weeks from now*). Words you can use include *after, ago, before, beforehand, beginning, end, ending, following, for, from, last, next, now, previous, start, that, this, through, till, tomorrow, yesterday, today,* and *until*.
- Spell out specific dates and times (for example, *August ninth, first of December, April 19th, midnight, noon, two twenty pm,* and *five o'clock a.m.*).
- Indicate holidays that fall on the same date every year (for example, *New Year's Eve, New Year's Day, Lincoln's Birthday, Valentine's Day, Washington's Birthday, St. Patrick's Day, Cinco de Mayo, Independence Day, Halloween, Veterans' Day, Christmas Eve, Christmas Day,* and *Boxing Day*).

TIP

Combine direct entry and form entry to get the benefits of both.

Make Appointments

Within the Calendar you can enter three types of activities:

- **Appointments** take time on your calendar, are less than 24 hours long, and do not require inviting others within Outlook to attend. Examples include a sales call, lunch with a buyer, and time you want to set aside to write a report.
- **Events** are 24 hours or longer, do not occupy time on your calendar, and appear as a banner on each day's calendar. Examples are conferences, trade shows, and your vacation.
- **Meetings** are appointments that require that others be invited and/or that resources be reserved. Meetings are set up using the Meeting form to identify participants, to send meeting requests to them, and to track the responses.

All three types of activities can be entered in several ways and with a number of options.

Create Appointments

Appointments can be entered in any view and in several different ways. Independent of the view, the ways can be grouped into direct entry and form entry. *Direct entry* means simply typing directly on the calendar, while *form entry* uses a form to gather the information, which is then displayed on the calendar. Direct entry is fast if you want to make a quick notation. Form entry allows you to select and set a number of options.

ENTER APPOINTMENTS DIRECTLY

You can directly enter an appointment on the calendar in Day/Week/Month view by clicking a time and typing in the description. If you want the entry longer or shorter than the default half hour (or whatever standard duration you have selected), just drag the top or bottom border up or down to change the time. If you want to move the appointment, simply drag it to where you want it in the current day or to another day in the Date Navigator. To change several properties of the appointment, right-click the appointment and open the context menu, where a number of properties can be set. To directly enter appointments:

1. With the Calendar open in Outlook in a Day/Week/Month view, select a day in the Date Navigator that you want to use, and click the time you want the appointment to start.

2. Type a short meeting description, and press **ENTER**.

3. Place the mouse pointer on the bottom edge of the appointment until you see a double-headed arrow appear, and drag the border down to the time you want the appointment to end. If you need to change the beginning time, then drag the top border up until it reflects the time interval you want.

4. Right-click the meeting to open the context menu. Here, you can open the appointment's form, print the form, forward the appointment to someone, make it private so anyone else looking at your calendar won't see it, determine how to show your time, add a colored label, apply automatic formatting, add categories, and delete the appointment.

	Open
🖨	Print
	Reply
	Reply to All
📧	Forward
	Private
	Show Time As ▶
	Label ▶
	Automatic Formatting...
	Categories...
✕	Delete

When you are directly working on the calendar, there are two modes:

- **Text mode** is for adding and removing text, such as entering and editing the description of an appointment. To use Text mode, click in the center area where the description is, wait (about 1/10th of a second) for the insertion point to appear, and then type.

  Dinner wt Jim at Tosca's

- **Object mode** is for working with the item itself, such as altering the duration or the start time. To use Object mode for sizing, move the mouse pointer to either the upper or the lower border of the appointment until the pointer becomes a vertical two-headed arrow, and then drag the border. To use Object mode for moving, point the mouse on the left border of the appointment until it becomes a four-headed arrow, and then drag the appointment where you want it.

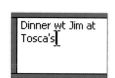

ENTER EVENTS DIRECTLY

An event is an activity that normally lasts at least 24 hours (although you can designate something as an event that lasts less than 24 hours but takes most of your time that day, such as a company picnic). Examples of events are conferences, seminars, and holidays. If events are tied to specific dates, they are Annual Events, such as a birthday or holiday. When you enter an event, it is considered free time, not busy. You create events differently than appointments. All events appear in the banner at the top of the daily schedule, while all appointments are on the calendar itself. To directly enter an event:

1. With the Calendar open in Outlook in Day/Week/Month view, select a day in the Date Navigator that you want to use.

2. Click in the dark gray area at the top of the daily schedule, just under the date header, to enter an event.

3. Type the event name and press **ENTER**.

ENTER APPOINTMENTS AND EVENTS ON A FORM

As an alternative to directly entering appointments and events, you can use an Appointment form to accomplish the same objective and immediately be able to enter a lot more information. The new Appointment form, which is shown in Figure 5-13, can be opened by:

- Double-clicking a time

  –Or–

- Clicking the **New Appointment** button in the Standard toolbar

  –Or–

- Clicking either the **File** or **Actions** menu and clicking **New Appointment**

Figure 5-13: The Appointment window, an example of a Calendar form, is used to set up or change an appointment.

In the new Appointment form, text added to the Subject text box becomes the description in the calendar, with the location added parenthetically and the date and time determining where the appointment goes on the calendar. For example, the appointment in Figure 5-13 creates this entry in the calendar:

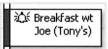

To create a new appointment:

1. Click **New Appointment** in the Standard toolbar to open the new appointment form, similar to what you saw in Figure 5-13.

2. Type the appointment name or description in the Subject text box, and press **TAB**. Type the Location, if appropriate, in its text box, and press **TAB** again. Select or type the start date, and press **TAB**. Then type the start time. Place a check mark in the Reminder check box to select it (or not, if you don't want a reminder—see "Use Reminders," later in this chapter. Choose among Busy, Free, Tentative, or Out Of Office in the Show Time As drop-down list. In the large text area, type the full description of what the appointment is for.

3. Click **Save And Close** in the Standard toolbar. You'll see your new appointment. If you can't see all of the subject and location, drag the bottom border down, and you can see the full location.

The only change needed to enter an all-day event is to check **All Day Event**. The title of the form changes from Appointment to Event; the start and end times disappear; the Reminder, by default, goes to 18 hours; and Show Time As changes to Free—as you can see in Figure 5-14.

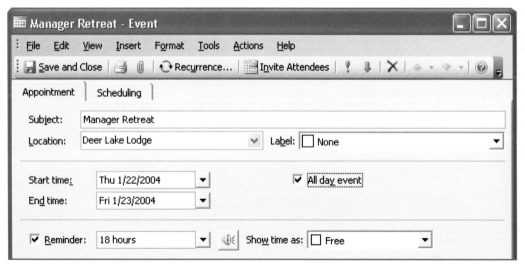

Figure 5-14: A new event is just a new appointment with All Day Event checked.

NOTE

During events your time is considered free and therefore won't show up in the Date Navigator. You need to set it to busy in the Show Time As drop-down list box in order for it to show up.

Enter Recurring Appointments

Often you'll have appointments and events that recur predictably, for example, a weekly staff meeting, a monthly planning meeting, a monthly lunch with a friend, and birthdays. You obviously do not want to re-enter these every week, month, or year. Outlook has a feature that allows you to enter these activities once and have them reappear on a given frequency for as long as you want.

1. Open a new Appointment form, and fill it out as described in the previous section.

2. Click **Recurrence** in the toolbar. The Appointment Recurrence dialog box opens, as shown in Figure 5-15.

3. Type the beginning and ending time of day, or select the duration from the drop-down list box.

4. Choose the recurrence pattern you want.

5. Click the range over which you want the recurrence perpetuated, and click **OK**. In the new Appointment form, you'll notice that the recurrence is now listed in place of the time.

Appointment	Scheduling
Subject:	Friday Poker Club
Location:	⌄ Label: ☐ None
Recurrence:	Occurs every Friday effective 1/23/2004 from 8:00 PM to 12:00 AM.

6. Click **Save And Close**. The recurring appointment reappears with an icon of two arrows in a circle. If you look on the calendar at the specified intervals, you'll see it reappear.

☼ Friday Poker
↻ Club

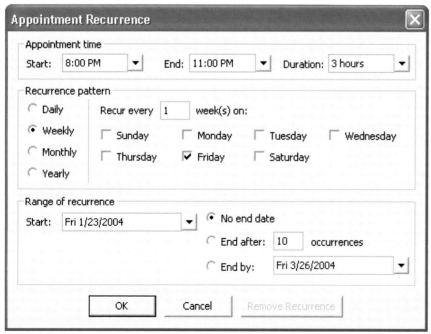

Figure 5-15: Appointment Recurrence allows you to schedule recurring appointments automatically.

EDIT RECURRING APPOINTMENTS

If you want to change the time of only one occurrence of a recurring appointment, you can drag it to another time slot, as long as you don't skip the next occurrence. You will be asked if you want to change all occurrences or just the single appointment. Click **OK** to change just the one appointment. However, to change something about all instances of a recurring series, double-click one of the appointments.

Open Recurring Item

⚠ "Friday Poker Club" is a recurring appointment. Do you want to open only this occurrence or the series?

⦿ Open this occurrence.

○ Open the series.

[OK]   [Cancel]

- Click **Open This Occurrence** to change something one time only.
- Click **Open The Series** to change something for all occurrences.

Move Appointments

If an appointment changes times within a day, you can move it to its new time by simply dragging it to that new time, as you saw earlier. If you entered an event on the wrong day or if an appointment changes days, you can drag it to the correct or new day in either a multiday Calendar view or in the Date Navigator. You cannot drag a recurring appointment to a date that skips over another occurrence of the same appointment. You can, however, change a recurring appointment to another date before the next one occurs. The different ways to move appointments or events are:

- Drag the appointment to the day you want in either a multiday calendar or the Date Navigator. If it is a recurring appointment, the message described earlier appears.
- You can drag an appointment anywhere in the calendar or Date Navigator by dragging the left side of the box using the four-headed arrow described earlier.
- When you drag an appointment to a new day, it will be placed in the same slot. You can also change the time by dragging it to the new time either before or after you move it to the new day.
- Double-click the appointment to open the form. Drag across the start date to change it, and type the new date to move it. Click **Save And Close** to return to the Calendar.

TIP

You can delete a single instance of a recurring activity without affecting the rest of the series. If you choose to delete a recurring activity, the dialog box asks if you want to delete the current instance of the activity or the entire series.

TIP

You can copy an activity by right-clicking and dragging it to where you want the copy and selecting **Copy** from the context menu that appears when you release the right mouse button.

Use Reminders

When you click the Reminder check box to turn it on, a Reminder dialog box appears at a designated time to remind you of the meeting. In dealing with a Reminder dialog box, you have three choices:

- **Dismiss** closes the reminder and tells it not to appear again.

- **Snooze** closes the reminder and tells it to appear again at the time indicated at the bottom of the dialog box.

- **Open Item** opens the appointment form that created the reminder, while leaving the reminder open. This gives you a chance to get additional information, possibly change the appointment, and then decide what to do about the reminder.

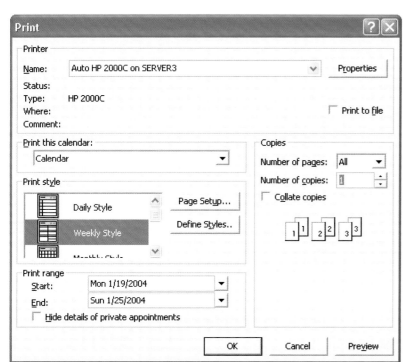

Figure 5-16

NOTE

Reminders are wonderful if they are used sparingly. If they are constantly going off and you dismiss them, then they are of little value. The default is for a reminder to be automatically turned on, so you must turn it off in a new appointment if you don't want it.

Print Calendars

When you have completed making entries on your calendar, you may want to take it with you, away from your computer, for reference and to jot new appointments on. For this reason, Outlook includes a number of printed formats that fit the various size binders made by several companies for such a purpose.

1. With the Outlook Calendar open, select the day, week, or month that you want to print. (You don't have to do this, since you can choose when you describe what to print, but selecting it prior to printing allows you to see what will print.)

2. Click **Print** in the Standard toolbar.
   –Or–
   Click the **File** menu and click **Print**. The Print dialog box opens, as shown in Figure 5-16.

Figure 5-16: The Print dialog box gives you considerable flexibility to change the print style, the format, paper specifications, and header/footer information.

3. Choose which print style you want by clicking **Define Styles**. Select a style (Weekly Style is used here), and click **Edit** to open the Page Setup dialog box (the same as if you had clicked **Page Setup** from the Print dialog box).

4. Click **Print Preview** to see what the report looks like with the default options. Click **Page Setup** in the toolbar to return to Page Setup. (Clicking **Close** escapes out of the Print function altogether.)

5. Accept or change the default setting in the Format tab.

6. Click the **Paper** tab. This tab, as you can see in Figure 5-17, allows you to select the type of paper or form you are using in your printer as well as the size and type of page you want printed on the paper.

7. On the Paper tab, adjust the margins and other settings as needed. Click the **Header/Footer** tab to see that the default is a footer with your name, page number, and date and time. Click **Print Preview** to see your page(s), and click **Actual Size** to see the detail.

Marty Matthews	1	1/24/2004 12:50 AM

8. Click **Print** to return to the Print dialog box, and click **OK** to print. Your results should duplicate the Print Preview screen, except that shading is added for a more finished look.

How your printed results look depends on your selection from among many different options and formats. Unless you have a particular format that you know you want to use, try printing in several formats, and see which works best for you.

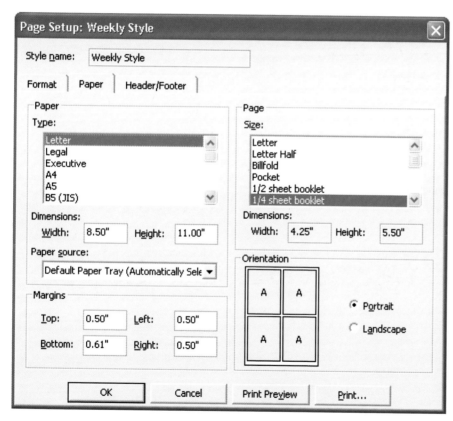

Figure 5-17: The Paper settings allow you to print forms for several brands of desk and pocket planners.

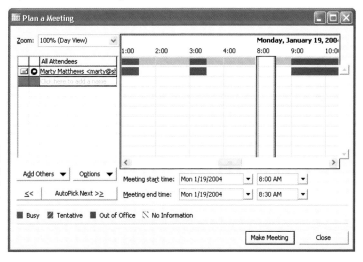
Plan Meetings and Request Attendance

In addition to scheduling appointments and events, you can also plan and schedule meetings. Meetings include inviting others or responding to invitations to meetings from others. Outlook can help you set up and manage meetings with the Meeting form. It allows you to identify the people you want to attend the meeting, send them e-mail requests to attend, reserve resources such as meeting rooms and projectors, and track the responses you get from the people you have invited.

Initiate a Meeting

You can plan and initiate a meeting with Outlook's help. Simply click **Plan A Meeting** on the toolbar or select **Plan A Meeting** in the Calendar menu. Here's how to do it:

1. In the Outlook Calendar, select a time you want the meeting to start, and click **Plan A Meeting** in the Standard toolbar. The Plan A Meeting dialog box opens, as shown in Figure 5-18.

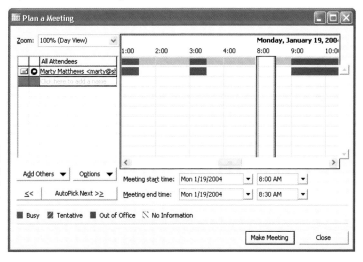

Figure 5-18: The Meeting form allows you to send out invitations, track who can attend, and schedule resources for the meeting.

NOTE

The Advanced button on the Select Attendees And Resources dialog box allows you to add new contacts who can then be added to the invitation list.

2. To specify people you want to invite, click **Add Others**, choose between your Address Book and a public folder with names and addresses, and select those to invite. Depending on how you are connected to the people you want to invite and the way you have your address book(s) organized, you may need to open several address sources.

3. From the address sources you have available, select the required and optional attendees. If you have a resource folder of meeting rooms and other resources, also select those. When you are done, your Select Attendees And Resources dialog box will look something like Figure 5-19.

Figure 5-19: The Select Attendees And Resources dialog box determines who will attend the meeting and, perhaps, where it will be held.

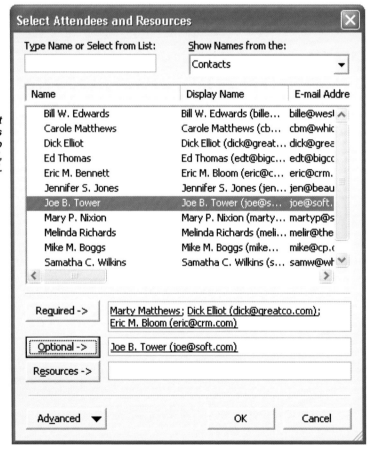

4. Click **OK** to return to the Plan A Meeting dialog box. You may be told that not all of the people you are inviting have free/busy information available to you and that you could all join Microsoft Office Internet Free/Busy Service. See the earlier discussion on this service.

5. Set the meeting times by entering the start and ending times. You can also drag the edges of the vertical meeting line to the time for the meeting to be held.

6. Click **AutoPick Next** to select the next available free time forward or back, depending on the direction of the arrows clicked.

7. Click **Make Meeting**, and a Meeting form opens. It looks very much like an Appointment form except that it has a To text box and therefore takes on message properties that allow it to be sent to those invited to the meeting. Fill in the subject of the meeting, its location, some comments about it, and possibly one or more categories. The attendees and meeting time are filled in automatically, as shown in Figure 5-20.

8. Click **Send** to send your meeting requests to the invitees.

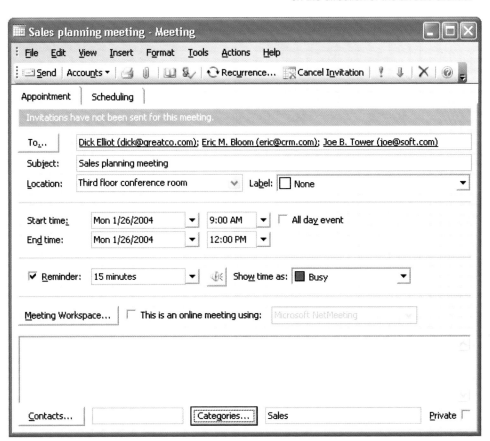

Figure 5-20: A Meeting form is similar to an Appointment form, but it lets you list potential attendees who will receive invitations.

Respond to an Invitation

When you receive a meeting request, a message appears in your Inbox with an icon that is different from the normal e-mail icon. When you open the message with Outlook, you will see an Appointment form similar to the one shown in Figure 5-21. This form has four unique buttons in the toolbar for accepting, tentatively accepting, declining, or proposing a new time for the meeting.

When you click one of the first three buttons to say whether you can attend the meeting, you are asked if you want to edit the automatic response, just send the automatic response, or not send a response. After determining whether to edit the reply or not, you can select **Send** and click **OK**.

If you click **Propose New Time**, the Meeting form will open and allow you to identify a new meeting time while looking at everybody's schedule. When you have selected a new time, click **Propose Time**. A special message form will open. You can add a comment and click **Send**.

NOTE

Closing the meeting appointment form not only sends the response and possibly adds the meeting to your calendar, but also automatically deletes the requesting message.

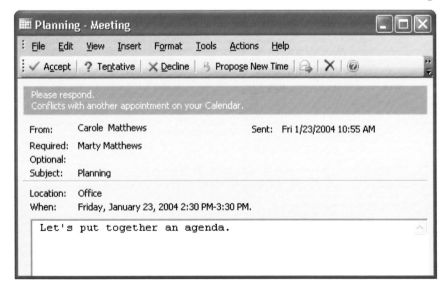

Figure 5-21: A meeting invitation message provides the means to respond in four different ways.

Manage Meeting Responses

You (the meeting originator) now receive the automatic reply in your Inbox. Again, the message has the unique icon that you saw earlier, and you can immediately see if it was accepted. In both the Reading pane and upon opening the message, you see the automatic information and any additional message that the respondent wanted to add. Note that each message you receive tallies the messages that have come before it. If you open the original Meeting form, you'll see a banner that tells you what the attendance count is. If you click the Tracking tab, you'll see the status of each invitee, as shown in Figure 5-22.

Change a Meeting

Once you have created a meeting and notified people about it, given human nature, you will need to change it in one or more ways. You have seen how easy it is to change an appointment; the only difference in changing a meeting is that you must notify and track the acceptance of the participants. The other unique characteristic about changing a meeting is the addition and removal of attendees.

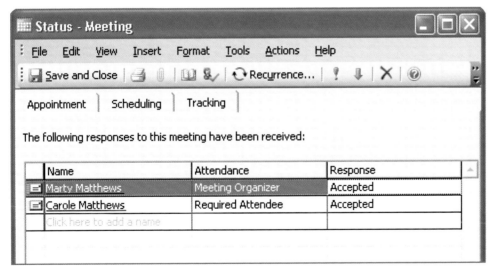

Figure 5-22: The Tracking tab of the meeting form automatically tallies responses as they are received.

RESCHEDULE A MEETING

To reschedule a meeting, you can use any of the techniques you saw earlier in the chapter to reschedule an appointment. You can drag the meeting to another time in the same day, you can drag it to a different day either in a multiday calendar or in the Date Navigator, or you can change the date and/or time in the Meeting form. When you change a meeting that you organized, you get a message asking if you want to send an update message to the attendees.

If you click Yes, the Meeting form is opened, allowing you to make any necessary changes or comments. When you close the form, you are asked if you want to send the revised form to the participants. Clicking **Yes** does that.

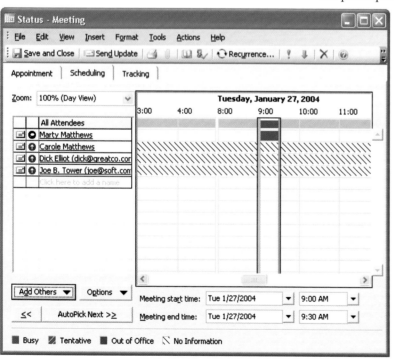

Figure 5-23: You can keep track of those you have invited and invite others to a meeting by using the Meeting form.

ADD ATTENDEES

To add people to a meeting:

1. Open the Meeting form by double-clicking the meeting in the calendar.

2. Click the **Scheduling** tab, shown in Figure 5-23.

3. Click **Add Others**, select **Address Book**, and the Select Attendees And Resources dialog box opens allowing you to select those you want to attend. When you have selected all you want to attend, click **OK**.

4. Click **Save And Close** to close the form.

5. You'll be asked if you want to notify the attendees of the changes. Clicking **Yes** sends a message to both the original and the new participants. If you remove participants from a meeting, you are again asked if you want to notify the participants, including those removed. In other words, if you make any change to the meeting, you'll be asked if you want to notify the participants of the change.

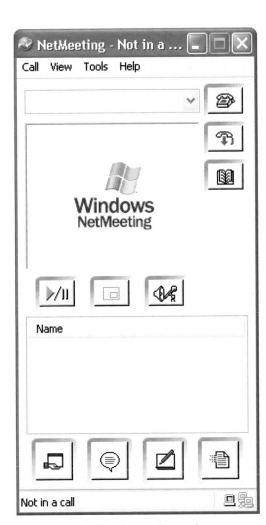

Figure 5-24: NetMeeting can be used independently of Outlook to chat (type messages back and forth) and to hold video and audio conferences.

Initiate an Online Meeting

Online meetings use Microsoft NetMeeting. NetMeeting is designed for online conferencing. It has a variety of services that you can use—everything from video and audio conferencing with multiple people using an electronic whiteboard to sketch out ideas, to a meeting of two persons typing text back and forth in real time for a chat.

SET UP NETMEETING

To use NetMeeting conferencing, you must have the appropriate hardware and software. For example, to use the video and audio features, you need a video camera, a video-capture card, and a sound card. However, to use the more limited types of online meetings, all you need is a modem, Internet Explorer, and your IP address.

NetMeeting is automatically installed with both Windows XP (Home and Professional) and Windows 2000 Professional, but unlike Windows 2000, it is hidden in Windows XP:

1. In Windows XP click **Start**, choose **All Programs | Accessories | Windows Explorer**, in the Folders pane open **My Computer | Local Disk (C:) | Program Files | NetMeeting**, and double-click **Conf.exe**.

   –Or–

   In Windows 2000 click **Start**, choose **Programs | Accessories | Communications**, and click **NetMeeting**.

2. Click **Next**, type your name and other information, and then click **Next** again.

3. Choose whether you want to log on to a directory server (you don't need to), the name of that server, whether you want your name listed, and once more click **Next**.

4. Select the speed of your communications link, and click **Next**.

5. Choose if you want a shortcut to NetMeeting on your desktop and/or on your quick launch toolbar, and click **Next**.

6. Test your microphone and record volume if you wish, click **Next** after each, and then click **Finish**. The NetMeeting window will open, as shown in Figure 5-24.

TESTING NETMEETING

Test NetMeeting with another computer on your network:

1. Set up NetMeeting on both computers as described in "Set Up NetMeeting."

2. Type the network name of the other computer in the address text box at the top of the NetMeeting window, and then click **Place Call**.

3. The other computer will hear a ring, and a message will appear asking if that person wants to accept the NetMeeting call or ignore it.

4. If the other person accepts the call, a meeting will commence.

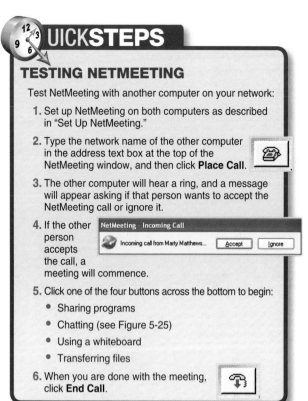

5. Click one of the four buttons across the bottom to begin:

   * Sharing programs
   * Chatting (see Figure 5-25)
   * Using a whiteboard
   * Transferring files

6. When you are done with the meeting, click **End Call**.

TIP

To quickly schedule a NetMeeting with a contact, click **Contacts** in the Navigation pane, click the contact, and select **Actions | Call Using NetMeeting** or click **Call Using NetMeeting** in the Advanced toolbar. NetMeeting will open.

Use NetMeeting

Planning an *online meeting* and then sending invitations works much the same as planning a regular meeting. Start as you normally would, with a Meeting form, and send and track invitations as with an ordinary meeting. In the process, though, indicate it will be an online meeting:

1. From the Calendar in Outlook, open the Meeting form (click **File | New | Meeting Request**).

2. Complete the Appointment tab as described earlier in "Initiate a Meeting." Use the Scheduling tab to add attendees.

3. Place a check mark next to **This Is An Online Meeting Using**. Complete the setting for NetMeeting that then becomes available. You can enter the server here or in the NetMeeting dialog box. If you don't have a server for your communications, it is easier to skip entering it now and specify the server later in the NetMeeting dialog box.

Figure 5-25: The simplest form of NetMeeting is to chat by typing messages back and forth.

4. To automatically start the meeting at a specific time, place a check mark next to **Automatically Start NetMeeting With Reminder**. Your Meeting form should look like Figure 5-26.

5. Click **Send** to schedule the meeting with attendees.

NOTE

To be included in a NetMeeting, a contact must have NetMeeting and must have the NetMeeting information set up in the Details tab of the Contacts form.

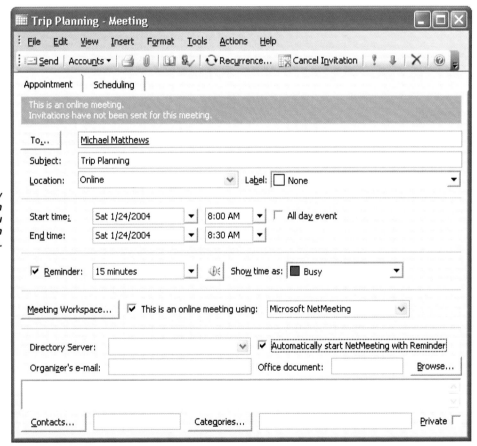

Figure 5-26: The only unique feature about an online meeting is that you provide specifications on how you will be online.

6. If you have chosen to start NetMeeting with the Reminder, when the reminder displays, you will see a unique icon indicating an online meeting. When you are ready to start, open the **Meeting Services** drop-down list, and click **Start NetMeeting**, as shown in Figure 5-27. This will open NetMeeting and automatically fill in the server address (if it is in the contact's record). Click **Place Call** to complete the process.

NOTE

To learn more about NetMeeting, open
http://www.microsoft.com/windows/netmeeting/.

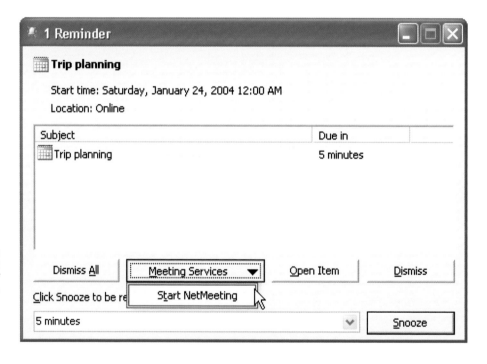

Figure 5-27: Start a NetMeeting from within the Calendar Reminder dialog box.

Chapter 6
Using Task Lists

Keeping organized and meeting appointments and deadlines is important to us all. Outlook can help you stay organized and can even alert you to events and appointments. In Outlook this feature is called Tasks, and you can create, manage, and use Tasks in a variety of ways to keep your business and personal life on track. In this chapter you will familiarize yourself with the Tasks folder, learn how to create tasks, and finally, you'll see how to manage your tasks.

Use the Tasks Folder

Tasks are Outlook items, just like e-mail and calendar entries, and when you create tasks, they are stored in a specific Outlook folder. The Tasks folder keeps all of your tasks in one place and automatically keeps them organized for you. In this section, you'll see how to use the Tasks folder and how to view tasks.

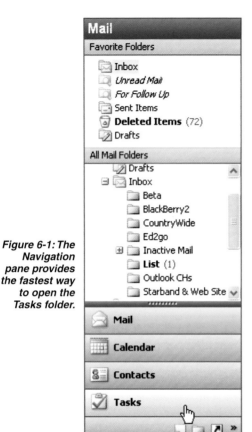

Figure 6-1: The Navigation pane provides the fastest way to open the Tasks folder.

Explore the Tasks Folder

You can easily access the Tasks folder and view your tasks:

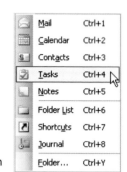

- Open **Outlook** as described in Chapter 1 if it is not already open.

- Click the **Go** menu and click **Tasks**.

  –Or–

  Access the Tasks folder by clicking the **Tasks** button either in the view bars or in the button bar of the Navigation pane, as shown in Figure 6-1.

Either way, the Tasks folder appears in the right side of the Outlook window, as you can see in Figure 6-2. Notice that the folder contains a listing of any existing tasks.

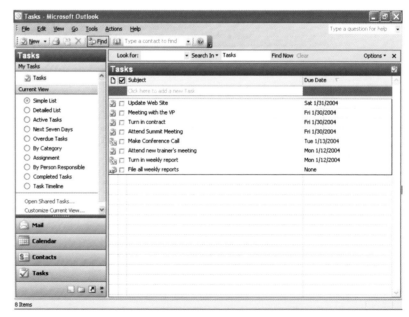

Figure 6-2: The Tasks folder provides both organization and the ability to store some information about your tasks.

NOTE

Although you can easily access the Tasks folder by simply clicking the **Tasks** icon under Personal Folders, if the Folder List is open, it doesn't open the Tasks Navigation pane, which gives you some important selection options. Using the Tasks view bar or choosing **Tasks** from the Go menu to open the Tasks folder opens the Tasks Navigation pane as well.

View Tasks

By default, Outlook gives you a simple list view of your tasks in the Tasks folder. You see the name of the task and the due date. However, you can re-sort these tasks in various ways using several different views, depending on the information you need, which can make your work easier.

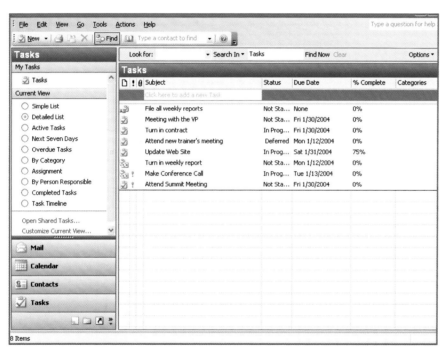

Figure 6-3: The Detailed List gives you additional information about the task.

1. Click **Tasks** in the Navigation pane to open the Tasks folder.

2. In the Navigation pane under Current View, notice that the Simple List is selected by default. However, you can change your view of the tasks by clicking the different options:

- **Simple List** displays a listing of your tasks and the due date

- **Detailed List**, as shown in Figure 6-3, displays the subject, status, due date, percent completed, and any categories that have been assigned to the task

- **Active Tasks**, same as the Detailed List, but only shows tasks that are currently active, that is, tasks that have not been deferred or completed

- **Next Seven Days**, same as the Detailed List, but only shows tasks for the next seven days

- **Overdue Tasks**, same as the Detailed List, but only shows tasks that are overdue

- **By Category**, same as the Detailed List, but the tasks are organized by the categories that have been assigned to the tasks.

- **Assignment** shows you tasks that have been assigned to others. The Tasks pane shows you the task, the owner, the due date, and the status of each task.

- **By Person Responsible** organizes your tasks into collections according to the person responsible for each task. You see the subject, who requested the task, the owner, the due date, and the status.

- **Completed Tasks** shows you all tasks that have been completed.

- **Task Timeline** turns the Tasks folder into a timeline view, where you can see the tasks that are due according to calendar dates, as shown in Figure 6-4.

TIP

You can toggle between any view at any time by simply clicking a different view option button.

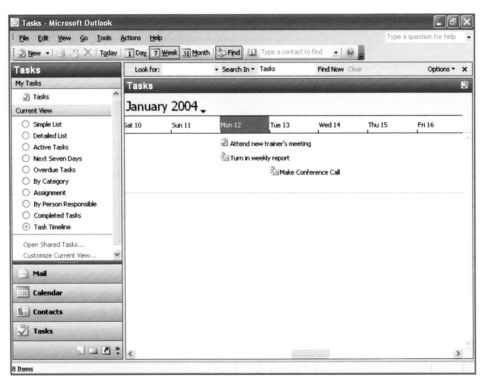

Figure 6-4: The timeline view gives you a quick look at the upcoming tasks.

QUICKSTEPS

CUSTOMIZING THE TASKS FOLDER

Customize the way the Tasks folder displays information by changing the default settings for the folder and changing the options of each task view as needed.

CHANGE BASIC TASKS FOLDER PROPERTIES

Change the Tasks folder properties:

1. Click the **Tools** menu and then click **Options**.

2. On the Preferences tab, under Tasks, click the **Reminder Time** drop-down menu, and choose an alternate time, as shown in Figure 6-5.

3. Click **Task Options**.

4. In the Task Options dialog box, change the Overdue Task Color and the Completed Task Color, if desired, by clicking the drop-down lists and choosing alternate colors, as shown in Figure 6-6. The new colors you select are applied to all overdue tasks and completed tasks.

5. Choose if you want to keep updated copies of your assigned tasks in the task list, send reports when tasks are completed, and set reminders on tasks with dates.

6. When you are done, click **OK** and click **OK** again in the Options dialog box.

Continued…

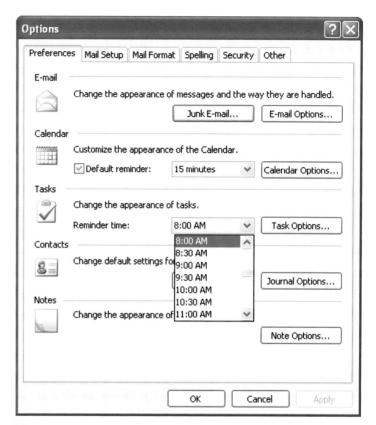

Figure 6-5: You can easily choose an alternate time on the Preferences tab.

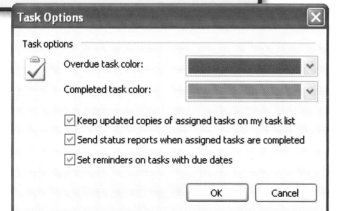

Figure 6-6: Change the color options with the drop-down lists.

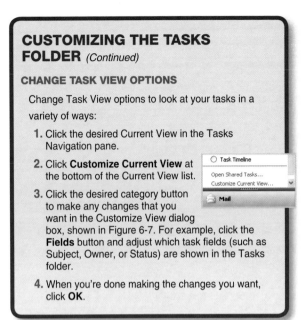

CUSTOMIZING THE TASKS FOLDER *(Continued)*

CHANGE TASK VIEW OPTIONS

Change Task View options to look at your tasks in a variety of ways:

1. Click the desired Current View in the Tasks Navigation pane.

2. Click **Customize Current View** at the bottom of the Current View list.

3. Click the desired category button to make any changes that you want in the Customize View dialog box, shown in Figure 6-7. For example, click the **Fields** button and adjust which task fields (such as Subject, Owner, or Status) are shown in the Tasks folder.

4. When you're done making the changes you want, click **OK**.

Figure 6-7:
You can make changes to any field by clicking the appropriate button.

Create Tasks

To use the Outlook Tasks feature, you'll have to create tasks as needed. As new appointments, jobs, and other tasks come your way, you can simply create a task in the Tasks folder so that you can keep your work organized and so Outlook can keep your deadlines on track. Creating and working with the tasks you create is rather easy, and in this section you'll see how to add a task, change a task, copy a task, make a recurring task, and more.

Add a Task

Your first step with Tasks is to create one. You create a new task by simply adding a task to your Tasks folder. From that point, you can further configure the task as needed and work with it. You can add a task in two different ways. First, you can add one directly within the Tasks folder itself:

1. Open the **Tasks** folder and choose the **Detailed List** Current View.

2. In the Tasks folder, click the **Click Here To Add A New Task** field, as shown in Figure 6-8.

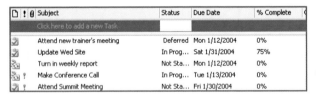

Figure 6-8: Enter a new task by simply clicking on the top line of the Tasks folder.

🗋	!	𝕌	Subject	Status	Due Date	% Complete	Categories
			Turn in contract	In Prog...	Fri 1/30/2004		
☑			Attend new trainer's meeting	Defe			
☑			Update Wed Site	In Pre		%	
☑			Turn in weekly report	Not S			
☑	!		Make Conference Call	In Pre			
☑	!		Attend Summit Meeting	Not S			

January 2004

S	M	T	W	T	F	S
28	29	30	31	1	2	3
4	5	6	7	8	9	10
11	12	13	14	15	16	17
18	19	20	21	22	23	24
25	26	27	28	29	30	31
1	2	3	4	5	6	7

Today   None

*Figure 6-9: Drop-down lists in many of the
fields assist in quickly entering a task.*

3. Type the name of the task, and use the field drop-down
lists to enter additional information as needed, as shown in
Figure 6-9.

4. When you're done, press **ENTER**, and the task is added to
your task list.

In addition to using the Tasks folder directly to add a task,
you can also use the Untitled Task window.

1. Open the **Tasks** folder.

2. Click **New** on the toolbar. The Untitled Task window appears.

3. As shown in Figure 6-10, type a task name (Subject), and
choose a Due Date, Start Date, Status, Priority, and other
fields as desired.

4. When you're done, click the **Save And Close** button. The
new task is added to your task list.

*Figure 6-10:
Complete the
desired task fields
to create your new
task.*

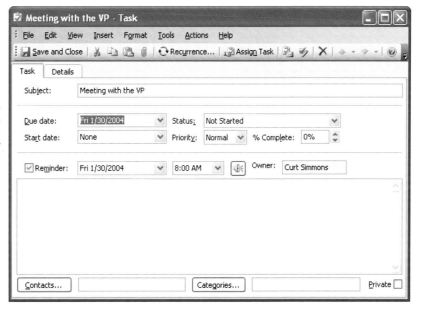

Change a Task

Some of the tasks that you create will change. The report that was due in a month is suddenly due in a week, and the conference call you had planned for 10 A.M. changes to 4 P.M. You can easily change your tasks and edit them. To change a task:

1. Open the **Tasks** folder.

2. In the Tasks folder, double-click the task that you want to change.

3. The window for the task appears. Make any desired changes to the task. For example, in Figure 6-11, I am changing the start date for the task.

4. When you're done, click **Save And Close**.

Figure 6-11: You can make any desired change to a task.

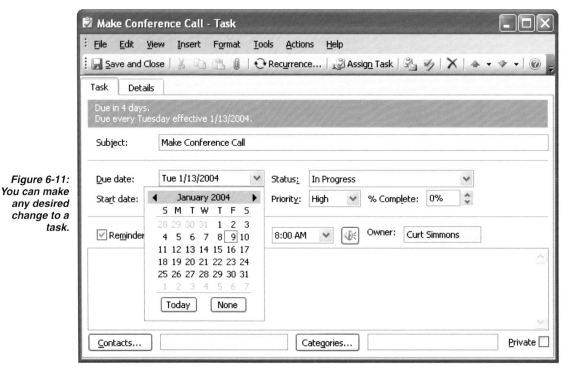

ASSIGNING TASKS TO OTHERS

You can easily create a task and assign it to someone else who is using Microsoft Outlook.

1. Using the Untitled Task window, create the task that you want to assign to someone else.

2. Click the **Assign Task** button on the toolbar, and then click **Save And Close**.

3. The Task window essentially changes to an e-mail message, as you can see in Figure 6-12. Type the addressee's e-mail address, and add your message.

4. You can choose to keep a copy of the task in your Tasks list that is updated as the task is completed, and you can also choose to have a status report sent to you when the task is completed. These two check box items are enabled by default, but you can disable them if you do not want to keep track of the task you are assigning.

5. Click **Send** to send the task to the individual.

TIP

The recipient must accept the task that you send in order for it to be added to his or her Tasks folder. You will receive an e-mail receipt from the recipient once the task is accepted.

TIP

You can assign the same task to several people by simply typing all e-mail addresses in the To text box, just as you would with any e-mail.

Add a Time Estimate

You can add a time estimate to any task by entering a due date and a start date. We call these "estimates" because they can be changed as needed. Keep in mind that you can change any configuration of a task by simply editing it at any time (see the previous section). With that in mind, you can make a time estimate for a task when you create it, or you can edit an existing task and make a time estimate.

1. Open the **Tasks** folder.

2. In the Tasks folder, double-click the task that you want to change, or click the **New** button if you are creating a new task. Either way, the window for the task opens.

3. Click the **Due Date** drop-down menu, and choose the desired due date from the calendar that appears.

4. Click the **Start Date** drop-down menu, and choose the desired start date from the calendar that appears.

5. When you're done, click **Save And Close**.

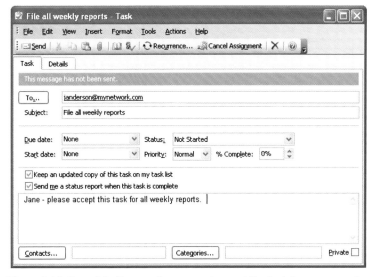

Figure 6-12: Complete the e-mail message to send the task to someone else.

Make a Task Recurring

You may have a task that recurs. For example, let's say that you must submit a team meeting report after each meeting. The meetings occur every Monday. Rather than create a new task in Outlook for each Monday report, you can simply create one task, and then have that task recur each Monday. Recurring tasks are time-savers, and you can easily create a recurring task, or can edit an existing task and make it recurring.

1. Create the task that you want to recur, or if the task already exists, double-click it in the Tasks folder. This action opens the configuration window for the task, as you saw in Figure 6-10.

2. Click the **Recurrence** button on the toolbar. ⟳ Recurrence...

   - In the Task Recurrence dialog box that appears, under Recurrence Pattern, choose how the task should recur. You can choose from Daily, Weekly, Monthly, and Yearly options, and then you can choose the recurrence cycle, such as the day(s) of the week on which the task recurs, as shown in Figure 6-13.

   - Under the Range Of Recurrence, select the start date and choose an end date if necessary.

   - Click **OK** when you're done, and click **Save And Close**.

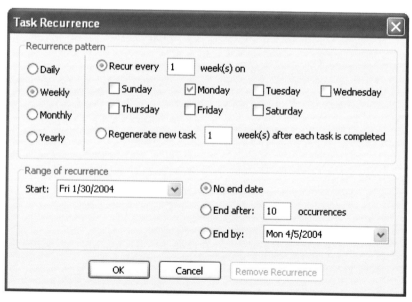

Figure 6-13: The Recurrence Pattern for the task can be from daily to yearly.

> **NOTE**
>
> If you want to remove the recurrence from the task without actually deleting the task, just double-click the task in the Tasks folder, click the **Recurrence** button on the toolbar, and then click the **Remove Recurrence** button in the Task Recurrence dialog box.

Prioritize a Task

By prioritizing a task, you designate a completion priority for that task. This feature enables you to further define your tasks and keep the high priority tasks at the forefront of your mind, while allowing low priority tasks to take a back seat. In short, the prioritize feature in Outlook simply helps you stay organized and on top of tasks that are urgent. You can easily set a priority for a new task that you are creating, or you can edit an existing task and choose a priority.

Figure 6-14: A task's priority can determine how noticeable it is on your list of tasks.

1. Click **New** to create the desired task, or double-click an existing task. This opens a configuration window for the task. Make any necessary entries or selections for the task.

2. Click the **Priority** drop-down menu, and choose **Low**, **Normal**, or **High**, as you can see in Figure 6-14. By default, all tasks are given a priority of Normal.

3. Click **Save And Close**.

Once you have set priorities on tasks, you'll see the priority settings by using the Detailed View in the Tasks folder. As you can see in Figure 6-15, Low priority tasks have a down arrow icon attached to them, Normal priority tasks have no icon, and High priority tasks have an exclamation mark icon.

However, like all things, the priority of a task may change. For example, notice in Figure 6-15 that the task "File all weekly reports" has a High priority. Let's say that priority falls to the Normal setting of other common tasks. You can easily change the priority of an existing task without having to edit it or re-create it.

Figure 6-15: Low and High priority tasks are noted in the Detailed View.

D	!	0	Subject	Status	Due Date	% Complete	Categories
			Click here to add a new Task				
	!		File all weekly reports	Not Sta...	None	0%	
			Meeting with the VP	Not Sta...	Fri 1/30/2004	0%	
			Turn in contract	In Prog...	Fri 1/30/2004	0%	
	↓		Attend new trainer's meeting	Deferred	Mon 1/12/2004	0%	
	↓		Update Web Site	In Prog...	Sat 1/31/2004	75%	
			Turn in weekly report	Not Sta...	Mon 1/19/2004	0%	
	!		Make Conference Call	In Prog...	Tue 1/13/2004	0%	
	!		Attend Summit Meeting	Not Sta...	Fri 1/30/2004	0%	

1. In the Tasks folder, click the **Detailed View** option in the Task pane.

2. Click the priority icon for the desired task, and the priority menu appears.

3. Select a different priority as desired.

Set a Reminder

Outlook can help keep you informed of upcoming tasks that are due with a feature called a Reminder. You set the reminder to let you know at a certain time before the due date that the task is about to be due. This quick and easy feature enables Outlook to make sure you don't forget an important task. You can set a reminder for a new task you create, or you can edit an existing task and set a reminder as well.

1. Create a new task, or select an existing task in the Task folder and double-click it. Either way, the configuration window for the task appears.

2. Note the Reminder section on the Task tab. To enable the reminder, select the **Reminder** check box, as you can see in Figure 6-16.

3. Click the drop-down menus to choose the date and time for the reminder. For example, if you have a task due on Friday, you might choose to configure a reminder for Thursday afternoon, Friday morning, or any other date and time that is helpful to you.

4. Click the **Sound** button. The Reminder Sound dialog box appears. Note that by default, Reminder.wav, an Outlook sound, is played. You can choose any other .wav file to play by clicking the **Browse** button and selecting an alternate .wav file. You may have additional .wav files on your computer that you would rather use, or can even download fun .wav files from the Internet! Click OK when you're done.

5. Click **Save And Close**.

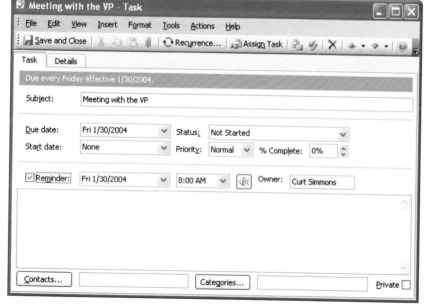

Figure 6-16: Choosing the Reminder check box will alert you when a task is coming due.

HANDLE A REMINDER

When the reminder appears, you'll see a simple dialog box that allows you to interact with the reminder. When the reminder time is met, you'll see a Reminder dialog box, as shown in Figure 6-17.

- If you want to open the task and look at it, just click the **Open Item** button.

- If you want to dismiss the reminder, or dismiss them all, click either **Dismiss** or **Dismiss All**.

- If you want the reminder to appear again, you can use the Snooze feature. Click the drop-down menu, choose a length of time for the snooze, and then click the **Snooze** button. The dialog box will disappear. Once the snooze time you selected is met, the reminder (and reminder sound, if configured) will appear again.

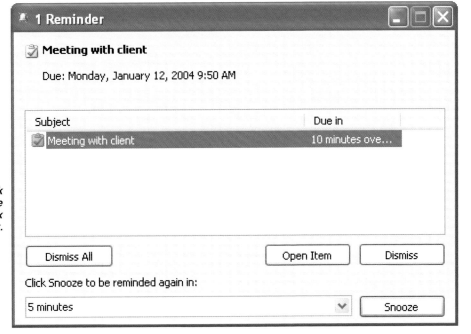

Figure 6-17: Click Open Item in the Reminder dialog box to open the task.

Set a Category

Outlook contains a Categories feature that enables you to label tasks with some basic categories, or you can even create your own. The Categories feature is simply another way Outlook can help you stay organized and make your tasks easier to locate, sort, and review. You can assign a category to any task that you create, or you can assign one to any task that has been previously created. To assign a category to a new task:

1. Click the **New** button and create the new task as described in "Add a Task," earlier in this chapter.

2. In the Task window, click the **Categories** button at the bottom of the configuration dialog box.

3. In the Categories dialog box that appears, choose the category you want to assign to the task by clicking the check box, as shown in Figure 6-18.

4. If you do not see a category that accurately identifies your task, click inside the text box at the top of the dialog box, type a new category name, and then click **Add To List**. Your new category will appear in your category list, and you can then select it.

5. Click **OK** and then click **Save And Close**. Your new task appears in your Tasks folder. If you choose the **Detailed View**, you can see the category you have assigned.

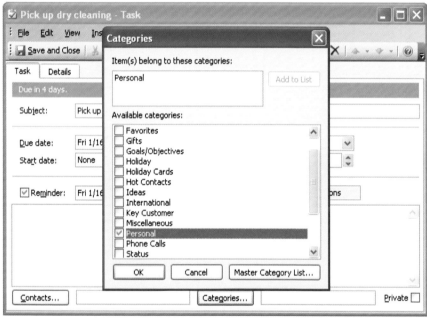

Figure 6-18: Categories allow you to group like tasks and to quickly locate tasks.

ADD A CATEGORY

Besides configuring a category when you first create a task, you can also add a category to a task at any time by simply typing the desired category name in the Tasks folder:

1. Choose the **Detailed View** option in the Navigation pane.
2. In the Tasks folder, notice the Categories column. You can enter a category name for any task by simply clicking in the category field for that item and typing the name.

Make a Task Private

In networks that use Microsoft Exchange Server, you can give other people access to your Tasks folder. For example, let's say that you are a team leader for a department. Within your department several department coordinators may need to access your Tasks folder to enter tasks that you need to complete. In networking environments you can give others access to your Tasks folder so that they can manipulate and change them, and you can, of course, work with tasks yourself.

However, in some instances you may create a task that you want to keep private in an environment like this. This action will keep people who have permission to view your Tasks folder from reading that particular task. To make a task private:

1. Create the new task or open an existing task as desired.
2. In the Task window, select the **Private** check box in the lower-right corner.

> ### TIP
>
> If you are a user on a private network or one who uses Outlook for Internet e-mail, there is no advantage to clicking the Private check box. This feature only works in networks where other users have specifically been granted Read permission for your Tasks, Calendar, and other Outlook features.

Mark a Task Completed

Once you finish a task, you can mark it as having been completed. The task will remain in your Tasks folder for future reference, but it will be marked as completed.

1. In the Tasks folder, right-click the task that you want to mark as completed, and click **Mark Complete**.

2. Once you mark a task complete, a line is drawn through the task.

	!	0	Subject	Status	Due Date	% Complete	Categories
			Click here to add a new Task				
			Meeting with the VP	Comple...	Fri 1/30/2004	100%	
			Pick up dry cleaning	Not Sta...	Fri 1/16/2004	0%	Personal

Delete a Task

Once a task has been completed, or should a task fall out of the scope of your responsibility, you can simply delete the task from your Tasks folder.

To delete a task:

- Right-click the task in the Tasks folder, and click **Delete**.

  –Or–

- Select the task in the Tasks folder, and click the **Delete** button on the toolbar.

  –Or–

- Select the task in the Tasks folder, click the **Edit** menu, and then click **Delete**.

QUICKSTEPS

MONITORING TASKS

You can monitor your tasks in two ways:

MONITOR WITH DETAILED LIST

Click **Detailed List** in the Tasks pane, and view the status of each task as well as the completion date, as shown in Figure 6-19. This feature gives you a quick view of all tasks.

USE THE READING PANE

The Reading pane works great with e-mail, but it also works great with your Tasks folder. You can simply turn on the Reading pane, browse your tasks, and see the details about those tasks.

1. Activate the Reading pane by clicking the **View** menu, choosing **Reading Pane**, and clicking **Right** or **Bottom**.

2. Then simply click on the task in the Tasks folder to read about it, as you can see in Figure 6-20.

Manage Tasks

Along with creating and working with individual tasks, several options are available to you for managing your tasks. These options enable you to track your progress on tasks, create status reports, share task information with others, and use the TaskPad.

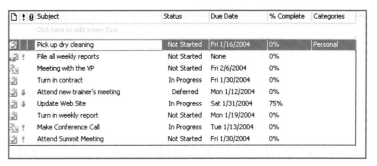

Figure 6-19: You can quickly monitor your tasks using Detailed List.

Figure 6-20: The Reading pane is a helpful way to monitor your tasks.

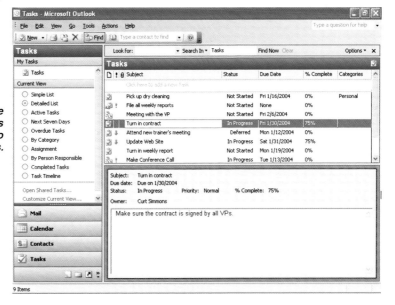

Create Status Reports

Outlook allows you to create a status report for a task which, in reality, is an e-mail message summarizing the status of your task. You can then send the e-mail to anyone who needs the status information. And you can also print a copy for your records.

1. In the Tasks folder, double-click the task on which you want to report.
2. In the Task window, click the **Details** tab and enter any pertinent information about the task.
3. Click the **Send Status Report** button on the toolbar.
4. Type the e-mail address(es) of the recipient(s). You can also add information in the message, just as you would in a normal e-mail, as shown in Figure 6-21.
5. Click **Send**.

NOTE

Just as with any e-mail message, you can also click the **View** menu and choose the **Bcc Field** option, should you want to send a blind copy to any recipients.

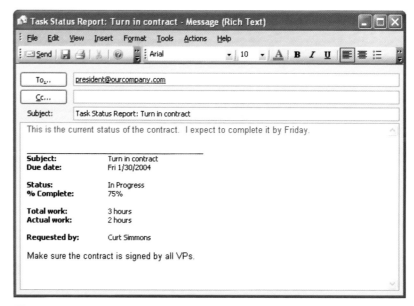

Figure 6-21: Task Status Report provides a fast and easy way to e-mail progress information on a task.

Share Task Information

If you work in a Microsoft Exchange environment, you can share your task information with other people. This feature actually shares your Tasks folder on the network, and others in your Microsoft Exchange environment can then access your Tasks folder and view information. This process gives the users Read permission, meaning they can view your tasks but not change them. To share your Tasks:

1. In the Tasks Navigation pane, click **Share My Tasks**.
2. To give anyone access, in the Name dialog box, select **Default**. From the Permissions menu, click **Read**.
3. To restrict access to certain persons, in the Name dialog box, click **Add**.
4. Click the **Type Name Or Select From List** text box, and type the network name of the person you want to give access, or you can select the person from the list.
5. Click **Add** and then click **OK**.
6. In the Name box, select the name of the person you added. Then, under Permissions, select the **Read** option.
7. Click **OK**.

If you want to access another person's tasks, you can do so directly within Outlook. Note that you must have permission to access another person's Tasks folder before you can do so. Also note that you must be connected to a Microsoft Exchange network in order for this option to work.

1. In the Tasks pane, click **Open Shared Tasks**.
2. In the Open Shared Tasks dialog box that appears, type the network name for the person whose tasks you want to access.

3. Click **OK**.
4. The person's Tasks folder is added to the Navigation pane.

QUICKSTEPS

USING THE TASKPAD

The TaskPad provides a helpful way to look at your tasks from within Calendar view. It helps you see your tasks in light of the calendar and provides a great way to get an overall perspective.

1. Click **Go** and then click **Calendar**.

2. Once the Calendar appears, click the **View** menu and click **TaskPad**. The TaskPad opens in the lower-right corner, as shown in Figure 6-22. By default, the TaskPad shows you all of the tasks for the selected day on the Calendar.

3. Click **View**, click **TaskPad View**, and then choose one of the following TaskPad views:

- **All Tasks** shows all of your tasks in the TaskPad.

- **Today's Tasks**, the default, shows all of the task entries for the current day.

- **Active Tasks For Selected Days** shows all of the tasks for the days you select.

- **Tasks For Next Seven Days** shows the active tasks that are due in the next seven days.

- **Overdue Tasks** shows all tasks that are overdue.

- **Tasks Completed On Selected Days** shows all of the tasks that were completed on the day you select.

- **Include Tasks With No Due Date** shows tasks in the TaskPad that have no due date assigned.

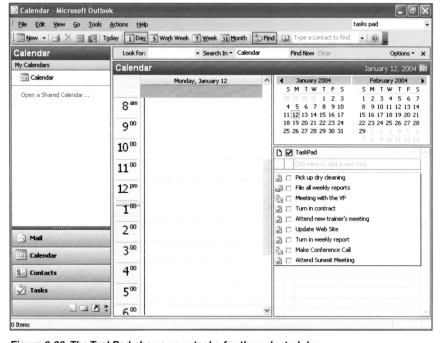

Figure 6-22: The TaskPad shows your tasks for the selected day.

How to...

Chapter 7

Using a Journal and Making Notes

Microsoft Outlook contains two important features that help you stay organized and that can help you manage various pieces of information. These features, Journal and Notes, are designed to help you manage information that you need to record, keep, and use in a variety of ways. In this chapter you'll learn how to use the Journal. You'll see how to work with journal entries, print your journal entries, and even share them. You'll also work with Notes in this chapter. You'll see how to organize your notes, print them, and use them with other Outlook features.

Use a Journal

The Outlook Journal is a great way to track and record different kinds of information. Designed for business use, the Journal can help you keep track of associated Office documents, e-mail to a certain contact, phone calls that you make, and other information. In other words, the Journal can help you keep track of your work flow so that you'll know what has been done. In this section you'll explore the Journal, set it up, work with Journal entries, and print and share your Journal.

Figure 7-1: The Navigation pane gives you some helpful view options for your Journal entries.

Explore the Journal

The Journal is a standard Outlook feature. You can easily access it from the Go menu and explore the basic structure of the Journal. As you'll see, the Journal looks and works much like Tasks, Calendar, and other Outlook features.

Click the **Go** menu and then click **Journal** (see the "Setting Up the Journal" QuickSteps). You see the following features:

TIP

You many need to click the **down arrow** on the menu to expand the Go menu so that the Journal option is visible.

NOTE

The Journal is not by default in the Outlook view bars or in the button bar at the bottom of the Navigation pane. You can, of course, access the Journal from the Go menu, or by using the keyboard shortcut CTRL+8. You can also change the Navigation pane to display the Journal by clicking **Configure Buttons** on the right of the button bar, clicking **Navigation Pane Options**, selecting **Journal** to display it on the button bar, and clicking **Move Up** to display the Journal in one of the Outlook view bars.

- **The Navigation pane**, on the left, as shown in Figure 7-1, has changed to the Journal features you can access, namely the Journal view options, which we'll explore later in this chapter.

- **The Reading pane**, on the right, by default gives you a timeline view and a listing of any existing Journal entries for the portion of the timeline you are looking at.

- **The Standard toolbar** gives you the option of selecting a day, week, or a month view. This feature enables you to move from a detail out to a broad view of your journal entries.

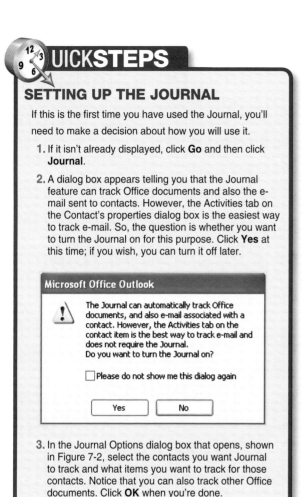

QUICKSTEPS

SETTING UP THE JOURNAL

If this is the first time you have used the Journal, you'll need to make a decision about how you will use it.

1. If it isn't already displayed, click **Go** and then click **Journal**.

2. A dialog box appears telling you that the Journal feature can track Office documents and also the e-mail sent to contacts. However, the Activities tab on the Contact's properties dialog box is the easiest way to track e-mail. So, the question is whether you want to turn the Journal on for this purpose. Click **Yes** at this time; if you wish, you can turn it off later.

Microsoft Office Outlook

⚠ The Journal can automatically track Office documents, and also e-mail associated with a contact. However, the Activities tab on the contact item is the best way to track e-mail and does not require the Journal.
Do you want to turn the Journal on?

☐ Please do not show me this dialog again

[Yes]   [No]

3. In the Journal Options dialog box that opens, shown in Figure 7-2, select the contacts you want Journal to track and what items you want to track for those contacts. Notice that you can also track other Office documents. Click **OK** when you're done.

TIP

You can make changes to these options at any time by clicking **Tools** and then clicking **Options**. In the Options window, click **Journal Options**. You'll see the dialog box in Figure 7-2.

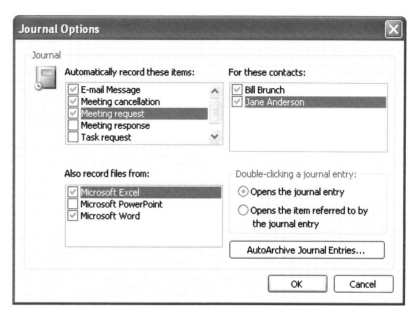

Figure 7-2: *You can select the items you want the Journal to track, including contact e-mail data.*

Add a Journal Entry

With the Journal open, you can quickly and easily add Journal entries as you need them.

1. Click the **New** button on the Standard toolbar.  New ▾

2. In the Journal Entry window, type a descriptive name for the Journal entry in the Subject text box, as shown in Figure 7-3.

Figure 7-3: Enter a short but descriptive name for the new Journal entry.

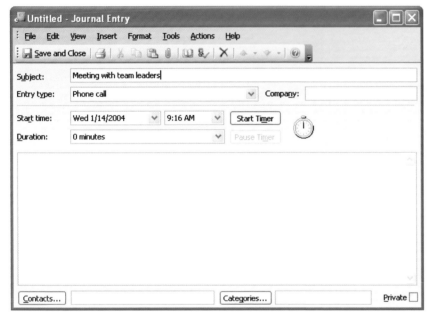

3. Click the **Entry Type** drop-down menu, and choose the type of entry you are creating.

Conversation
Document
E-mail Message
Fax
Letter
Meeting
Meeting cancellation
Meeting request
Meeting response
Microsoft Excel
Microsoft PowerPoint
Microsoft Word
Note
Phone call
Remote session
Task
Task request
Task response

4. Use the available drop-down menus to select the start date and time. You can also use the drop-down menu to choose the duration of the entry, if desired.

5. If you want to time the entry, such as in the case of a telephone call or meeting, click the **Start Timer** button.

6. Click **Save And Close**. The new Journal entry appears in your Journal.

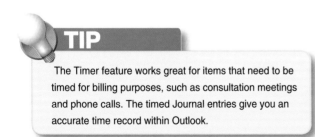

TIP

The Timer feature works great for items that need to be timed for billing purposes, such as consultation meetings and phone calls. The timed Journal entries give you an accurate time record within Outlook.

Change a Journal Entry

Journal entries, like most anything else you might record in Outlook, may need to be changed. To do that:

1. In your Journal, right-click the entry you want to change, and click **Open Journal Entry**, as shown in Figure 7-4.

2. The Journal Entry window appears. Make any desired changes to the Journal entry.

3. Click **Save And Close**.

Delete a Journal Entry

You can easily and permanently remove Journal entries from Journal. You can do this by simply deleting the entry item. To delete a Journal entry:

- Right-click the entry in the Journal, and click **Delete**.

  –Or–

- Select the entry in the Journal, and click the **Delete** button on the toolbar.

  –Or–

- Select the entry in the Journal, click the **Edit** menu, and then click **Delete**.

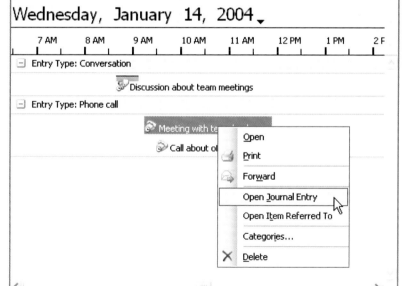

Figure 7-4: Right-click the entry and select Open Journal Entry, or just double-click the entry.

Move a Journal Entry

The time and date values placed on Journal entries might change. For example, the phone call you were going to make at 10:00 A.M. was moved to 4:00 P.M., and meeting times and dates are certainly subject to change, along with most other Journal items. You cannot directly drag items onto the Journal itself, but you can easily change the start date and time for an entry, thus moving it on the timeline.

1. In your Journal right-click the entry you want to edit, and click **Open Journal Entry**, or you can just double-click the entry.

2. In the Journal Entry window, change the start date and time as needed.

3. Click **Save And Close**. The entry item will be updated on the timeline.

NOTE

Moving a Journal entry does not change the start time of the item, document, or contact for that item.

Attach Journal Entries to Contacts

You can directly attach a contact to a Journal entry as you are creating a new entry, or you can decide to attach a contact later.

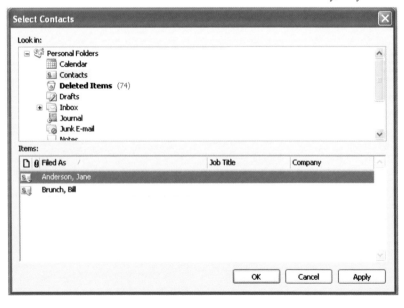

1. For an existing entry, double-click the entry in the Journal. If you are creating a new entry, click the **New** button on the toolbar.

2. In the entry window, click the **Contacts** button. | Contacts... |

3. In the Select Contacts window, shown in Figure 7-5, make sure the **Contacts** folder is selected under Look In. In the Items field, select the desired contact.

4. Click **OK** and then click **Save And Close**.

Figure 7-5: Choose the contact you want to associate with the Journal entry.

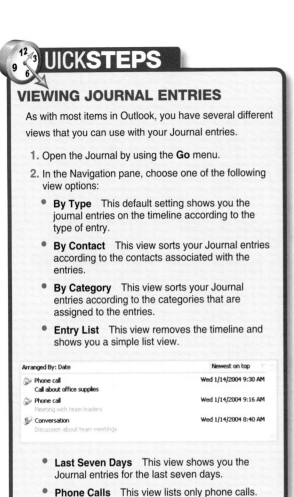

VIEWING JOURNAL ENTRIES

As with most items in Outlook, you have several different views that you can use with your Journal entries.

1. Open the Journal by using the **Go** menu.

2. In the Navigation pane, choose one of the following view options:

   - **By Type** This default setting shows you the journal entries on the timeline according to the type of entry.

   - **By Contact** This view sorts your Journal entries according to the contacts associated with the entries.

   - **By Category** This view sorts your Journal entries according to the categories that are assigned to the entries.

   - **Entry List** This view removes the timeline and shows you a simple list view.

Arranged By: Date	Newest on top
Phone call Call about office supplies	Wed 1/14/2004 9:30 AM
Phone call Meeting with team leaders	Wed 1/14/2004 9:16 AM
Conversation Discussion about team meetings	Wed 1/14/2004 8:40 AM

   - **Last Seven Days** This view shows you the Journal entries for the last seven days.

   - **Phone Calls** This view lists only phone calls.

Assign a Category

As with Tasks, you can assign categories to a Journal entry. This feature makes it easier for you to keep track of the specific nature of the Journal entries.

1. For a new Journal entry, click the **Categories** button at the bottom-right of the new entry window.

2. For an existing Journal entry, right-click the entry in the Journal, and click **Categories**. Either way, you see the same Categories dialog box, as shown in Figure 7-6.

3. In the Categories dialog box, choose the desired category or categories you want to assign to the task by selecting the appropriate check box.

4. If you do not see a category that accurately identifies your task, click inside the text box at the top, type a new category name, and then click **Add To List**. Your new category will appear in your category list, and you can then select it.

5. Click **OK** and then click **Save And Close**.

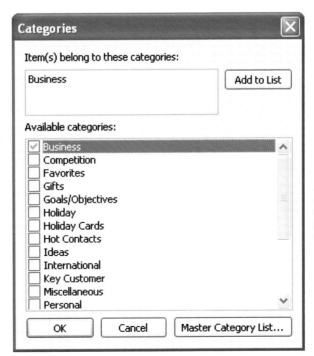

Figure 7-6: Assigning categories to Journal entries allows you to group entries and more easily find them.

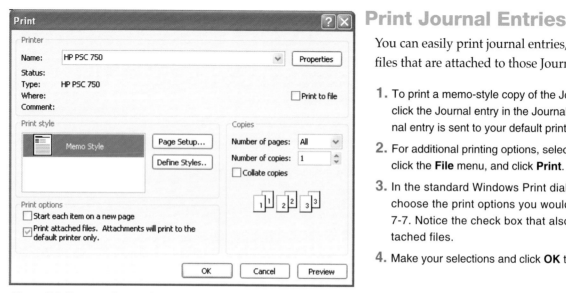

Figure 7-7: You can change the default print options as desired.

Print Journal Entries

You can easily print journal entries, and you can also print files that are attached to those Journal entries.

1. To print a memo-style copy of the Journal entry, simply right-click the Journal entry in the Journal, and click **Print**. The Journal entry is sent to your default printer.

2. For additional printing options, select the entry in the Journal, click the **File** menu, and click **Print**.

3. In the standard Windows Print dialog box that appears, choose the print options you would like, as shown in Figure 7-7. Notice the check box that also allows you to print attached files.

4. Make your selections and click **OK** to start printing.

Share Journals

If you use Outlook on a Microsoft Exchange network, you can share your Journal with others and also access the shared Journals of other Outlook users for which you have permission. To share your Journal:

1. In the Journal Navigation pane, click **Share My Journal**.

2. To give anyone access, in the Name dialog box, select **Default**. From the Permissions menu, choose **Read**.

3. To restrict access to certain persons, in the Name dialog box, click **Add**.

4. In the Type Name Or Select From List box, type the network name of the person you want to give access, or you can select the person from the list.

5. Click **Add** and then click **OK**.

6. In the Name box, select the name of the person you added. Then, under Permissions, select the **Read** option.

7. Click **OK**.

NOTE

You cannot share journal entries unless you are on a Microsoft Exchange network.

NOTE

If **Share My Journal** is not available on the Navigation pane, then you are not connected to a Microsoft Exchange network.

TIP

You may need to drag the menu up a bit to see the Notes option.

If you want to access another person's Journal, you can do so directly within Outlook. You must have permission to access another person's Journal, and you must be connected to a Microsoft Exchange network in order for this option to work.

1. In the Navigation pane, click **Open A Shared Journal**.

2. In the Open A Shared Journal dialog box that appears, enter the network name of the person whose Journal you want to access.

3. Click **OK**.

4. The user's Journal is added to the Navigation pane.

Make Notes

If you are like most of us, notes are a way of life. Your desk might be littered with scraps of paper where you can scribble important things quickly. Of course, finding the note you need is another story. The great news is that you can keep all of the notes you want, and simply let Outlook take care of them. Instead of scribbled notes on paper, you can use Outlook's Notes feature to collect and organize them all. In this section you'll learn how to create, manage, and work with your notes.

Explore Notes

The Notes feature in Outlook is easy to use. To explore the Notes feature:

1. Click **Go** and then click **Notes**.

   –Or–

   Click the **Notes** button on the Navigation pane.

2. The Notes folder appears in the right pane. If you have any notes written, they will appear in the task pane. Select **Icons** view, if it isn't currently selected.

QUICKSTEPS

SETTING UP NOTES

You can make some quick and easy changes to the way notes look:

1. Click **Notes**.

2. Click **Tools** and then click **Options**.

3. In the **Options** dialog box, shown in Figure 7-8, click the **Note Options** button.

4. In the Notes Options dialog box, click the **Color** drop-down menu, and choose a color for your notes. The default is yellow.

5. Click the **Size** drop-down menu, and choose the note size you want. The default size is Medium.

6. Click the **Font** button to select a different font. In the **Font** window that appears, as shown in Figure 7-9, you can choose the font, font style, size, and any effects you might want to use. Make your selections and click **OK**.

7. Click **OK** on the Notes Options dialog box and **OK** on the Options dialog box.

3. On the toolbar you can change the icon size of the notes from large icons to small icons, and even to a simple list. You can easily switch between these icon views as desired.

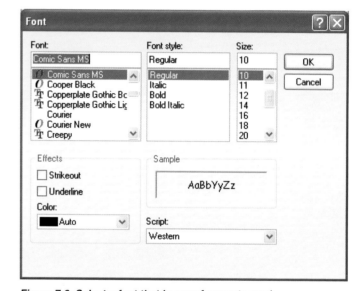

Figure 7-9: Select a font that is easy for you to read.

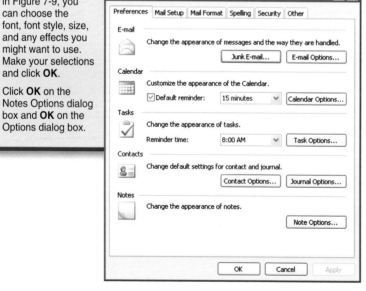

Figure 7-8: Note Options gives you quick access to Outlook configuration features.

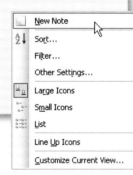

Use Notes

Notes are easy to use, and you can quickly create, modify, and add them as you need.

ADD A NOTE

You can quickly and easily create a note whenever you need to. To add a note to your Notes folder:

1. Click the **New** button on the Standard toolbar.

2. The note appears. Type the information you want directly on the note.

3. When you're done, click the **Close** button on the note. The note now appears in your Notes folder.

CHANGE A NOTE

Editing a note is quick and easy. This feature allows you to change and update information on any note.

1. In the Notes folder, double-click the desired note.

2. Retype or change the information on the note.

3. Click the **Close** button on the note.

DELETE A NOTE

Notes are designed to be pieces of information that help you stay organized. As such, you'll probably need to update, change, and delete old notes fairly often. To delete a note:

- Right-click the note in the Notes folder, and click **Delete**.

  –Or–

- Select the note and click the **Delete** button on the Standard toolbar.

  –Or–

- Select the note and click the **Edit** menu, and then click **Delete**.

CATEGORIZE NOTES

As with other Outlook items, you can also attach categories to your notes. When you use a category view (which you'll explore later in this chapter), you can easily keep business notes separate from personal notes, and so on. To categorize a note:

1. In the Notes folder, right-click the note and click **Categories**.

2. In the Categories dialog box that appears, choose the category you want to assign to the note by clicking the check box.

3. If you do not see a category that accurately identifies your note, click in the text box at the top, type a new category name, and then click **Add To List**. Your new category will appear in your category list, and you can then select it.

4. Click **OK** when you're done.

CHANGE A NOTE'S COLOR

By default your notes are all the same color, depending on the color you chose in the Notes Options dialog box. However, you can override this default setting for any note you choose. This feature allows you to color-code your notes. You might choose to color-code all of your business notes, or perhaps all of your personal notes. Or, you might want to assign a certain color to urgent notes. No matter what your selection, you can easily change a note's color at any time.

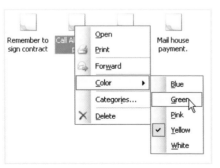

1. In the Notes folder, right-click the desired note.

2. On the context menu that appears, point to **Color**, and then click the color that you want to assign to the note.

3. You can repeat these steps for any other note, or to change the color again on a previously edited note.

FW: Remember to sign contract - Message (HTML)

File Edit View Insert Format Tools Actions Help

Send   Arial   ▼ 10 ▼ A **B** *I* U ≡ ≡ ≡ ≔

To...   janderson@mynetwork.com;

Cc...

Subject: FW: Remember to sign contract

Attach...   Remember to sign contract

Hi Jane:
See this note about contract signatures.

Thanks!

Figure 7-10: A note can be automatically added to an e-mail message as an attachment.

1
2
3
4
5
6
7
8
9
10

FORWARD A NOTE

The notes you create in Outlook can easily be used as e-mail attachments to other Outlook users. This feature enables you to easily share information with someone over e-mail without having to retype the information in the e-mail or having to cut and paste the information. To forward a note:

1. In the Notes folder, right-click the note and click **Forward**.

2. A new e-mail message appears, with the note included as an attachment, as you can see in Figure 7-10. Enter the recipient's e-mail address, and type your message.

   Open
   Print
   Forward
   Color   ▶
   Categories...
   ✕ Delete

3. Click **Send**.

VIEW NOTES

The Notes feature gives you five important options for viewing your notes in the Navigation pane:

- **Icons** This default feature gives you an icon view of your notes seen earlier in this section.
- **Notes List** View your notes as a list of items.
- **Last Seven Days** View the last seven days of notes.
- **By Category** See your notes organized by category.
- **By Color** See your notes organized by color.

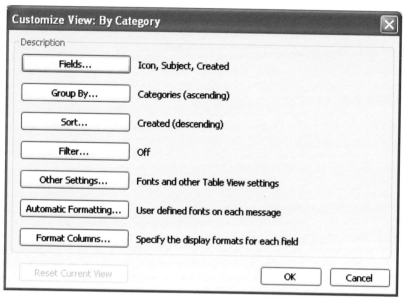

Figure 7-11: You can change the display options by clicking an option button.

CUSTOMIZE CURRENT VIEW

You can also customize the current view by working with the field options for the notes.

1. Click the desired Current View in the Notes Navigation pane.

2. Click **Customize Current View** at the bottom of the Current View list.

3. Click the desired category button to make any changes that you want in the Customize View dialog box, shown in Figure 7-11.

4. When you're done making your changes, click **OK**.

USE THE READING PANE

The Reading pane works with most Outlook features, including notes. The Reading pane allows you to easily switch between notes and read the full content of the note without having to open it (see Figure 7-12). To use the Reading pane with notes:

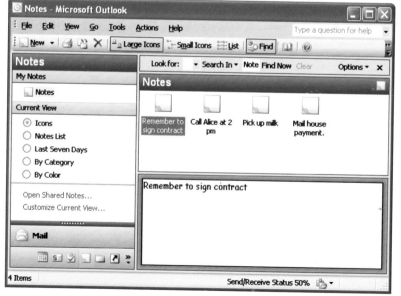

1. Click the **View** menu and then **Reading Pane**. Choose **Right** or **Bottom** for the location.

2. Select a note in order to view the note's text in the Reading pane.

Figure 7-12: You can easily read your notes by turning on the Reading pane.

Share Notes

You can share notes with other users on a Microsoft Exchange network, just as you can share Calendar information, Tasks, and Journal entries. You can also access the notes of others for which you have been granted permission.

1. In the Notes Navigation pane, click **Share My Notes**.
2. To give anyone access, in the Name dialog box, select **Default**. From the Permissions menu, choose **Read**.
3. To restrict access to certain persons, in the Name dialog box, click **Add**.
4. In the Type Name Or Select From List box, type the network name of the person you want to give access, or you can select the person from the list.
5. Click **Add** and then click **OK**.
6. In the Name box, select the name of the person you added. Then, under Permissions, select the **Read** option.
7. Click **OK**.

ACCESS ANOTHER PERSON'S NOTES

If you want to access another person's Notes, you can do so within Outlook. You first must have permission to access another person's Notes, and you must be connected to a Microsoft Exchange network in order for this option to work.

1. In the Navigation pane, click **Open Shared Notes**.
2. In the Name dialog box that appears, enter the network name of the person whose Notes you want to access.
3. Click **OK**.
4. The user's notes are added to the Navigation pane.

NOTE

If **Share My Notes** is not available on the Navigation pane, you are not connected to a Microsoft Exchange network.

Print Notes

You can easily print your notes, when desired.

1. To print a memo-style copy of the Journal entry, simply right-click the note, and click **Print**. The note is sent to your default printer.

2. For additional printing options, select the note you want to print in the Notes folder, click **File**, and then click **Print**.

3. In the standard Windows Print dialog box that appears (see Figure 7-13), choose the print options you would like, such as the style, the number of copies, the default printer, and so forth.

4. Make your selections and click **OK** to start printing.

TIP

You can print multiple notes at the same time. In the Notes folder, hold down the **CTRL** key on your keyboard, and select the notes you want to print. This creates a "multiple selection" of notes, which you can then print together.

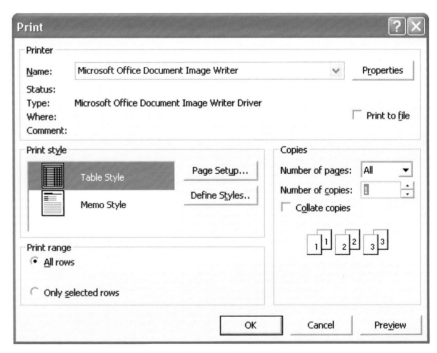

Figure 7-13: You can print notes in either table or memo style.

QUICKSTEPS

USING NOTES IN OTHER OUTLOOK AREAS

You can use your notes by simply dragging and dropping them to other areas of Microsoft Outlook:

1. To automatically create an e-mail message using a note, drag the desired note to the Mail selection button on the Navigation pane, as shown in Figure 7-14.

2. To send a note to your calendar, drag the note to the Calendar button on the Navigation pane. The note is converted to a Calendar item, which you can configure as needed, as shown in Figure 7-15.

3. Repeat this same process to turn a note into a Task or a Contact.

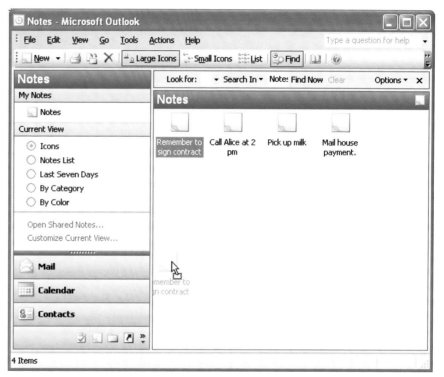

Figure 7-14: You can drag the note to any Navigation pane option.

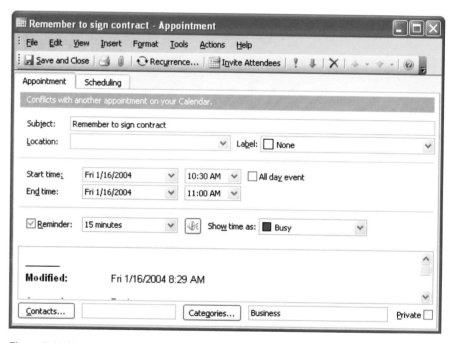

Figure 7-15: Your note instantly turns into a Calendar item.

Chapter 8
Managing Files and Folders

As you send and receive e-mail and work with your Outlook data, you'll need to organize and work with data files. Microsoft Outlook makes data management easy. In this chapter you'll see how to work with folders and manipulate files in Outlook. You'll also see how to make Outlook secure by setting security options and encrypting private messages.

Work with Folders

Outlook manages data by storing information in folders, specifically your Personal Folders. When you use e-mail, you see folders such as your Inbox, Outbox, Deleted Items, Sent Items, and so forth. However, you are not limited to these basic folders. Instead, you can create and work with additional folders so that you can easily store e-mail messages and files in an organizational system that works best for you. In this section you'll see how to create different kinds of folders, share them, and work with them in a variety of ways.

Create a Normal Folder

You can create basic folders within Outlook so that you can store e-mail messages and files. You may wish to create folders based on work and family correspondence, or you can create any structure that is helpful and meaningful to you. To create a normal folder:

- Click the **File** menu, point to **Folder**, and then click **New Folder**.

    –Or–

    Right-click your **Inbox**, and on the context menu, click **New Folder**.

- In the Create New Folder dialog box, shown in Figure 8-1, enter a name for the folder. Click the **Folder Contains** drop-down menu, and choose the type of items you will store in the folder, such as Mail And Post Items. Finally, select the location where you want to store the folder, such as a subfolder in your Inbox.

When you're done, click **OK**. The folder will appear in the place where you chose to store it.

Figure 8-1: A new Outlook folder can contain only a specific kind of information and must be located within Outlook's Personal Folders hierarchy.

Create a Search Folder

Search folders are a very helpful feature of Outlook. Using search folders, you can store messages and easily search them for certain types of content, or based on the sender or another attribute. In short, search folders enable you not only to store mass amounts of messages, but also to sort easily through and find certain kinds of messages.

Search folders aren't really folders at all. They are virtual folders that search all of your other Outlook folders and give you a report of the messages and information you are looking for, rather than being just a collection of messages that are in one place at one time. This feature allows you to find any message that you want and to show it in the search folder, although the original message isn't actually moved there. To create a search folder:

Figure 8-2: Search folders allow you to search Outlook folders for a wide variety of criteria and to create your own folders.

Click **File | New | Search Folder**.

In the New Search Folder window, shown in Figure 8-2, you can choose one of the following options:

- **Reading Mail:**

  - **Unread Mail** shows you any mail you have not read in any folder.

  - **Mail Flagged For Follow-Up** shows you any mail that is flagged for follow-up in any folder.

  - **Mail Either Unread Or Flagged For Follow-Up** locates unread mail or mail that has been flagged for follow-up in any folder.

  - **Important Mail** locates mail that has been sent with high importance.

- **Mail From People And Lists:**

  - **Mail From And To Specific People** locates mail from and to specific people in any folder.

  - **Mail From Specific People** locates mail from specific people in any folder.

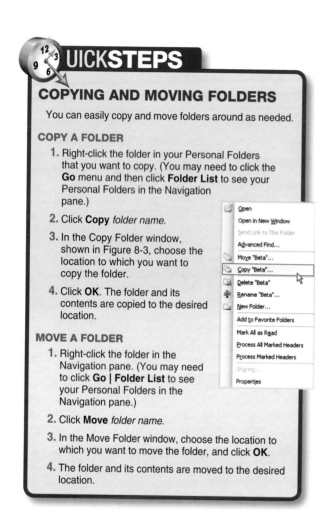

COPYING AND MOVING FOLDERS

You can easily copy and move folders around as needed.

COPY A FOLDER

1. Right-click the folder in your Personal Folders that you want to copy. (You may need to click the **Go** menu and then click **Folder List** to see your Personal Folders in the Navigation pane.)

2. Click **Copy** folder name.

3. In the Copy Folder window, shown in Figure 8-3, choose the location to which you want to copy the folder.

4. Click **OK**. The folder and its contents are copied to the desired location.

MOVE A FOLDER

1. Right-click the folder in the Navigation pane. (You may need to click **Go | Folder List** to see your Personal Folders in the Navigation pane.)

2. Click **Move** folder name.

3. In the Move Folder window, choose the location to which you want to move the folder, and click **OK**.

4. The folder and its contents are moved to the desired location.

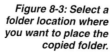

Once you have used search folders, you can simply access your search in the Navigation pane and click on it to perform the search again. The search folder is located in your Personal Folders.

- **Mail Sent Directly To Me** locates mail that was sent directly to you (rather than by means of a distribution list or as a Cc or Bcc).

- **Mail Sent To Distribution Lists** locates mail that was sent to a distribution list.

- **Organizing Mail:**

  - **Large Mail** locates messages above a specific file size.

  - **Old Mail** locates all old mail beyond a specific date.

  - **Mail With Attachments** locates all mail that has an attachment.

  - **Mail Received This Week** shows you all mail that you have received this week.

  - **Mail With Specific Words** locates mail that contains specific words.

- **Custom:**

  - **Create A Custom Search Folder** allows you to create a custom folder that searches for the parameters you specify.

Once you have selected the kind of search folder you want, click **OK**. The type of mail you searched for will appear in the Reading pane.

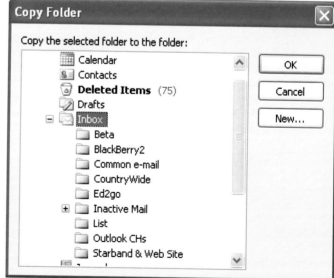

Figure 8-3: Select a folder location where you want to place the copied folder.

Rename Folders

Folder names should be easily recognizable. To that end, you can change a folder's name at any time.

1. Right-click the folder in the Navigation pane, and click **Rename** *folder name*. (You may need to click **Go | Folder List** to see your Personal Folders in the Navigation pane.) Your cursor appears on the folder name.

2. Type a new name for the folder and press **ENTER**.

Share Folders

If your computer resides on a Microsoft Exchange network, you can share any of your folders, allowing other users on your network to access specific personal folders. When you share a folder, you can set permissions allowing certain network users access to your folders and specifying the permissions they have with your folders. Table 8-1 shows the permissions that you can assign.

TABLE 8-1: OUTLOOK PERMISSIONS

PERMISSION	EXPLANATION
Owner	"Owns" the folder and can essentially do any task, including create, read, modify, delete, and create subfolders. Can also assign other rights to individuals
Publishing Editor	Can create, read, modify, and delete all items and files as well as create subfolders
Editor	Can create, read, modify, and delete all items and files
Publishing Author	Can create and read items and files, create subfolders, and modify and delete only own items and files
Author	Can create items and files, read all items and files, create subfolders, and modify and delete only own items and files
Editor	Can create and read files and modify or delete only own items and files
Contributor	Can only create items and files. Cannot read or see items in the folder
Reviewer	Can only read items and files
Custom	Folder owner defines activities for this permission
None	No access to the folder

TIP

If the Sharing option is grayed out, you are not connected to a Microsoft Exchange network.

Keep in mind that you must be on a Microsoft Exchange network to share a folder. To share a folder:

1. In the Navigation pane, right-click the desired folder and click **Sharing**. (You may need to click **Go | Folder List** to see your Personal Folders in the Navigation pane.)
2. Click the **Sharing** tab and click **Share This Folder**.
3. Click the **Permissions** tab. Choose the permission you want to assign for the users on your network by using the **Name** dialog box.
4. Click **OK**.

There may come a time when you need to modify shared permissions. You can easily make those changes as needed:

1. In the Navigation pane, right-click the desired folder and click **Sharing**. (You may need to click **Go | Folder List** to see your Personal Folders in the Navigation pane.)
2. Click the **Permissions** tab. In the Name dialog box, click the name of the person for whom you want to remove permissions.
3. Click the **Remove** button.

Delete Folders

When deleting a folder, you can move all of the folder's contents to another folder if you still want the folder contents. If not, then the folder contents are moved to the Deleted Items folder.

1. In the Navigation pane, right-click the desired folder and click **Delete** *folder name*. (You may need to click **Go | Folder List** to see your Personal Folders in the Navigation pane.)
2. Click **Yes** in response to the warning message that appears.

Figure 8-4: You can get basic information about your folder on the General tab.

Set Folder Properties

Like all folder in Windows, Outlook folders have some basic properties you can configure as needed.

1. Click **Go** | **Folders List**.

2. Right-click the desired folder and click **Properties**.

You have the following options:

- On the **General** tab, shown in Figure 8-4, you see the name of the folder and its general properties. You can choose to show all items in the folder or the number of unread items in the folder. By default, Microsoft Exchange views are automatically set to be created, and you can click **Folder Size** to find out how much disk space your folder is taking up.

- The **Home Page** tab allows you to configure a default home page for the folder if your folders are Web enabled (which is common for folders found on a company intranet).

- On the **AutoArchive** tab, shown in Figure 8-5, you can choose the Auto-Archive method you want to use with this folder. By default, no AutoArchive setting is configured. However, you can choose to automatically have the folder AutoArchive based on Outlook's default settings, or you can configure your own AutoArchive settings for the folder, as you can see in Figure 8-5.

- On the **Administration** tab, the basic folder view is the Normal setting, which is probably your best configuration. The other options on this tab are only available if you are on a Microsoft Exchange network.

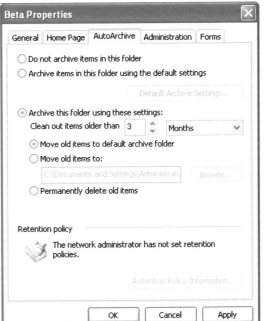

Figure 8-5: The AutoArchive settings give you the flexibility to AutoArchive the folder items in a way that works best for you.

QUICKSTEPS

COPYING AND MOVING FILES

You can easily copy and move files between Outlook folders as you do standard Windows files.

COPYING FILES

1. Click **Go | Folders List**. In the Navigation pane, expand and select the desired folder. The folder contents appear in the Folder pane.

2. Select the file that you want to copy, click the **Edit** menu, and click **Copy**, as shown in Figure 8-6.

You can now paste the copied file into any Windows folder by clicking **Edit | Paste**.

MOVING FILES

1. Click **Go | Folders List**. In the Navigation pane, expand the desired folder and select it. The folder contents appear in the Folder pane.

2. Select the folder that contains the file you want to move.

3. In the Folder pane, right-click the file you want to move, and on the context menu that appears, click **Move To Folder**. The Move Items dialog box will open.

4. In the Move Items window, choose the Outlook folder where you want to move the file, and click **OK**.

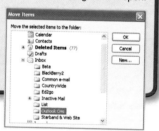

TIP

You can also copy a file by selecting it and pressing **CTRL+C**.

- On the **Forms** tab you can choose to associate any default forms or forms you have created (see Chapter 9) with this folder. Click **Manage** to choose the forms you want to associate.

3. Click **OK** when you are done making any desired changes.

Manipulate Files

Just as you can work with individual folders in Outlook, you can also work with individual and groups of files that are stored in those folders. In this section, you'll see how to manipulate files and work with them by copying, renaming, sharing, deleting, grouping, and sorting files. You'll also see how to import and export files in Outlook.

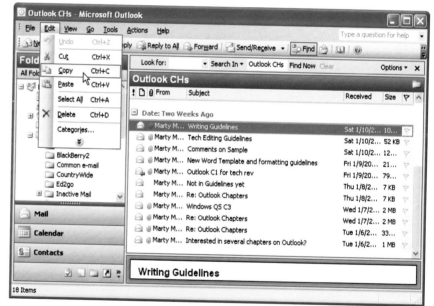

Figure 8-6: Select the file you want to copy, and use the Edit menu.

VIEWING FILES

You can easily view the files within your Outlook folders and then view the file contents in several ways:

- Select the folder in the Folder List, and then select the file in the Folder pane. You can then see the file's contents in the Reading pane.

- Double-click the file. This opens the file in a separate window so that you can view it.

- Right-click the file and click **Open**. This will also open the file in a separate window, just as does double-clicking it.

NOTE

Once again, remember that you cannot share any files with other users from within Outlook unless you are connected to a Microsoft Exchange network.

TIP

You can also select the file and press **CTRL+D** on your keyboard to delete the file.

Share Files

To share files, you'll need to share a folder and place the files that you want to share in that folder. As is typical in Microsoft networking, you do not share individual files, but rather you share folders that contain the files you want to share.

If your computer is on a Microsoft Exchange network and you want to share Outlook files with others, see the earlier section "Share Folders," and then simply move any files that you want to share into the shared folder.

	Open
🖨	Print
📧	Reply
📧	Reply to All
📧	Forward
	Follow Up ▸
✉	Mark as Unread
	Categories...
	Find All ▸
📩	Create Rule...
	Junk E-mail ▸
✕	Delete
🗂	Move to Folder...
📋	Options...

Delete Files

You can delete individual files from within Outlook as needed. Let's say you have a folder that contains a number of older e-mail messages. You do not want to delete the entire folder, but you do want to delete several unnecessary messages from the folder. In this case, you can individually select the messages that you want to delete. Deleted messages are moved to your Deleted Items folder.

1. In the Navigation pane, select the folder that contains the file you want to delete. You may need to click **Go | Folder List** to see your Personal Folders in the Navigation pane.

2. In the Reading pane, right-click the file and click **Delete** or click **Edit | Delete**.

Group Files

You can have Outlook automatically group files for you as a part of Outlook's standard grouping arrangement, or you can manually group items. For example, you might want all e-mail from a specific person grouped into one folder, or you might want e-mail that contains attachments to be grouped into one folder. The choice is yours, but you can easily group items in almost any way that you need.

Figure 8-7: You can group files by up to four items, such as attachments and categories.

Figure 8-8: You can sort files in any folder by up to four levels of criteria.

1. Click the **View** menu, click **Arrange By**, and then click **Custom**.

2. In the Customize View dialog box, click **Group By**.

3. In the Group By dialog box, clear the first check box, the one for automatic arrangement. Then select the desired check boxes, and use the drop-down menus to determine how you want to group items within Outlook, as shown in Figure 8-7.

4. Click **OK** when you're done.

UNGROUP ITEMS

Should you need to ungroup items at any time, you can easily do so.

1. Click **View | Arrange By | Custom**.

2. In the Customize View dialog box, click **Group By**.

3. In the Group By dialog box, click the **Group Items By** drop-down menu, and choose **None**.

Sort Files

Outlook has the capability to sort files that you receive in your Inbox. This feature can automatically help you manage your e-mail and is particularly helpful if you receive a large volume of e-mail.

1. Click **View | Arrange By | Custom**.

2. In the Customize View dialog box, click **Sort**.

3. In the Sort dialog box, shown in Figure 8-8, do the following:

   • Choose a sort item from the drop-down menu, such as Attachment, Contacts, Cc, and so on.

   • Choose more sort criteria in the additional drop-down list boxes as needed.

4. Click **OK** when you are done, and click **OK** again on the **Customize View** window. Your items in the current view are now sorted as you specified.

NOTE

The features you see in "Sort Files" and Figure 8-8 allow you to sort by different criteria levels. For example, you can sort the current view so that all attachments that you are Cc'd on are sorted. This sorting feature allows you to sort items according to several different criteria needs, which can be helpful in locating items.

Import and Export Files

You can import and explore Outlook files from a variety of sources and in a variety of formats.

IMPORT FILES

1. Click **File** and then click **Import/Export**.

2. In the Import and Export Wizard, choose what you would like to import, as shown in Figure 8-9. Make your selection and click **Next**. You have the following options:

- **Import A VCARD File (.vcf)** allows you to import an Outlook vCard that you have received from someone else.

  - **Import An iCalendar Or vCalendar File (.vcs)** imports information from an iCalendar or vCalendar file directly into your Calendar.

  - **Import From Another Program Or File** allows you to import items from other e-mail programs, such as ACT!, Lotus, and so forth. You can also import standard text files and Personal Folders from another Outlook program.

  - **Import Internet Mail Account Settings** allows you to import settings from Outlook Express or Eudora e-mail programs.

  - **Import Internet Mail And Addresses** allows you to import Internet mail and e-mail addresses directly from Outlook Express or Eudora e-mail programs.

3. Complete the steps as instructed by the wizard to import the desired files.

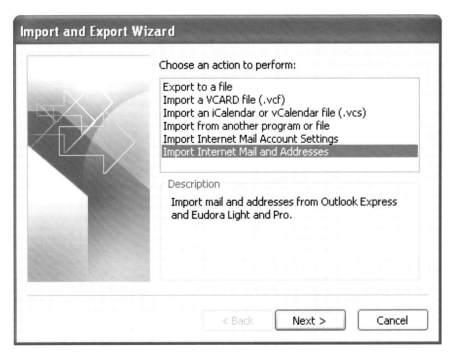

Figure 8-9: You can import a number of different kinds of files, including those created by Outlook Express, Eudora, ACT!, and Lotus Organizer.

Just as you can import files, you can also export files so that they can be used with other programs or as a way to back up your Outlook files.

1. Click **File | Import/Export**.

2. In the Import and Export Wizard, choose **Export To A File**. Click **Next**.

3. Choose the kind of file you want to export to, and click **OK**. You can choose Personal Folder File (.pst), which allows your files to be imported to other Outlook programs, or you can choose file types for other e-mail programs. See the other e-mail program for details about the kinds of files it will import so that you make the best decision for what you want to do.

4. Select the folder within Outlook that you want to export, as shown in Figure 8-10. Notice you may have the option to include subfolders of the primary folder you select. Click that check box if you want to enable the Include Subfolders feature.

Figure 8-10: You can choose to export both individual folders and a folder with all of its subfolders.

5. If you want to filter out some of the messages that you are exporting, click **Filter**, which opens the Filter window. Here, you can search for particular works in specified fields in order to filter out certain messages. For example, you can filter out messages that have certain subjects in the Subject line or messages sent directly to you, and so on. Click the **More Options** tab for additional filtering options, and then click **OK** when you're done.

6. Click **Next**. Choose an export location for the file, which is your Desktop by default. Choose how you want to replace previously exported items and duplicate items, and click **Finish**.

7. The Create Microsoft Personal Folders dialog box appears so that you can choose to create the desired folder where the items will be exported. If you want to accept the default name, just click **OK**. Also, notice that you can encrypt the exported file so that no one can open it without your user name and password. Make your selections and click **OK**.

8. The files are exported. This process may take some time, depending on the number of files that must be exported.

Make Outlook Secure

Outlook 2003 has some important security options that you can configure to keep your e-mail, Calendar, Journal, and other Outlook items secure. In this section you'll see how to set the security options, how to encrypt messages, and how to protect your computer against viruses that may be transmitted through e-mail.

Set Security Options

Outlook is already set with default security options when you first install it. It is important to understand that Outlook provides security with three basic approaches: zone security, encryption security, and minimal protection against viruses. We'll explore encryption settings and virus protection options in the next section and in the upcoming QuickSteps, but this section explores the basic zone settings.

First, it is important to note that zone security affects Outlook, Outlook Express, and Internet Explorer. In other words, if you change zone security settings, you change them for all three programs. Windows uses four different zones to provide basic protection against Internet hackers and intrusion programs:

- **Internet** protects against basic Internet programming languages that can be used to transmit viruses or for hacking purposes. By default, the Medium setting is used, which provides you with basic Internet access capabilities, but unsigned ActiveX controls are not permitted. This setting combines flexibility with security.

- **Local Intranet** protects against basic threats you might find on a local intranet. The default setting is Medium-Low, since most intranets are considered safer than the Internet; however, unsigned ActiveX controls are still not permitted.

- **Trusted Sites** allows you to configure sites that you trust. As such, the security setting is Low.

- **Restricted Sites** allows you to configure sites that are restricted. The default setting for these sites is High.

NOTE

It is important to point out that the security provided by Windows is basic security against threats from the Internet. You may also wish to enable Windows Personal Firewall (see the companion book, *Windows XP QuickSteps*, for further information on firewalls), or you may wish to purchase additional firewall software or hardware for maximum protection from companies such as McAfee, Symantec, or Zone Alarm.

As noted, the zones affect Outlook, Outlook Express, and Internet Explorer, and as a general rule, the default settings are all you need. However, you easily can change the zone settings directly within Outlook if you desire.

1. Click the **Tools** menu and then click **Options**. In the Options dialog box that opens, click the **Security** tab.

2. On the Security tab, in the Security Zones section, click **Zones Settings**.

3. Click **OK** to the warning message that appears.

4. Also on the Security tab, shown in Figure 8-11, select the security zone, and then use the slider bar to adjust the amount of security. Be sure to read the notes for each zone so you will understand how the different settings affect your use of the Internet. The higher the setting, the higher the security, but the more restrictions that are placed on Internet usage.

5. Adjust the other security zones as desired, and then click **OK** when you are done. Click **OK** on the Options dialog box.

Internet Options

General | Security | Privacy | Content | Connections | Programs | Advanced

Select a Web content zone to specify its security settings.

| Internet | Local intranet | Trusted sites | Restricted sites |

Internet

This zone contains all Web sites you haven't placed in other zones

Sites...

Security level for this zone

Move the slider to set the security level for this zone.

Medium
- Safe browsing and still functional
- Prompts before downloading potentially unsafe content
- Unsigned ActiveX controls will not be downloaded
- Appropriate for most Internet sites

Custom Level...   Default Level

OK   Cancel   Apply

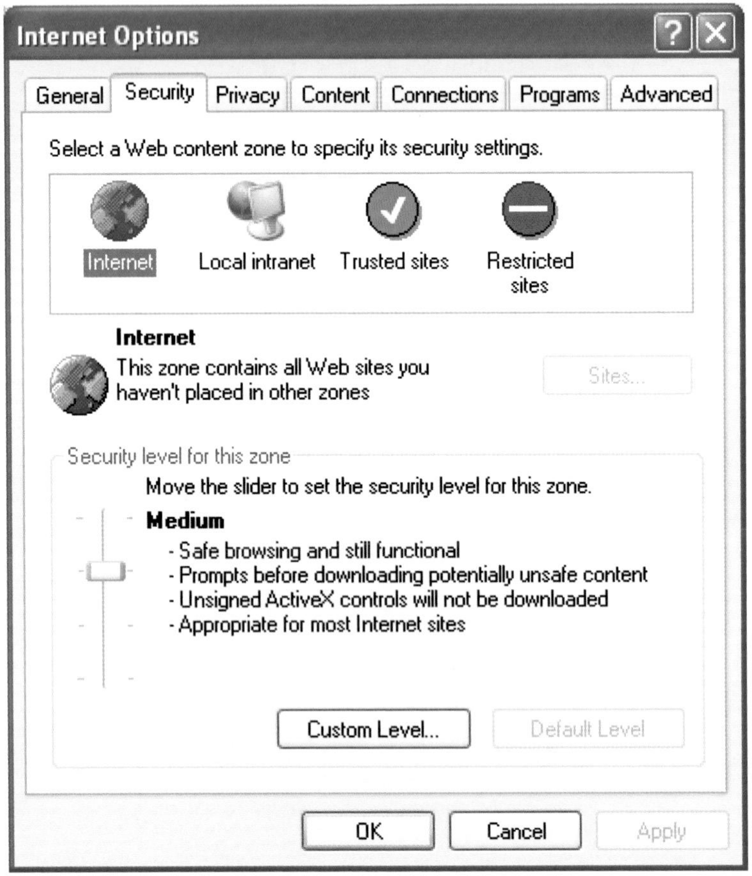

Figure 8-11: For each security zone, you can choose a level of security and then assign sites to the zone to provide the selected level of protection at that site.

Encrypt Messages

Encryption is the process of making an e-mail message unreadable to anyone who is not authorized to view the message. Encryption takes a plain text e-mail message and scrambles it so that it is unreadable. Your recipient must have a private key that matches a public key you used to write the message in order to decrypt and read the message.

If you are on a private Microsoft Exchange network, messages can be encrypted and sent and automatically decrypted by other users on your network. However, if you are sending messages over the Internet to another Outlook user, that user must have a private key that matches your public key in order to read the message. You can do this in a few different ways:

- **Send a digitally signed message** to the recipient. The recipient can then add your e-mail name to Contacts, which imports your certificate with a private key.

- **Attach your certificate** (.cer) file to a message you send to the recipient. The recipient can then import the .cer file and add it your contact card. The certificate can be used to exchange keys.

- **Create a contact with your .cer file,** and then send the contact card to the recipient.

No matter which way you choose to go, the recipient must have your .cer file in his or her Outlook program so Outlook can use that to exchange keys to decrypt any encrypted messages you send.

TIP

In case you are wondering, Outlook uses the 3DES encryption algorithm, which is a standard form of encryption used in the United States and other countries. You can find out more about 3DES encryption at http://kingkong.me.berkeley.edu/~kenneth/courses/sims250/des.html

ENCRYPT MESSAGES ON A PER MESSAGE BASIS

You can choose to encrypt messages on a per message basis so that you can encrypt various messages as needed.

1. Create a new e-mail message addressed to the desired recipient.

2. In the message click **Options** on the Standard toolbar.

3. In the Message Options dialog box that appears, click **Security Settings**, as shown in Figure 8-12.

4. Select the **Encrypt Message Contents And Attachments** check box.

5. Click **OK** three times to return to your message.

6. Send your message. The message will be encrypted and sent.

NOTE

If you attempt to send a message and you do not have a certificate, you will get a message that Outlook could not send the message for that reason. The message will also tell you to open the **Tools** menu, click the **Security** tab, and click **Get A Digital ID**, or to use a different mail account that has a certificate.

Figure 8-12: You can encrypt an individual message through the Message Options dialog box.

QUICKSTEPS

PROTECTING AGAINST VIRUSES

Computer viruses are a major headache in the computing world, and e-mail and Internet usage are major pathways for your computer to become infected. Outlook provides *minimal* protection against viruses. Outlook is not equipped to scan your e-mail and remove viruses, so when Outlook tells you that it can help with virus protection, it really does mean that it "helps" only.

Outlook provides virus protection mainly through macro security levels. Different files, especially Microsoft Word files, can contain *macros,* which are little programs, and viruses can be implanted in the macros. This is a common way for viruses to be spread. Outlook's macro security simply disables macros that are not from secure or trusted sources, thus reducing the likelihood of getting a macro virus. But beware, Outlook will not detect any virus that you actually get.

The good news is, Outlook provides macro security by default and sets it to a high level. You can change it if you like:

1. In Outlook click **Tools** | **Macro**, and then click **Security**.

2. In the Security dialog box, choose a security level, as shown in Figure 8-13. Notice that by default, the High setting is configured.

3. Click **OK**.

TIP

The High setting gives you the best protection. You can still use macros, but they are not allowed from untrusted sources. Think carefully before you choose a lower security setting.

Figure 8-13: Using a high level of macro security is your best protection.

ENCRYPT ALL OUTGOING E-MAIL

You can also choose to encrypt all outgoing mail, which saves you from having to configure each e-mail message with encryption. However, keep in mind that this setting will encrypt every e-mail that you send.

1. In Outlook click **Tools | Options**, and click the **Security** tab.

2. On the Security tab under Encrypted E-Mail, choose the **Encrypt Contents And Attachments For Outgoing Messages** check box.

3. Click **OK**.

Chapter 9
Using Forms, Labels, and Mail Merge

You've seen that Outlook is a lot more than a mail program. In this chapter you'll see that Outlook is much more than just its features in the Navigation pane. You'll see how to modify existing forms and create custom forms, how to create and use templates in many Outlook views, and how to set up Outlook to perform a mail merge and print both labels and envelopes.

Use Forms

Much of Outlook is built around forms: message forms, appointment forms, contact forms, and many others. *Forms* provide the means to collect information. Forms are built around *fields,* which are individual pieces of information collected by the form, such as the addressee and subject in the e-mail message form shown in Figure 9-1.

Explore Outlook Forms

In earlier chapters you saw how to use various forms from within each of the views. You can also see all the forms together:

1. Open **Outlook** in one of the ways described in Chapter 1.

2. Click the **Tools** menu, select **Forms**, and click **Choose Form**. The Choose Form dialog box will open, as shown in Figure 9-2.

3. Click one of the forms, and click **Advanced**. You'll see a description of the form, who created it, tion of the form, who created it, and the message class, which is used in programming for Outlook.

4. Open a form by clicking it and clicking **Open**.

   –Or–

   Double-click the form.

5. Click **Close** to close the Choose Form dialog box.

Figure 9-1: Most of what is done in Outlook is done with forms.

Figure 9-2: Outlook uses 11 standard forms to perform its functions.

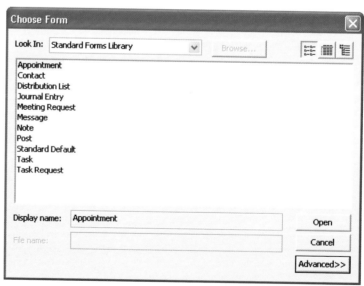

Modify a Standard Form

You can modify any of the standard forms and then use a revised form in the same way you used it before it was modified.

1. From Outlook click the **Tools** menu, select **Forms**, and click **Design A Form**.

2. Open the **Look In** drop-down list, and select the folder that holds the form you want to use. (This is particularly useful for the Message form, which is used in several different folders.)

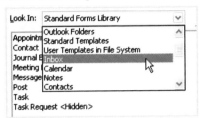

3. Select the form you want to modify, and click **Open**. The form will open in Design mode with the Field Chooser dialog box open beside it (see Figure 9-3).

Add pages

Design-related menus

Add predefined fields

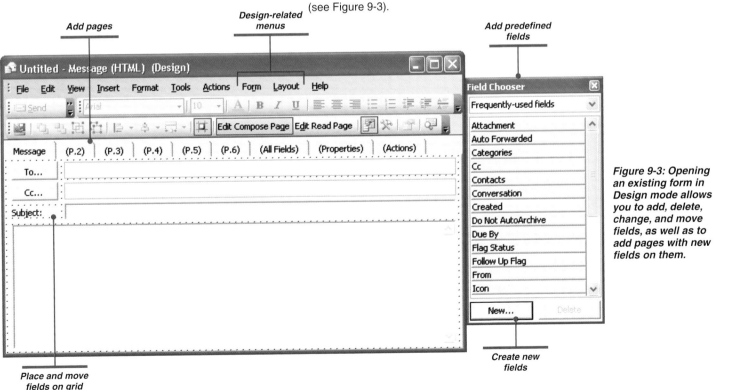

Place and move fields on grid

Create new fields

Figure 9-3: Opening an existing form in Design mode allows you to add, delete, change, and move fields, as well as to add pages with new fields on them.

NOTE

Before you can modify any of the existing standard forms, you must turn off Word as the e-mail editor. From Outlook click **Tools | Options | Mail Format | Use Microsoft Office Word 2003 To Edit E-Mail Messages | OK**.

TIP

See both "Modify a Standard Form" and "Create a Custom Form" for the full range of modifications you can make to a form.

4. Select whether you want to change the form as the sender will see it (click **Edit Compose Page**), or as the recipient will see it (click **Edit Read Page**).

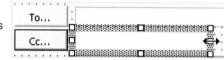

5. Select a field whose size you want to change. A shaded border with *sizing handles* (small black or white squares) appears around the field. Drag one of the sizing handles to change the size of the field.

6. Select a field you want to delete, and press **DELETE**.

7. Open the **field categories** drop-down list at the top of the Field Chooser dialog box, click a category, and drag a predefined field to the place on the form where you want it.

8. Click **New** in the Field Chooser. Enter a name, select a type and format, and click **OK** in the New Field dialog box. Drag the new field to the place on the form where you want it.

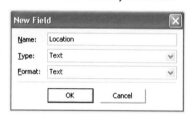

9. Click the **File** menu and click **Save As**. Open the **Save In** drop-down list, and select the folder in which you want to save the form. Enter the name for the form, click **Save**, and close the form.

Create a Custom Form

Creating a custom form is the same as modifying a form, because Outlook does not allow you to start with a blank form. You can do that very easily, though, by starting with an existing form, deleting all the fields you don't want—possibly all of them—and adding the fields you want. Also, there are a number of additional tools you can use to customize a form, including the Form Design toolbar, the design tabs, the design menus, and the Controls Toolbox.

USE THE FORM DESIGN TOOLBAR

The Form Design window has a toolbar, shown in Figure 9-4, that allows you to perform the following functions:

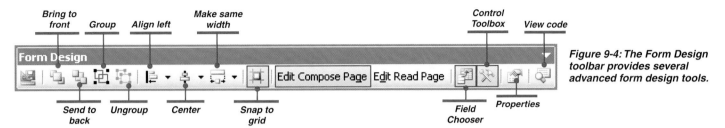

Figure 9-4: The Form Design toolbar provides several advanced form design tools.

- Publish the form so you or anyone else with access can use it.
- Position and align fields.
- Choose to edit the page as the sender will see it (compose) or to edit the page as the reader will see it (read).
- Open and close the Field Chooser and the Controls Toolbox.
- Open the Properties dialog box for a field.
- View Visual Basic Script code you have added to the form.

To align two fields, use first the Properties dialog box and then the alignment tools on the Form Design toolbar:

1. From Outlook click the **Tools** menu, select **Forms**, and click **Design A Form**. Double-click the existing form that will be the foundation of a new form.

2. Delete any existing fields you do not need. Drag two new fields from the Field Chooser to the new form, and purposely make them unaligned and of different sizes.

TIP

You can use either **CTRL** or **SHIFT** to select multiple fields, but there is a difference. When you use **CTRL**, the first field selected is the one that will move when you align the fields, and it will have black selection handles after both fields are selected, while the fixed field will have white selection handles. If you use **SHIFT** to select multiple fields, the last field selected is the one that will move and will have the black selection handles.

3. Select the field that will remain in its current position, and make sure its left edge is where you want it. Click **Properties** on the Form Design toolbar to open that dialog box, as shown in Figure 9-5.

4. Note the four position numbers, and close the dialog box. Select the other field, click **Properties**, enter all but the top position from the first field, and click **OK**. The fields will look alike.

5. Once again make the fields unaligned and different sizes.

6. Select the field that will remain in its current position, and make sure its left edge is where you want it. Press and hold **SHIFT** while clicking the second field. Note the first field has white selection handles, while the second field has black selection handles.

7. Click **Align Left** and then click **Make Same Width**, both on the Form Design toolbar. Note that the field with the black handles was the one that moved in both instances.

USE THE DESIGN TABS

The Form Design window has eight new tabs in addition to the tabs that are in the standard form. Of the eight new tabs, five are additional blank pages for the form. The three other tabs specify additional aspects of the form:

- **All Fields** lists the initial values of the fields available for the form and allows you to define new fields.

- **Properties** allows you to specify the form's categories, version, form number, icons, contact, and description.

- **Actions** contains the user actions that are implemented for the form, such as Reply and Forward.

Figure 9-5: You can align and similarly size two fields by making all but one of their coordinates the same.

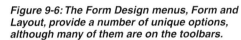

USE THE DESIGN MENUS

The Form Design window has two unique menus (see Figure 9-6), Form and Layout—each with several unique options, most of which are reflected in the toolbar. The more important and unique options are the following:

Form menu:

Figure 9-6: The Form Design menus, Form and Layout, provide a number of unique options, although many of them are on the toolbars.

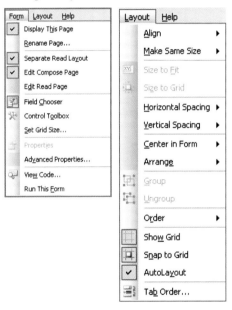

- **Display This Page** and **Rename Page** allow you to turn on or off the use of the Message page as well as P.2 through P.6 (which are off by default, indicated by the parentheses) and to rename them from "Message" and "P.x" to your choice.

- **Separate Read Layout**, when on (which is the default), specifies a separate layout for the page as it will be read upon receipt, distinct from the layout for the page displayed while the sender is creating it. When this is off, only one layout is used—the compose page, as the sender will see it. If you turn this option off and then back on, both layouts are the same (they are the compose page).

- **Properties** and **Advanced Properties** allow you to enter detail specifications, including the name, position, font, color, initial value, and any validation rules you want to establish for a field.

- **View Code** allows you to enter and edit any Visual Basic Script code that you want to attach to the form.

- **Run This Form** switches out of Design view and lets you test the form you are designing.

Layout menu:

- **Arrange** allows you to arrange the position of objects, such as a command button, within set boundaries. For example, create a frame, put a command button within the frame, and then select **Layout | Arrange Right**; the button will move to the top-right. If you choose Layout | Arrange Bottom, the button will move to the bottom left.

- **Group** and **Ungroup** allow you to combine two or more fields, and then to move and place them without disturbing the layout within the group.

- **Order** allows you to stack fields or groups of fields on top of one another and then to change their placement in the stack.

- **Snap To Grid** turns on a "magnetic" property of the grid so that fields are automatically drawn to the nearest grid intersections.

- **AutoLayout** turns on or off the automatic alignment of fields that you drag from the Field Chooser onto the form. With AutoLayout on, if you drop a field between two others, AutoLayout will move one of them out of the way to make room for the new one. AutoLayout will either shift controls down or to the right, but all fields will be aligned on the left. AutoLayout affects only fields from the Field Chooser and not controls dragged from the Toolbox.

- **Tab Order** allows you to specify the order in which the user will progress from one field to the next.

Use the Controls Toolbox

The Controls Toolbox is used to add new fields and labels to a form. The Controls Toolbox is opened with the Controls Toolbox button in the Design toolbar and contains 15 tools, as shown in Figure 9-7. Use the Controls Toolbox to create a combo box and a label.

1. In Outlook click the **Tools** menu, and click **Forms | Design A Form**. Double-click the existing form that will be the foundation of a new form.

2. Delete any existing fields you do not need and otherwise make room, such as moving fields, to add a new label and combo box. Click the **Controls Toolbox** icon on the Forms Design toolbar.

3. Click the **Label** tool and then place the label by clicking your form to the left of where you will want the combo box to be.

4. With the label selected, click the label again, drag across the existing text and type over it to change it to what you want.

5. In the Controls Toolbox, click the **Combo Box** tool, and drag a combo box from the right edge of the label you just placed to make a box, about 2 inches × ¼ inch.

6. Right-click in the new combo box, and select **Properties** from the context menu to open the Properties dialog box. In the Display tab, type the name you want in the Name text box.

Figure 9-7: Controls and features are added to a new form from the Controls Toolbox.

Select object — Text label
Text box — Combo box
List box — Check box
Option button — On/off button
Group items — Command button
Tab strip — Multiple pages
Scroll bar — Spinner
Image

7. Click the **Value** tab, and click the **New** button to create a new field in the Outlook database. In the New Field dialog box, type the field name in the Name text box, select the type of field in the Type drop-down list, and choose the format you want from the Format drop-down list.

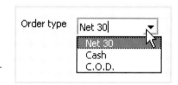

New Field

Name:	Order Type
Type:	Text
Format:	Text

OK   Cancel

8. Click **OK** to close the New Field dialog box. Back in the Properties dialog box, in the Value tab, click inside the Possible Values text box, and type the values that are to be displayed in the drop-down list, separated by semicolons.

9. Select the **Set The Initial Value Of This Field To** check box, click inside the text box, and type the value from the drop-down list that you want to be the default. If you have numbers in the default value, place quotation marks around the value. When you are done, your dialog box should look something like Figure 9-8.

10. Click **OK** to close the Properties dialog box. To see how your new combo box works, click the **Form** menu and click **Run This Form**. You should see the default value in the combo box, and if you open the box, you should see the alternatives that you have entered. This is what ours looked like:

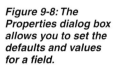

Order type   Net 30
Net 30
Cash
C.O.D.

11. Close the form sample that you opened and return to the Design view. With the new combo box still selected, hold down CTRL and click the field's label. Click **Layout** menu and click **Horizontal Spacing | Remove** to remove the horizontal space between the fields. Click the **Align Left down arrow** on the Design toolbar, and select **Middle**. Click the **Group** toolbar button to group the label and the combo box together.

12. Click **File**, click **Save As**, locate the folder in which you want to save the form, type a name for the form, and click **Save**.

Enter the initial or default value.

Enter values to be displayed in the drop-down list separated by commas.

Create a new database field.

Properties

Display | Value | Validation

Field and Format of Control

Choose Field ▼   Order Type   New...

Type: Text

Format: Text

List Type: Dropdown ▼

Property to use: Value

Possible values: Net 30; Cash; C.O.D.

Initial Value

☑ Set the initial value of this field to:

"Net 30"   Edit...

● Calculate this formula when I compose a new form

○ Calculate this formula automatically

OK   Cancel   Apply

Figure 9-8: The Properties dialog box allows you to set the defaults and values for a field.

Change the Tab Order

The tab order of a form is the order in which you go from field to field as you are filling out the form. How this works is important because the tab order should follow, as much as possible, how users would logically move through the form if they were to click on each field.

1. Click the **Layout** menu and click **Tab Order** to open that dialog box. In the Tab Order dialog box, the fields in a form are listed in the order in which they will be selected as you go through the form. You can change the order by moving fields up and down the list.

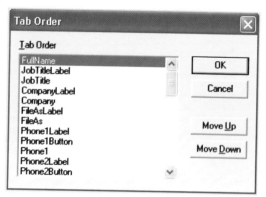

2. Select a field whose order you want to change, and move it by clicking **Move Down** or **Move Up**.

3. Click **OK** to close the Tab Order dialog box.

Use Separate Compose and Read Layouts

Outlook allows you to have a form for the person who initially fills it out be different from the form for the person who reads it. When you create a form, you can choose to have the *compose page*—the form the way you fill it out— different from the *read page*—the form the way it will be read. You can initiate this feature in the Design view window by clicking the **Form** menu and clicking **Separate Read Layout**. When this is selected, you will have two buttons on the Design toolbar that allow you to switch between the compose page and the read page.

NOTE

Separate read and compose layouts allow you to tailor a form to a very specific audience and to add features that are important to either the person filling out the form or the person reading it, but not to both.

The easiest way to see the difference between a compose page and a read page
is to use the standard Outlook e-mail message form. You first see the form in
Design view as the compose page, as shown in Figure 9-9. If you click **Edit Read
Page**, you will see a number of changes,
as shown in Figure 9-10.

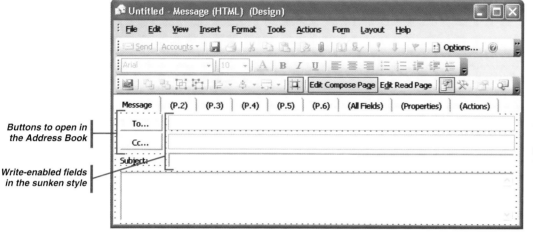

Buttons to open in
the Address Book

Write-enabled fields
in the sunken style

*Figure 9-9: A message
form in compose layout
provides special fields
useful to the writer.*

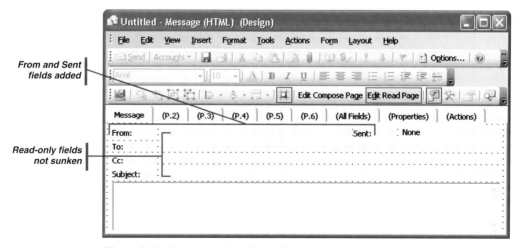

From and Sent
fields added

Read-only fields
not sunken

Figure 9-10: A message form in read layout allows it to be tailored for the reader.

Publish a Form

When you are ready for people to start using a form, you need to *publish* it. Publishing a form puts it into a different state than just saving it. When you save a form and then reopen and use it, you are using the original and only copy of the form. If you publish the form and then open and use it, you are using a copy and not the original. Every time you use a published form, you are using a copy of the form. To publish a form:

1. Click the **Publish Form** button on the left of the Design toolbar.

2. As shown in Figure 9-11, select the folder you want to use (Personal Forms Library is recommended), type the name of the form in Display Name (it is automatically repeated in Form Name, but you can change it), and click **Publish**.

3. If you are asked if you want to save the form definition with the form, click **Yes**. (It's very important to save the form definition information with the message if you're going to send it to someone who doesn't have the form and is not connected to your Exchange Server.)

4. When you are done, close your Form Design window, answering **Yes** when asked if you want to save your changes.

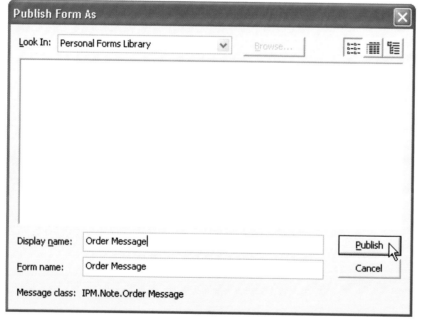

Figure 9-11:
Publishing a form allows it to be used over and over again.

You can enter this information in the form's Properties dialog box.

Figure 9-12: *The default is to store custom forms in the Personal Forms Library.*

TIP

You can do many things with forms when they are tied to one or more of the Outlook views. For example, you can tie a schedule reminder message to the Calendar or tie a task list confirmation to Tasks.

Use a Custom Form

Using a custom form is easy:

1. In the Outlook window with the Inbox open, click the **New Mail Message down arrow** on the toolbar, and select **Choose Form**. Open the **Look In** drop-down list, select **Personal Forms Library**, and you will see the display name of your custom form, as shown in Figure 9-12.

2. Double-click your form and it will open, ready to fill in, as you can see in Figure 9-13.

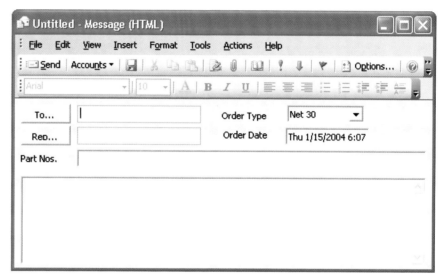

Figure 9-13: *Custom forms can be very handy for such things as order confirmation.*

CREATING AND USING A TEMPLATE

A *template* is a blank message form with custom text in the body of the message that can be used as a standard e-mail message for some task. For instance, you might set up a standard reply to professional inquiries you receive. A template uses the same fields as the standard form, whereas the custom forms we've been discussing change those fields.

CREATE A TEMPLATE

Templates are an easy way to send a lot of repetitive e-mail. If you are sending the same message to three or more people, you should probably create a template:

● From the Outlook window with the Inbox open, click the **New Mail Message** toolbar button to open a new Message window.

● Leave the To and Cc text boxes blank, type the **Subject** text, and type the template's message text.

● Click the **File** menu and click **Save As**. In the Save In drop-down list, select your templates folder (this often is C:\Documents and Settings*yourname*\\Application Data\Microsoft\\Templates).

● Accept the text from your template's Subject field as the file name. Under Save As Type, select **Outlook Template (*.oft)**, and click **Save**. The new template will be saved.

● Click **Close** to close your Message window, and answer **No** when asked if you want to save the file (that is, unless you want to save it in your Inbox, which you don't—you've already saved it as a template).

Continued...

Perform a Mail Merge

Performing a mail merge allows you to merge a form letter with your Outlook contacts, thereby sending each contact a unique letter addressed just to him or her. This can be done with all contacts in a folder or just a subset of them. This section discusses sending form letters to a subset of your contacts, although the steps for sending form letters to all your contacts are much the same—and simpler.

There are three steps to performing a mail merge using Outlook Contacts with a Word document. First, within Outlook you prepare the contacts you wish to use in the mail merge and then export them in a form that Word can use with its Mail Merge function. Second, in Word you create the document that will be used to perform the mail merge. Finally, you perform the mail merge itself in Word.

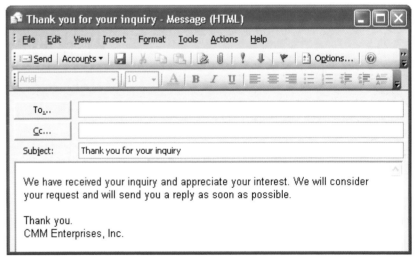

Figure 9-14: Templates can speed the handling of a large volume of e-mail.

CREATING AND USING A TEMPLATE *(Continued)*

USE A TEMPLATE

1. Click the **New Mail Message down arrow** in the toolbar, and select **Choose Form**. The Choose Form dialog box opens.

2. From the Look In drop-down list, select **User Templates In File System**. Your template named for the subject should be visible to you.

3. Double-click your template name, and it opens as a new Message window with the subject and body filled in as you left them. All you need to do is fill in the To information and click **Send**, as you can see in Figure 9-14.

TIP

Any of the built-in Outlook forms you see by clicking **New | Choose Form** can be customized by you and then saved under a new template name.

NOTE

If your contacts are in more than one folder, either you will need to perform multiple mail merges (one with each of the folders designated as the data source), or you must create one folder to combine the contacts, either by merging the folders or by creating a new folder and copying the contacts to it.

Prepare Contacts

If you are only going to perform a mail merge on some of your contacts, it is a good idea to first create a new folder to hold only the contacts you wish to include in the mail merge. Then, in Word you select that folder as your data source. To create a new folder and export it:

1. In Outlook click **Contacts** in the Outlook view bars.

2. Click the **New Contact down arrow** and click **Folder**. The Create New Folder dialog box will open.

3. Type the name for the new folder, and make sure **Contact Items** is selected under Folder Contains and that **Contacts** is highlighted under Select Where To Place the Folder, as shown in Figure 9-15.

4. Click **OK**. Your new folder appears in the list of Contacts folders at the top of the Folder List.

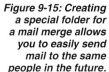

Figure 9-15: Creating a special folder for a mail merge allows you to easily send mail to the same people in the future.

UICKSTEPS

SELECTING CONTACTS

You can select contacts to use in a mail merge in four ways: manually, or with Outlook's Mail Merge, Outlook's filters, or Word's Mail Merge. The first three are discussed here.

SELECT CONTACTS MANUALLY

Right-drag contacts from your main Contacts folder to your new mail merge folder, and choose **Copy**.

–Or–

Select a number of contacts either by holding down **CTRL** while clicking on a number of contacts or by holding down **SHIFT** while clicking the first and last members of a contiguous range of contacts. These can then be dragged to the new folder or used directly in Outlook's Mail Merge.

USE OUTLOOK'S MAIL MERGE

Outlook's built-in mail merge doesn't need a new folder, but it is useful.

1. Click the **Tools** menu and click **Mail Merge**, which opens as shown in Figure 9-17.

2. Either click **All Contacts In Current View**, which can be filtered (see the following "Use Outlook Filtering"), or click **Only Selected Contacts** when contacts have been manually selected (see preceding "Select Contacts Manually").

3. Select either **New Document** or an **Existing Document**.

4. Click **Permanent File** and browse to or type the file name you wish to use.

5. Select the merge options that are correct for you, and click **OK**.

Outlook will prepare your contact data, open Microsoft Word, and create a new mail merge document linked to your contact data and ready for you to type in the contents. See "Prepare a Word Merge Document" later in this chapter.

Continued...

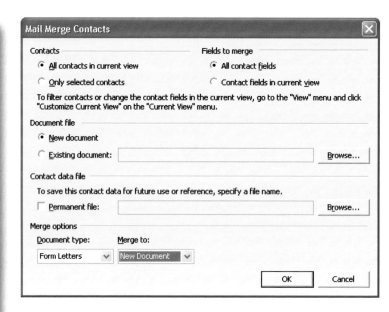

Figure 9-16: Outlook will help you set up your contacts for a mail merge and then will open Word to create the document and do the merge.

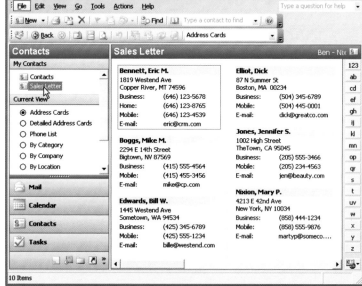

Figure 9-17: Use one of several ways within Outlook to select contacts to use in a mail merge.

Prepare a Word Merge Document

You can approach mail merge from Outlook and use Word to produce a document, or you can start from Word and use Outlook to supply the contacts. Since this book is on Outlook, we will use the first approach and assume you have used the Outlook Mail Merge function to prepare your contacts, open Word, and create a new Word mail merge document. You should, therefore, have Word open on your screen, ready for you to type the document and place field names where you want the Outlook contact information.

1. Type a new letter or paste an existing one that you want to send to your selected contacts. Leave blank the areas that will contain the recipient's name and address.

2. When the body of the letter is the way you want it, return to the top of the page, and click **Insert Address Block** (the fourth icon from the left on the Mail Merge toolbar). The Insert Address Block dialog box opens.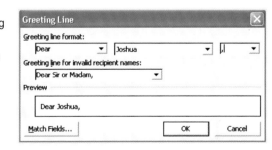

3. Review the defaults. In most cases they work well. Click **Match Fields**. Make sure the field on the right matches the required information on the left. (I found that I needed to open the drop-down list opposite Postal Code and select ZIPPostal_Code.) Click **OK** twice when ready.

4. Under the Address Block that just appeared, leave a blank line or two, and then click **Insert Greeting Line** (the fifth icon from the left on the Mail Merge toolbar). The Greeting Line dialog box opens. Select the options that are correct for you, and click **OK**.

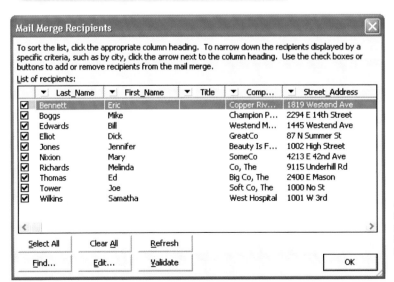

Figure 9-18: Word provides a means of filtering, sorting, and selecting contacts in the Mail Merge Recipients dialog box.

5. Click **Mail Merge Recipients** (the third icon from the left on the Mail Merge toolbar). Here you can make a final selection of your recipients, as shown in Figure 9-18. Use the check boxes on the left to select individuals; click a column heading to sort the list on that column; click the drop-down arrow in a column heading to select a particular entry in the column, including "blanks" and "nonblanks"; and click **Edit** to change an individual record. When you have the recipients the way you want them, click **OK**.

6. Click **View Merged Data** (the eighth icon from the left on the Mail Merge toolbar) to display your contacts merged with the letter, as shown in Figure 9-19. Use the arrows in the middle of the Mail Merge toolbar to look at more contacts.

7. When the document is as you want it, click **Save** on the Standard toolbar.

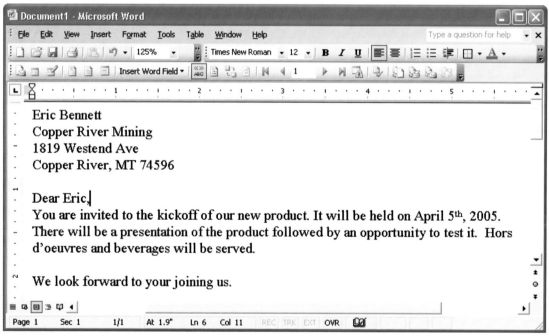

Figure 9-19: A well-done mail merge letter is impossible to tell from an individually typed letter.

Perform a Mail Merge

With the document and contacts the way you want them, run tests—first of the data, and then of the merge—to see if any data is missing and if the merge is picking up the right fields. When you are satisfied with the tests, to print the actual letters:

1. Click **Check For Errors** (fifth from the right on the Mail Merge toolbar) to see if there are any needed fields missing. Click **Simulate The Merge And Report Errors In A New Document**, and click **OK**. You will get either a message of errors in the data or a message that there are no errors.

2. After you have fixed any errors, click **Merge To New Document** (fourth from the right on the Mail Merge toolbar), accept the **ALL** default to merge all records, and click **OK**. A new document will be created containing all of the letters you want created. Use the **Next Page** and **Previous Page** controls in the lower-right of the Word window to look at the succession of letters you have created. Next Page

3. When you are ready to print your merged letters, click **Print** on the Standard toolbar of the new merged document you created in Step 2.

   –Or–

   Click **Merge To Printer** (third from the right on the Mail Merge toolbar).

4. If you wish, save your new merged document, and once more save the original mail merge document.

Print Mailing Labels

Printing labels is done the same way as the mail merge. First, prepare your data file in Outlook (which you've already done while preparing for the mail merge). Then switch to Word, create a blank document, and perform a mail merge.

1. If you haven't already prepared a contacts file for the mail merge, follow the steps described in "Prepare Contacts" and the "Selecting Contacts" QuickSteps, earlier in this chapter, to learn how to create a data file for the names and addresses.

2. In Word open a new, blank document, click the **Tools** menu, and click **Letters And Mailings | Mail Merge** to open the Mail Merge pane.

3. In the Select Document Type section, click **Labels**, and then click **Next**. Keep **Change Document Layout**, click **Label Options**, and click **Next**. The Label Options dialog box will open.

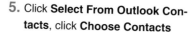

4. Select the labels you want to use (Avery 5160 or its equivalent is the most common), and click **OK**.

5. Click **Select From Outlook Contacts**, click **Choose Contacts Folder**, double-click the contacts folder you want to use. If needed, select the profile you want, and click **OK**. The Mail Merge Recipients dialog box, shown in Figure 9-18, will open. Make any needed changes, click **OK**, and click **Next**.

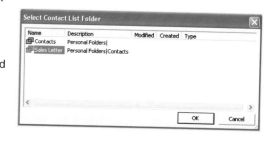

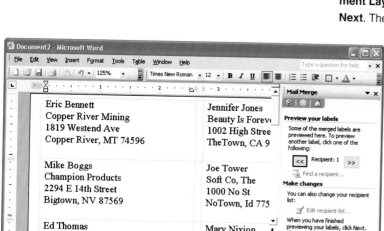

Figure 9-20: Word's Mail Merge pane is a wizard that can lead you through all types of mail merge, including letters, labels, and envelopes.

6. Click in the top-left corner label (the first label on the sheet), and then click **Address Block** in the Mail Merge pane. Make any needed changes to the address block, check for any unmatched fields, and click **OK**.

7. Scroll the **Mail Merge** pane, and click **Update All Labels**. The address block will be added to all labels. Click **Next**, and you will see the labels populated with your contact list, as you can see in Figure 9-20.

8. Scroll the **Mail Merge** pane, click **Next**, and after making sure your labels are correctly loaded in your printer, click **Print**. If you want to save your label merge document for later use, click **Save** in the Standard toolbar, enter a name, select a folder, and click **Save**.

Print Envelopes

As with the mail merge and printing labels, printing envelopes first requires that you create a contacts file (described earlier in "Prepare Contacts" and the "Selecting Contacts" QuickSteps), then create a word merge document:

1. In Word, open a new, blank document, click the **Tools** menu, and click **Letters And Mailings | Mail Merge** to open the Mail Merge pane.

2. In the Select Document Type section, click **Envelopes**, and then click **Next**. Keep **Change Document Layout**, click **Envelope Options**, and click **Next**. The Envelope Options dialog box will open.

3. Make any needed changes, click **OK**, and click **Next**.

4. Click **Select From Outlook Contacts**, click **Choose Contacts Folder**, double-click the contacts folder you want to use, if needed select the profile you want, and click **OK**. The Mail Merge Recipients dialog box (shown earlier in Figure 9-18) will open. Make any necessary changes, click **OK**, and click **Next**.

5. Click in the upper-left corner of the envelope displayed in Word, and type the return address if the envelopes aren't preprinted.

6. Click in the lower-middle of the envelope, and then click **Address Block** in the Mail Merge pane. The Insert Address Block dialog box will open, as shown in Figure 9-21. Make any needed changes to the address block, check for any unmatched fields, and click **OK**. Press **ENTER** twice and then click **Postal Bar Code**. Confirm the ZIP code and street address fields, and click **OK**.

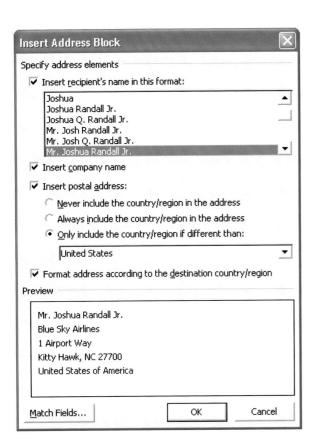

Figure 9-21: Word provides a number of ways of formatting the address block and selecting its components.

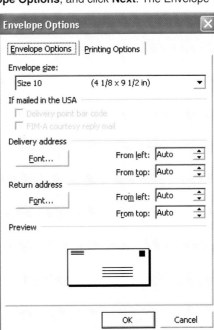

7. Click **Next** and you will see the envelope appear with your first recipient, as shown in Figure 9-22.

8. Scroll the **Mail Merge** pane, click **Next**, and after making sure your envelopes are loaded correctly in your printer, click **Print**. If you want, click **Save** in the Standard toolbar, type a name, select a folder, and click **Save**.

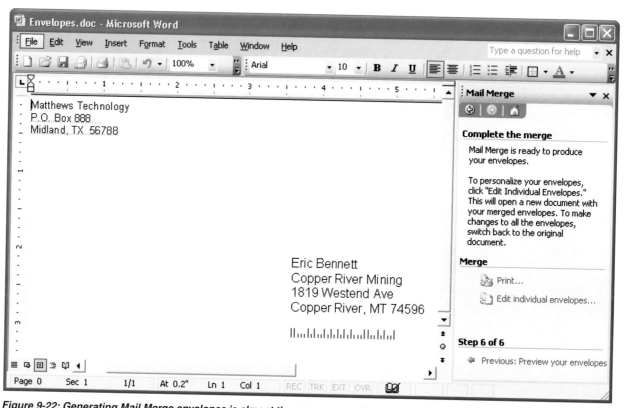

Figure 9-22: Generating Mail Merge envelopes is almost the same as creating labels.

Chapter 10

Using Outlook in Other Ways

Being a part of Microsoft Office and the Microsoft family brings a number features and capabilities to Outlook that extend what it can do and how it functions. In this chapter you'll see some of those features and capabilities—including using Outlook with instant messaging, with PDAs (personal digital assistants), and with a potpourri of extensions. These supplementary applications, such as Office Clipboard and handwriting recognition, help integrate Outlook with the other members of the Office suite; or, in the case of using Outlook as a Web browser, with the Windows product line.

Use Instant Messaging with Outlook

If you're addicted to instant messaging, you'll be glad to know that Outlook can launch you right into a conversation. If you've never used instant messaging, now's the time to try it because Outlook 2003 has instant messaging built into it.

You just might get hooked on this quick and easy tool for making plans, solving problems, or catching up. You can use it with one person or several at a time. If you have a .NET Passport or Hotmail account, as explained in Chapter 2, "Receiving and Handling E-Mail," you're ready to go. If not, get one and come back when you're ready.

Set Up Instant Messaging

Get some IM-savvy friends to send you their .NET Passport e-mail addresses, and if an address is different from the person's regular e-mail address, enter it in his or her Outlook Contact IM Address field. Send yours to him or her, of course. Once you have done that, you can proceed to enter the world of IM-ing. If you haven't used Windows Messenger, now's the time to start.

LOG ON TO WINDOWS MESSENGER

1. Click **Start**, select **All Programs**, and click **Windows Messenger**.

2. Click the available sign-in option, and type your .NET Passport and password, as is shown in Figure 10-1, and click **OK**. The Windows Messenger window opens (see Figure 10-2).

Signs in default account automatically

Lets another account log on

Eliminates need to type password

.NET Messenger Service

Please sign in with your .NET Passport to see your online contacts, have online conversations, and receive alerts.

E-mail address: kellen_diagonal@passport.co

Password: ••••••••

☑ Sign me in automatically

OK   Cancel

Get a .NET Passport   Help

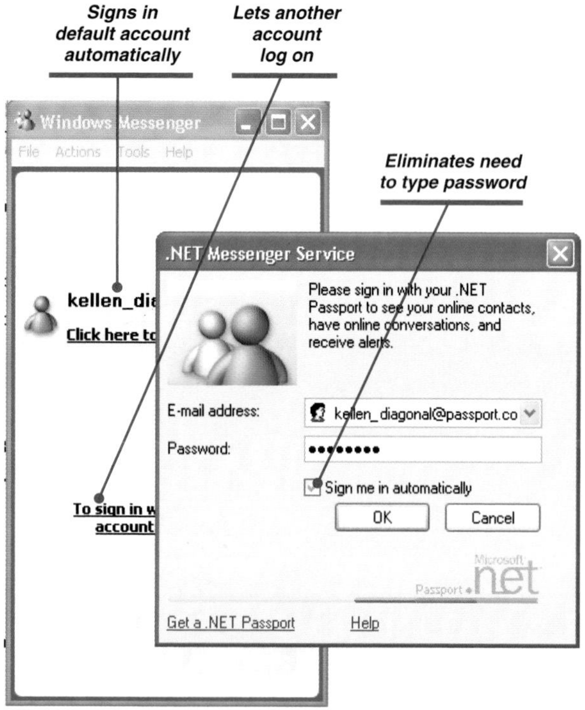

Figure 10-1: Other persons using the same computer can use their own Passports to sign on to instant messaging.

Figure 10-2: Windows Messenger offers access to video, audio, games, telephone service, and a whiteboard for online meetings.

NOTE

As you create IM contacts, each person will be notified that you have done so, and he or she will get the option to add you to his or her list of contacts.

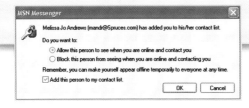

CREATE AN IM CONTACT

1. Click **Add A Contact** under I Want To in the Windows Messenger window. The Add A Contact dialog box opens.

2. Choose whether to add one manually or to search for one in your Outlook Contacts, and click **Next**.

3. If you chose to add the person manually, type the .NET Passport address, and click **Next**.

4. If you chose to find the person in your Outlook Contacts, type the person's first and last names as they appear in any of the name fields in Contacts, select **Address Book On This Computer**, click **Next**, select the name in the list, click **Next**, and click **Finish**.

Activate IM in Outlook

As great as IM is by itself, using it from within Outlook makes it even better. Start by activating IM in Outlook.

1. Start **Outlook**, click the **Tools** menu, select **Options**, and click the **Other** tab.

2. Under Person Names, check the **Enable The Person Names Smart Tag** and the **Display Messenger Status In The From Field** check boxes, and click **OK**.

Instant Messaging from Outlook

Instant messaging begins by seeing if your contact is online. You then can start a conversation and add other people to it. Finally, you can control your online availability.

SEE IF YOUR CONTACT IS ONLINE

See if the person is online, by pointing to his or her name in any of these locations:

- New message window
- Reading pane return address
- Opened message

NOTE

A smart tag is a small button that appears in Microsoft Office products to allow you to perform some function related to a piece of information next to the button. Here, we are talking about a Windows Messaging button that appears next to a person's name if that person has been identified as an IM contact. Pointing at the button tells you if the person is online. Clicking the button opens a menu of various options including sending an instant message.

1. Right-click a smart tag for someone who is online, and select **Send Instant Message**.

2. Start typing a greeting or message, and press **ENTER**.

3. When you're finished, close the window.

MAKE IT A PARTY

Several persons can talk at a time when you are using IM. Get a conversation going with one other person, and then:

1. Click **Invite Someone To This Conversation** in the Conversation window. The dialog box lets you see which of your IM contacts is currently online.

2. Select the person and click **OK**.

3. Continue conversing as before.

STATE YOUR AVAILABILITY

Click the **down arrow** left of your display name, and select a status.

Use Outlook with PDAs

A PDA, or personal digital assistant, is a handheld computer that performs many of the functions found in Outlook. If you use a PDA and either a desktop or laptop computer with Outlook installed on it, you naturally want the information to be the same on both, and you want to transfer information between the two easily. How to do that is the subject of this section.

Most PDAs use one of two operating systems, Palm or Pocket PC.

- If you are using a Palm device, many of the later models transfer information to and synchronize with Outlook 2003, using either Palm or third-party software packages. See the Palm web site (http://www.palmone.com/us/support/outlooksupport.html) for more information.

- If you are using Pocket PC, you have Pocket Outlook, which includes the pocket versions of Calendar, Contacts, Inbox, Notes, and Tasks. Also, PDAs with Pocket PC normally come with a CD containing Microsoft ActiveSync, which will install on Windows-based PCs and provide the ability to transfer and automatically synchronize information between Outlook on your PC and Pocket Outlook on your Pocket PC PDA. (*Synchronization* compares the information on the PC with that on the PDA and updates the older information with the newer information, independent of which device it is on.)

In this section you'll see how to set up a PDA with Pocket PC, how to set up ActiveSync on a desktop or laptop PC, how to transfer information between them, and how to synchronize the two. You'll also explore ways to use this combination.

Set Up a PDA with Pocket PC

The setup of a PDA with Pocket PC is simple. When you first receive it, you want to:

1. Connect the PDA to a power source, using the cable that comes with it, and charge the batteries overnight before doing anything else.

NOTE

This discussion of Pocket PC and ActiveSync is based upon Pocket PC 2002, ActiveSync 3.5, and a Toshiba e330 PDA. Therefore, you will need to adjust for any variation you have from these products.

2. Leave the PDA disconnected from (*not* connected to) the PC during all of the steps to set up the PDA and all of the steps to set up ActiveSync until you are specifically told to connect the PDA to the PC.

3. With the PDA charged, but still disconnected from the PC, turn it on and follow the instructions on the PDA's screen to perform the initial setup. This may include:

- Align the screen by tapping in five specific locations.
- Select your time zone.
- Set your current time and date.
- Enter your name, address, and other information.

4. When you have completed all the initial setup tasks, turn off the PDA and set it aside (do not connect it to the PC).

Set Up ActiveSync

ActiveSync is already installed on your PDA as a part of the Pocket PC operating system. You'll need to use the CD that came with your PDA to install ActiveSync on your desktop or laptop computer.

1. Insert the Power PC CD in its drive. The install program will automatically start. Follow the instructions on the screen to start the process, as you can see in Figure 10-3.

CAUTION

It is important that you leave the Pocket PC PDA and its cradle disconnected from the PC and ActiveSync until you are specifically told to connect them. Connecting them too soon will cause problems with ActiveSync installation.

Figure 10-3: The initial Pocket PC Getting Started screen will vary among PDAs, but all should have a "Start Here" or "Begin" button for you to click.

2. Since you probably already have Outlook installed, you can skip that and click **Install ActiveSync 3.5.** (Note the warning to make sure that the Pocket PC cradle is un-plugged.)

3. Read the **Product Details And Installation Guidelines**, and then click **Install**. Follow the instructions on your screen to begin the installation.

4. When you see the Get Connected dialog box, follow the instructions to connect your cradle and/or PDA to your desktop or laptop computer. The Found New Hardware Wizard should open.

5. Leave the **Install The Software Automatically** option selected, and click **Next** on the Found New Hardware Wizard. When the wizard tells you it has finished, click **Finish**.

6. Back in the Get Connected dialog box, click **Next**. The New Partnership dialog box will open to set up the part-nership between your PDA and your laptop or desktop computer.

Figure 10-4: ActiveSync also allows you to synchronize several files outside of Outlook.

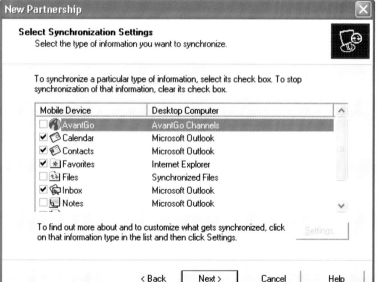

7. Read the descrip-tions of the Stan-dard and Guest partnerships, select the one that is correct for you, and click **Next**.

8. Choose between synchronizing with just this computer or synchronizing with both this com-puter and a Microsoft Mobile Information Server. Click **Next**.

9. Select the particular type of information you want synchronized between the two devices (as shown in Figure 10-4), click **Next**, and then click **Finish**.

Synchronize with a PDA

When you complete the installation of ActiveSync, ActiveSync will automatically start and begin the process of synchronizing your files. When it is finished, you should see a status of "Synchronized" for all the information types.

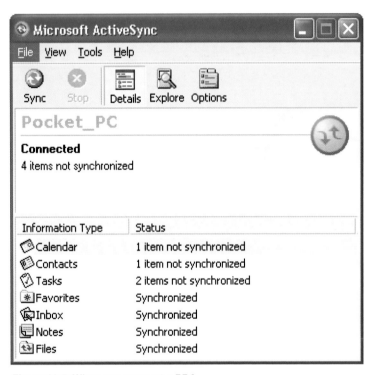

Figure 10-5: When you connect a PDA to a PC, ActiveSync goes through both devices, comparing files and identifying which file on which device needs to be updated. It then does the updating.

On a day-to-day basis, as you use your PDA and Outlook on your desktop or laptop computer, each device will have changes made to it. When you connect the PDA to the PC, ActiveSync automatically will open and synchronize both devices, as shown in Figure 10-5. You have to do nothing more than connect them. All comparison of the files, looking at the modification dates, and updating the oldest one is automatically handled for you.

Transfer Information with a PDA

In addition to the automatic synchronization that transfers information between your PDA and PC, you can manually transfer information between the two just as if your PDA were another disk drive with a number of folders on it.

1. Connect your PDA to your PC. If ActiveSync does not automatically open, click its icon in the notification area on the right of the taskbar.

2. Click **Explore** on ActiveSync's toolbar. Windows Explorer will open as it would for any folder on a disk drive.

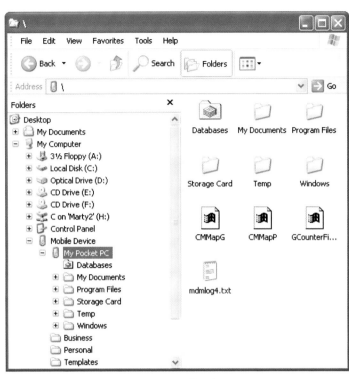

Figure 10-6: Looking at the files on a PDA is very similar to looking across a network at the files on another computer.

3. Click **Folders** on the toolbar. In the Folders pane, open **Mobile Device**, **My Pocket PC**, and several other folders to see what is there, as shown in Figure 10-6.

4. Identify a small Word and a small Excel file on your PC, and drag them to one of the general-purpose folders (Temp, Business, or Personal) on your PDA. A message will open, telling you that the files may need to be converted. Click **OK**.

5. Disconnect the PDA from the PC and, on the PDA, open the folder in which you stored the files. You should see the files.

6. Start Pocket Word or Pocket Excel. The files that you moved to the PDA should be listed in their respective programs. Click a file to open it. Make some change to the file. Save and close the file.

7. Reconnect the PDA to the PC. When ActiveSync looks for changes, it should find the two new files and automatically copy them to your Pocket_PC My Documents folder on your PC. This folder is in your normal My Documents folder, as shown in Figure 10-7.

Figure 10-7: ActiveSync creates a folder on the PC named "Pocket_PC My Documents" and uses that folder to store non-Outlook files that are being synchronized with a PDA.

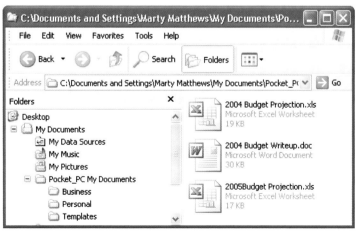

QUICKSTEPS

MANAGING A PDA AND ACTIVESYNC

ActiveSync provides a number of tools to manage both your PDA and ActiveSync, as shown in Figure 10-8.

SYNC OPTIONS

Sync Options determines what information is synchronized.

1. On your PC open **Start | All Programs | Microsoft ActiveSync**. The ActiveSync window will open.

2. Click **Options** in the toolbar. The Options dialog box will open with Sync Options.

3. Select each of the information areas—**Calendar**, **Contacts**, and so on—and for each, click **Settings**. Make any desired adjustments and then click **OK**.

SCHEDULE

The Schedule tab determines under what conditions and how frequently the synchronization is carried out.

1. Click the **Schedule** tab. Determine which of the three modes of synchronization you want to use.

2. Determine if you want to synchronize when you are connected to your PC and if so, how often.

3. If you have a wireless PDA, determine if you want to synchronize when you are not connected.

RULES

The Rules tab determines under what circumstances and to which party the synchronization will take place.

1. Determine how to resolve the conflict when the same information in both the PDA and the PC have changed (there is no easy answer to this question).

2. Click **Conversion Settings** and determine how files will be converted going in each direction by file type. Click **OK** when finished.

3. Determine how the PC will be used to allow the PDA to connect to the Internet or a network server.

4. When you have completed configuring the synchronization rules, click **OK**.

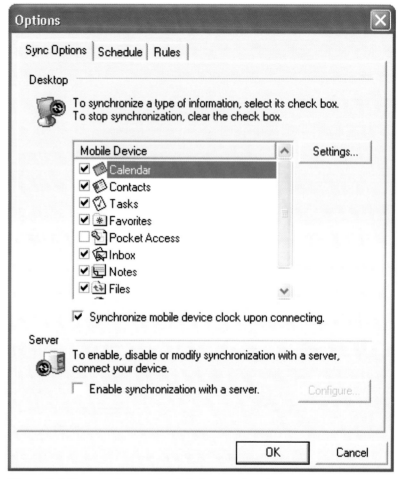

Figure 10-8: You can change what is being synchronized, when it will happen, and which rules it will follow, in ActiveSync's Options dialog box.

Back Up a PDA

The information on a PDA can be backed up in two ways: to a removable memory card in your PDA and to your PC, using ActiveSync.

BACK UP TO REMOVABLE MEMORY

Many Power PC PDAs come with the ability to add a removable memory card. This can be very handy for backing up the memory in the PDA.

1. Turn on the PDA, tap **Start**, tap **Programs**, and tap **Data Backup**. The Data Backup program will open and show you the size of the files on the PDA and the amount of unused space on the removable memory card.

2. Tap **Backup**. You will get a message to close all programs that are running on the PDA, to not use the PDA or remove the memory card while backup is in progress, and then you are asked if you are sure you want to do the backup.

3. Tap **Yes**. The backup will start. You will see the progress in a bar on the screen. When it is completed, you will be informed of the time it took. Tap **OK** twice to return to the Programs screen.

BACK UP TO A PC

Even if you have a removable memory card, and especially if you don't, it is important to back up your PDA on your PC in case something happens to your PDA. The backup will create a file on your PC of all the files, along with other information from the PDA.

1. With your PDA connected to your PC and ActiveSync open on your screen, click the **Tools** menu and click **Backup/Restore**. The Backup/Restore dialog box will open, as you can see in Figure 10-9.

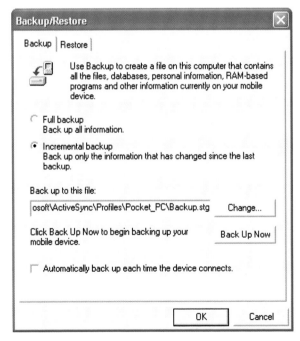

Figure 10-9: Backing up to your PC allows you to recover the data stored on your PDA should it be stolen.

Do not insert or remove removable memory while your PDA is turned on.

10

2. The first time you do a backup, choose **Full Backup**. Then you can do several incremental backups before you need to do a full backup again.

3. Note where the backup will be stored. If you wish to change this (and I would, because the default is buried six folders beneath Documents And Settings), click **Change.**

4. Create or select the folder you want to use for the backup (I created a new folder, "Pocket PC Backup"), type the file name you want, and click **Save**.

5. In the Backup/Restore dialog box, click **Back Up Now**. The Backup In Progress dialog box will open and show you how the backup is going. When it is complete, you will get a message to that effect. Click **OK**.

NOTE

When using ActiveSync, and especially in the Options dialog box, the term "server" refers to a separate Microsoft Mobile Information Server that is on the network to which the PDA is connected, but not necessarily directly connected to it. It is important to differentiate between the directly connected computer and the server, and to determine which of the two, or possibly both, will be synchronized with the PDA.

Other Extensions of Outlook

Looking across the Office and Microsoft family of products, you can see there are many that add features to Outlook. Among those discussed here are the Office Clipboard, using Word as an e-mail editor, and using handwriting in Outlook.

Use the Office Clipboard

The Microsoft Office Clipboard connects all the programs in the Office suite, letting you copy items from various programs and paste them into others. That means you can lift a paragraph and a picture out of Word, a slide out of a PowerPoint presentation, or a graph from Excel and then select from the clipboard the items that best serve your needs and paste them into an Outlook message.

NOTE

When you copy items from more than one Office program, the Clipboard only displays in the first program until you double-click the Clipboard icon in the notification area of the taskbar. However, copying an item from another Office program still places it on the Clipboard and indicates the new item with an alert on the taskbar

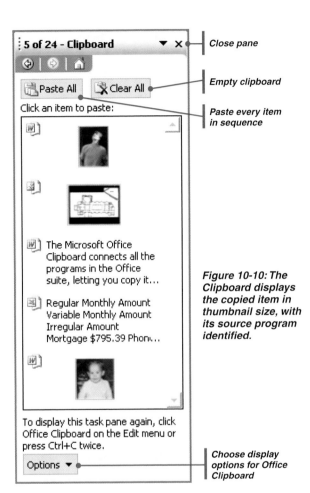

Close pane

Empty clipboard

Paste every item
in sequence

Click an item to paste:

*Figure 10-10: The
Clipboard displays
the copied item in
thumbnail size, with
its source program
identified.*

Choose display
options for Office
Clipboard

1. Start **Outlook**.

2. Start another Microsoft Office 2003 program, and open a saved document with that program:

   - **Excel** workbook

   - **Word** document

   - **Publisher** publication

   - **FrontPage** Web page

   - **Access** database

3. Click **Edit** and select **Office Clipboard**. The Clipboard opens as a pane on the right, as shown in Figure 10-10.

4. Select an item in the document you opened, and copy it, using either:

   - Click **Edit** and select **Copy**.

     –Or–

   - Press **CTRL+C**.

5. Click **Outlook** on the taskbar, and then click **New** in the Mail workspace.

6. Click in the message body.

7. Double-click the **Clipboard** icon in the notification area on the right of the taskbar. The Clipboard opens next to the message.

8. Click the desired item on the Clipboard. This "pastes" the item into the message where the cursor was located.

QUICKSTEPS

EDITING E-MAIL WITH WORD

Utilizing tools available in other Microsoft Office programs, such as Microsoft Word, gives you access to features not available in the Outlook e-mail editor. See Chapter 3, "Creating and Sending E-Mail," for basic e-mail editing and to make Word the editor (Tools | Options | Mail Format tab). Several of the more useful Word features are AutoCorrect, AutoFormat, and table making.

USE AUTOCORRECT

AutoCorrect, which automatically corrects many common typing and spelling errors, is turned on from the Word new message window:

1. Click the **Tools** menu and click **AutoCorrect Options**.

2. Click **Show AutoCorrect Options Buttons** if you want to be able to point to an affected word, see the bar indicating a correction, and be able to select other options.

3. Check any of the other options for correction conventions.

4. Scroll to view the list of common typographical errors, and check **Replace Text As You Type** to use them.

5. Type common personal typos and their corrections in the Replace and With text boxes, and press **ENTER**.

USE AUTOFORMAT

In the AutoCorrect Options dialog box, click the other tabs to see other popular options, such as:

- **AutoFormat**, for automatic application of typographical quotation marks, superscripted ordinals (1st), fraction characters (½), and dashes (—)

- **AutoText**, for suggestions based on common openings and closings and ones you've used elsewhere in Word

Continued...

CLEAR ITEMS FROM THE CLIPBOARD

Though the clipboard holds up to 24 items at a time, you might want to discard some items as you go.

1. Point to an item that you want to remove, and click the **down arrow** that appears.

2. Click **Delete**.

3. To remove all items from the clipboard, click **Clear All**.

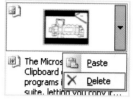

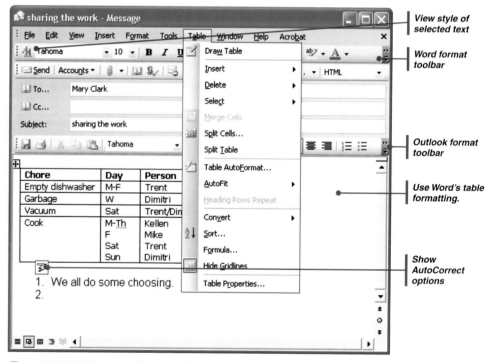

Figure 10-11: While using Word to edit e-mail, you can remove Outlook's formatting toolbar by opening the View menu and deselecting E-Mail on the Toolbars list.

EDITING E-MAIL WITH WORD
(Continued)

- **AutoFormat As You Type**, for defining styles based on formatting you set, automatically creating bulleted and numbered lists, and turning e-mail addresses and URLs into hyperlinks when you press **SPACEBAR**

President@whitehouse.gov

President@whitehouse.gov

MAKE A TABLE

Use Word's Table menu to organize information into a grid that will display properly even for recipients who don't use Word:

Click the **Table** menu, select **Insert**, click **Table**, type or use the spinner to enter numbers of columns and rows to start with, and click **OK**. You can add or delete columns and rows from the Table menu and format the data right on the toolbar (see Figure 10-11).

CAUTION

Large items like spreadsheets and big graphics can make for very slow going as you wait for them to paste. Also, there's a bug preventing PowerPoint items on the clipboard from pasting into Outlook.

NOTE

Placing characters in parentheses "(1/4)" as you type shields them from AutoFormat, so add the parentheses after you type characters that you want changed (¼).

Browse the Web with Outlook

Use the Outlook folder pane as a browser window and gain immediate access to the Internet by adding the Web toolbar.

1. Click the **View** menu, click **Toolbars**, and click **Web**.

2. Type the URL for an Internet site in the address text box, and then press **ENTER**. The folder pane becomes a browser window displaying Web pages, as shown in Figure 10-12.

3. Return to an Outlook view by clicking any folder or button in the Navigation pane.

4. Remove the Web toolbar by clicking **View | Toolbars** and clicking **Web**.

Go to previous view Stop loading Web page Reload Web page Go to home page Start search engine

Recent Internet sites visited

URL or Internet address

Figure 10-12: Click any address in the Internet address drop-down list to return to that Web page.

NOTE

If you have both Word and Outlook running, and a number of other programs and folders on the taskbar, minimizing an Outlook message that uses Word as its editor places the message under Word on the taskbar, not under Outlook.

NOTE

The Language bar contains five modes of entry: the on-screen keyboards (standard and symbol), which give new meaning to hunt and peck; writing and drawing pads, which let you scribble off to one side; and Write Anywhere, which lets you do just that.

Use Handwriting in Outlook

Microsoft Office 2003 contains handwriting recognition software called "Ink," which recognizes marks made by a digital pen or mouse and translates those marks into typed text or drawings. Outlook can utilize Ink, which would allow you to sketch a remodeling idea with annotating text on an e-mail message.

To utilize Ink, you will need to install it, and then you need to make Word your e-mail editor, as explained in Chapter 3, "Creating and Sending E-Mail."

INSTALL HANDWRITING RECOGNITION

Have your Office CD ready in case the installation calls for it.

1. Click **Start** and click **Control Panel**.
2. Click **Add Or Remove Programs**. The Add Or Remove Programs dialog box opens.
3. Scroll the Currently Installed Programs list, click **Microsoft Office 2003**, and then click **Change**. The Microsoft 2003 Setup Wizard opens.
4. Choose **Add Or Remove Features**, and click **Next**.
5. Click **Choose Advanced Customization Of Applications**, and click **Next**.
6. Click the expand button (⊞) beside **Office Shared Features**.
7. Click the expand button beside **Alternative User Input**.

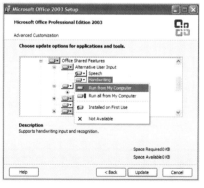

8. Click the **Handwriting down arrow**, and select **Run From My Computer**.
9. Click **Update**.
10. Insert the Office 2003 CD, if and when it is requested, and click **OK**.
11. When installation is successful, click **OK**, click **Close** on the Add Or Remove Programs dialog box, click **Close** on the Control Panel.
12. If it's open, close and restart Outlook (otherwise, just start Outlook), and then click **New** in any workspace. The Language bar opens in the upper-right part of the screen.

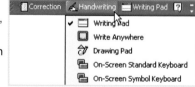

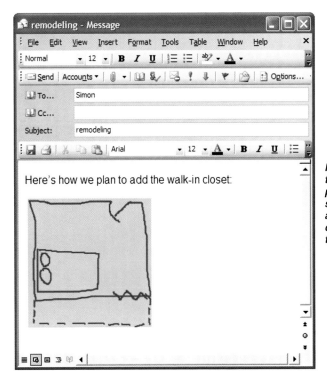

Select options

Delete and switch to Writing Pad

Clear entire drawing

Copy to Clipboard

Copy to Clipboard

Insert drawing

Figure 10-13: The options down arrow opens the way for changing ink color and line thickness.

DRAW WITH INK

1. Click **New** to open a new message, task, or other Outlook item.

2. Create the item and click the cursor where you want the drawing to appear.

3. Click **Handwriting** on the Language bar, and select **Drawing Pad** from the drop-down list. The Drawing Pad, as shown in Figure 10-13, opens on screen.

4. Click in the Drawing Pad workspace, and draw the item using your mouse.

5. As soon as you are satisfied with the image, click the **Copy To Clipboard** button to avoid accidentally deleting your work, and then click the **Insert Drawing** button. The image displays wherever the cursor is in the Outlook item (see Figure 10-14).

6. Complete and save or send the item as usual.

Figure 10-14: After the drawing is in place, you can still enter text and anything else that can be inserted into the Outlook item.

WRITE WITH INK

Outlook can convert your handwriting to typed characters. The primary limitation here is that Outlook will be able to read your handwriting only if it is readable to other persons.

1. Click **New** to open a new message, task, or other Outlook item.

2. Click **Handwriting** and select **Write Anywhere**. The Write Anywhere toolbox opens.

3. Click to place the cursor wherever you want the text to appear—even text fields are okay—and begin writing with the mouse. At each pause, Outlook will attempt to convert the writing to text, as shown in Figure 10-15.

4. Complete and then save or send the item as usual.

Figure 10-15: Each Handwriting toolbox allows you to switch to any other toolbox.

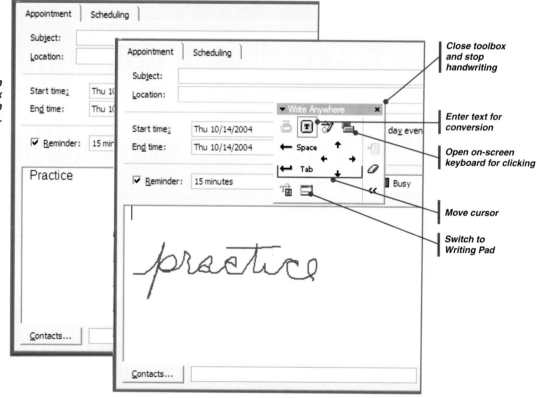

Close toolbox and stop handwriting

Enter text for conversion

Open on-screen keyboard for clicking

Move cursor

Switch to Writing Pad

D

Date Navigator, 87-88, 91
date/time, 103
deleting
  custom menus, 22
  custom toolbars, 20
  e-mail, 42
  files, 167
  items, 17
  Journal entries, 145
  task lists, 136
dictionary, 15, 58
digital certificates, 56-57, 67, 69
digital signatures, 56-57, 62
distribution lists, 48, 72-74, 75

E

embedded attachments, 44
e-mail
  account information, 29
  adding categories to, 39
  Address Book, 30, 47
  addressing, 47-49
  archiving, 41-42
  arranging the Inbox, 39
  attachments, 43-44, 53-55
  Bcc fields on, 48-49, 74, 138
  blocking pictures,
  categories, 39
  checking, 31
  creating, 45-46, 157
  delay sending, 64
  deleting messages, 42
  digital signatures in, 56-57,
  downloading headers only in, 33-34
  editing, 49-51
  editor, Microsoft Word as, 50, 212-213
  encryption, 62-63, 173-176
  finding a message, 41-42
  flagging, 37-38
  formatting, 46, 49-51
  forwarding, 61
  Hotmail, 4, 29

hyperlinks, 53
importance, setting, 61
importing from Outlook Express, 4-5
junk. *See* spam
marking, 37
pictures in, embedding, 55
printing, 44
protection levels, 35-36
reading, 32
receipts, 63
receiving, 30, 31-32
removing accounts, 30
replying to, 59-60
security, 62-63
sending, 59-62
setting up, 25-26
signatures, 55-56
spell checking, 58
stationery, 46, 51-54
templates, 191-192
unblocking picture downloads in, 35
See also accounts, filter lists, rules
encryption, 62-63, 173-176
envelopes, printing 197-198
events, Calendar, 93, 103, 105-106
Exchange. *See* Microsoft Exchange Server
exit Outlook, 5
exporting files, 169-170

F

files
  adding to contacts, 71
  attaching to e-mail, 53-55
  exporting, 169-170
  importing, 4-5, 169
  manipulating, 166-168
  sharing, 167
  views of, 168
filter
  contacts in mail merge, 193
  lists, 35-37
  See also sorting
Find, 30
  using for contacts, 77

using for e-mail , 41
flagging
  colors for, 38
  contacts, 77-78
  e-mail, 32, 37-38
folder pane, 30
folders
  creating, 160-162
  Delete, 42
  deleting, 164
  list, 6, 7, 9
  mail merge, 191-192
  manipulating, 162-164
  Notes, 149, 151
  opening, 9
  properties of, 165-166
  sharing, 163-164
  Tasks, 121-126
fonts, 32, 51
formats, email, 46, 49-51
Form Design toolbar, 181-182
forms
  about, 177
  appointment, 105-106
  Business Contact Manager record, 83-84
  compose/read layouts of, 186-187
  Contacts, 67-69
  Controls Toolbox for, 181, 184-185
  creating, 180-187
  customizing, 179-180
  custom, using, 189
  publishing, 188
  tab order on, 186
forwarding
  e-mail, 61
  notes, 153

G

graphics. *See* pictures

H

handwriting recognition, 214-216
headers, downloading, 33
Help, 13-14
holidays, adding to Calendar, 97, 103
Hotmail, 4, 29
HTML format, 49, 53
HTTP, 4, 26, 29
hyperlinks in email, 53

I

image files. *See* pictures
IMAP, 4, 29
importance, setting e-mail, 61
importing,
   Address Book, the, 4
   files, 4-5, 169
   Outlook Express files, 5
Inbox arrangements, 39
Ink, 215-216
installing
   Business Contact Manager, 82-83
   e-mail accounts, 29-30
   handwriting recognition, 214
   See also setting up
instant messaging (IM), 68, 199-202
Internet
   browsing the, 213
   Free/Busy, Microsoft Office, 97-99
   mail, importing, 4
ISPs (Internet service providers), 26-27

J

Journal
   about the, 141-142
   entries, 144-147
   printing from the, 148
   setting up, 143
   sharing the, 148-149
junk e-mail. *See* spam

K

keyboard
   open menu with, 11
   shortcuts for Contacts, 82

L

labels, printing, 195-196
Language bar, 214
letters, composing to a contact, 81
lists
   filter, 35, 37
   folder, 6-7, 9
   task, 123

M

macros, viruses in, 175
Mail. *See* e-mail
mail merge
   contacts, preparing/selecting, 191-193
   documents, preparing, 193-194
   envelopes, printing, 197-198
   labels, printing, 195-196
   Outlook filtering for, 193
   performing, 195
mail servers, 4
MAPI, 26
maps, adding to Contacts, 71
marking
   headers, 33
   messages, 37
menu(s)
   Control, 6-7
   customizing, 21-22
   dragging to a toolbar, 20
   resetting, 19
   Start, 2
   using, 11
messages. *See* e-mail
meetings
   attendees, adding, 116

changing/rescheduling, 115-116
initiating, 111-113
invitations, responding to, 114
online meetings. *See* NetMeeting
responses, managing, 115
See also appointments, Calendar
Microsoft Exchange Server, 4, 26
   calendar sharing on, 102
   e-mail voting on, 55
   file sharing on, 167
   folder sharing on, 163-164
   group schedules on, 111
   Internet Free/Busy on, 97-98
   Journal sharing on, 148-149
   notes sharing on, 155
   task sharing on, 139
Microsoft Office Word
   documents for mail merge, 193-194
   signatures for e-mail, 56
   stationery themes from, 54
   using to edit e-mail, 49, 50
   writing letters to Contacts with, 81
Microsoft Referral Service, 26-28
multiple profiles, 22-23

N

.NET Passport, 28-29, 99, 200-201
Navigation pane, 6-7, 9-11
   contents on the, 17
   Journal, setting up the, 142
   Notes, exploring the, 153
   Tasks folder, opening the, 122-124
   using the, 9-11
NetMeeting, 117-120
New Connection Wizard, 26-29
New Letter Wizard, 81
Notes
   about, 149-150
   categorizing, 150
   colors for, 150
   creating Outlook items with, 157-158
   current view, customizing, 154
   forwarding, 153
   printing, 156

Reading pane, using, 142
setting up, 150
sharing, 155
using, 151-153
viewing, 153

O

Office Assistant, 14, 15-16
Office Clipboard, 210-212
Outlook
starting, 1-3
updates, 23
window, the, 6-7, 87-88
Web browsing from, 213
Outlook Express
importing files from, 4-5
upgrading from, 1, 3, 4-5
Outlook Today, 11-13

P

Palm, 203
panes
folder
Journal, 142
Navigation, 6-7, 9-11
Reading, 31-32, 115, 137, 142, 154
Research, 15
Search Results, 14
passwords, 28-30
PDAs (personal digital assistants), 203-210
phoning contacts, 80
pictures
adding to contacts, 71
embedding in e-mails, 55
unblocking in downloads, 35
plain text format, 49
Planner options, 97
Pocket PC, 203-204
POP3, 3, 26, 29, 33
preferences
e-mail, 31

print, 44
security, 18
setting, 17-18
printing
Calendars, 109-110
contact information, 79
e-mail, 44
envelopes, 197-198
Help, 14
Journal entries, 148
labels, 195-196
notes, 156
priority. *See* importance
profiles, 22-23
protection levels, 35-36
publishing forms, 188

Q

Quick Launch toolbar, 2

R

receipts, 63, 129
recurring
appointments, 107-108
tasks, 130
reminders, 109, 132-133
replying to e-mail, 59-60
reports
Business Contact Manager, 85-86
task status, 125, 129, 138
Research, 15
resource scheduling, 100
rich text format, 49-50
rules
importing, 4
creating, 32, 40-42
synchronization, 208
to delay e-mail delivery, 64
Rules Wizard, 16-17

S

schedules
e-mail, 62
free/busy options, 97-99
group, 111
on a PDA, 208
resource, 100
Search folders, 161-162
security
and attachments, 43
e-mail, 62-63
making tasks private, 135
options, 18
updating, 23
zones, 18, 171-172
See also encryption
Send/Receive, 6-7
setting up
ActiveSync, 204-205
a dial-up connection, 26-29
Business Contact Manager, 82-83
e-mail accounts, 22, 29-30
instant messaging, 200-201
NetMeeting, 117
Pocket PC, 203-204
shortcuts
keyboard, 82
to starting Outlook, 2
signatures
digital, 56-57
e-mail closing, 55-56
Snooze, 133
sorting
contacts, 75-76
files, 168
spam,
filtering, 25, 35
protection levels against, 35-36
spell checking, e-mail, 58
Standard toolbar
in the Outlook window, 6-7
on the Calendar, 88, 90-92
Startup Wizard, 3
stationery (e-mail), 46, 51-54
synchronizing with a PDA, 206

T

tab order, 186
TaskPad, 87-89, 91, 140
task pane
    Help, 13
    Research, 15
Tasks
    add a time estimate, 129
    adding, 126-127
    assigning tasks to others, 124, 129
    categories for, 134-135
    completing, 136
    customizing 125-126
    deleting, 136
    sharing information on, 139-140
    private, 135
    monitoring, 137
    prioritizing, 131
    Reading pane, 137
    receipts, 129
    recurring, 130
    reminders about, 132-133
    status reports on, 125, 129, 138
    TaskPad with, using, 140
    viewing, 123-125
templates e-mail, 190-191
thesaurus, 15
time zones, setting 101
toolbar(s), 6-8
    Advanced, 6-8, 18
    customizing, 17, 19-20
    deleting, 20
    Form Design, 181-182
    Quick Launch, 2
    Standard, 6-7, 87, 92
tracking
    accounts in Business Contact Manager, 85
    e-mail. *See* receipts
transferring data with a PDA, 206-208

U

unblock picture downloads, 35
update
    contacts, 74, 80
    lists, 35
    Outlook, 23

V

vCards, 44, 72
view bars, 9-10
views
    Calendar, 91-95; 140
    Contacts, 76
    file, 168
    Journal, 147
    Mail, 39
    Tasks, 123, 131
    TaskPad, 140
    selecting, 9
virus protection, 171, 175
voting buttons, 55

W

Web. *See* Internet
Word. *See* Microsoft Office Word

Z

zone security, 18, 171-172
Zone Settings, 18

International Contact Information

AUSTRALIA
McGraw-Hill Book Company Australia Pty. Ltd.
TEL +61-2-9900-1800
FAX +61-2-9878-8881
http://www.mcgraw-hill.com.au
books-it_sydney@mcgraw-hill.com

CANADA
McGraw-Hill Ryerson Ltd.
TEL +905-430-5000
FAX +905-430-5020
http://www.mcgraw-hill.ca

GREECE, MIDDLE EAST, & AFRICA
(Excluding South Africa)
McGraw-Hill Hellas
TEL +30-210-6560-990
TEL +30-210-6560-993
TEL +30-210-6560-994
FAX +30-210-6545-525

MEXICO (Also serving Latin America)
McGraw-Hill Interamericana Editores S.A. de C.V.
TEL +525-1500-5108
FAX +525-117-1589
http://www.mcgraw-hill.com.mx
carlos_ruiz@mcgraw-hill.com

SINGAPORE (Serving Asia)
McGraw-Hill Book Company
TEL +65-6863-1580
FAX +65-6862-3354
http://www.mcgraw-hill.com.sg
mghasia@mcgraw-hill.com

SOUTH AFRICA
McGraw-Hill South Africa
TEL +27-11-622-7512
FAX +27-11-622-9045
robyn_swanepoel@mcgraw-hill.com

SPAIN
McGraw-Hill/Interamericana de España, S.A.U.
TEL +34-91-180-3000
FAX +34-91-372-8513
http://www.mcgraw-hill.es
professional@mcgraw-hill.es

UNITED KINGDOM, NORTHERN, EASTERN, & CENTRAL EUROPE
McGraw-Hill Education Europe
TEL +44-1-628-502500
FAX +44-1-628-770224
http://www.mcgraw-hill.co.uk
emea_queries@mcgraw-hill.com

ALL OTHER INQUIRIES Contact:
McGraw-Hill/Osborne
TEL +1-510-420-7700
FAX +1-510-420-7703
http://www.osborne.com
omg_international@mcgraw-hill.com